THE TRAUMA MODEL

A Solution to The Problem of Comorbidity in Psychiatry

Colin A. Ross, M.D.

Manitou Communications, Inc.

Also By The Author

Northern Studies (1975)

Portrait Of Norman Wells (1979)

Adenocarcinoma And Other Poems (1984)

The Osiris Complex: Case Studies In Multiple Personality Disorder (1994)

Satanic Ritual Abuse: Principles Of Treatment (1995)

Pseudoscience In Biological Psychiatry (1995)

Dissociative Identity Disorder: Diagnosis, Clinical Features, And Treatment Of Multiple Personality, Second Edition (1997)

Schizophrenia: Innovations In Diagnosis and Treatment (2004)

Songs For Two Children: On Dissociation And Human Energy Fields (2004)

Spirit Power Drawings: The Foundation Of a New Science (2004)

The C.I.A. Doctors: Human Rights Violations By American Psychiatrists (2006)
[Originally published as BLUEBIRD (2000)]

TABLE OF CONTENTS

V.   CONCLUSIONS

VI.   APPENDIX

REFERENCES

INDEX

ACKNOWLEDGMENTS

The Trauma Model is the outcome of twenty-one years of work in medicine and psychiatry. During this period, from 1979 to 2000, I have studied my patients very carefully. They taught me the principles of the trauma model.

Tere Kole worked tirelessly on preparation of the manuscript and the mechanics of publication. Melissa Caldwell listened to me think out loud on countless flights to workshops and our Trauma Programs, and provided cogent feedback and ideas of her own, especially the principle that, in trauma therapy, everything boils down to avoidance. Joan Ellason did a lot of work gathering and analyzing data, and writing papers. Thank you, Tere, Joan and Melissa.

INTRODUCTION

Twenty-one years ago, in 1979, I did my clinical rotation in psychiatry as a medical student at the University of Alberta, in Edmonton, Canada. I noticed then that psychiatric inpatients tended to have many different diagnoses. They would be admitted and treated for depression on one occasion, and for a psychotic disorder another time, and often would have numerous admissions. The current diagnosis was always the correct one, but at some point in the future it would become a past incorrect diagnosis. I was most troubled when I saw the diagnosis change several times in a single admission. Not uncommonly, the diagnosis was changed in order to provide a rationale for prescribing a new medication.

Some psychiatrists were simply sloppy diagnosticians and irrational polypharmacists. Others were careful, conscientious and reasonable. The problem was that the patients did not fit the conceptual system of late twentieth century psychiatry. Even when the conceptual system was applied consistently, it did not work. The patients were too polymorphous, variable, complicated and, often, uncooperative. I was taught that sometimes this was because the patient was "borderline." Borderlines, I was taught, display pan-anxiety, pan-sexuality, and polymorphous perversity. Those terms conveyed to me the frustration generated by the conceptual system.

Even if the "borderline" patients were set aside, the problem persisted. On the inpatient wards, the norm was extensive comorbidity. I have been thinking about this problem for twenty-one years, and have devised a solution for it, which I call *the trauma model*. The purpose of this book is to define the problem of comorbidity, and then to describe its solution through the trauma model. The trauma model is a comprehensive, testable scientific theory of mental illness.

The polydiagnostic patient with extensive comorbidity is the major recipient of inpatient psychiatric treatment. In managed care terms, this is the high-cost, high-utilization, high-recidivism patient. There is no scientific model in psychiatry which accounts for this patient, even though he or she is the major consumer of psychiatric services. The dominant model in contemporary psychiatry is the single gene-single disease model. Insurance policies which have expanded their coverage for serious mental illness include disorders assumed to be distinct genetic biomedical brain diseases within contemporary psychiatry;

schizophrenia, unipolar and bipolar depression, obsessive-compulsive disorder, and substance abuse.

Yet, the patients requiring expensive psychiatric care, for the most part, do not fit the single gene-single disease model. They meet DSM-IV-TR (American Psychiatric Association, 2000) criteria for many different disorders and are often given many different clinical diagnoses over time. The separate diseases model simply cannot account for the clinical data. The problem of comorbidity, from a financial perspective, is the core clinical problem in psychiatry. The solution for the problem of comorbidity adopted by psychiatry over the next ten years will set the tone for research, theory, clinical practice and health care coverage in the twenty-first century. In this book, I propose the trauma model as a scientifically testable solution to the problem of comorbidity.

In the first section of the book, the clinical origins and a formal scientific statement of the problem of comorbidity are presented. In the second section, key assumptions of the model are outlined in detail. The third section begins with a description of some general principles of the model, then takes up each of the major sections of DSM-IV-TR. In each of these chapters I describe the specific research predictions arising from the trauma model. These are divided into subsections on phenomenology, natural history, epidemiology, twin and adoption studies, biology, treatment outcome, and revisions to DSM-IV-TR.

In the fourth section of the book, trauma therapy is described. The basic principles and techniques in the psychotherapy of the extensively comorbid patient are outlined. These tend to be cognitive-behavioral in form. As in the rest of the book, the therapy is grounded in relevant bodies of science wherever possible. The testability of the therapy is dealt with in the separate chapters of the previous section.

In the final chapter, the trauma model is discussed from the perspective of the structure of scientific revolutions (Kuhn, 1962). Adoption of the trauma model by mainstream psychiatry would represent a major paradigm shift. At present, the trauma model is marginalized and has no impact on the majority of research, clinical practice and theory in psychiatry. This fact presents an interesting opportunity for anyone interested in scientific paradigm shifts. Major paradigm shifts do not occur every decade in a given field, or even every century. Here we have one in progress. Or, alternatively, one that will fail. Either way, the fate of the trauma model will provide interesting lessons about the balance of science and politics in psychiatry.

I have made no effort to be comprehensive in my references because there is no point. Since the trauma model is a general model of mental illness, I would have to master and reference the literatures on all the major sections of DSM-IV-TR, in order to be comprehensive. That is an impossible task. Fortunately, it is also an irrelevant task. The purpose of the book is to outline the model and the specific scientific predictions that follow from it, then describe the principles of trauma therapy. I have therefore decided not to be exhaustive in my referencing of the content of psychiatry. The reader can consult any of the major comprehensive textbooks of psychiatry for this content. For an inventory of measures relevant to the predictions of the trauma model, I refer the reader to the *Handbook of Psychiatric Measures* (Pincus, Rush, First, and McQueen, 2000).

The references in this book are illustrative only. I have used my own published research to illustrate some points because I am familiar with it, and because it was carried out within the trauma model. Particular data are used only to illustrate the logic of the model, not to prove it.

The trauma model is constructed to be falsifiable. Therefore it could be wrong. That is how it is with scientific models. Ideological objections to the model are irrelevant. What counts are the data. There will be no single crucial experiment. The predictions of the trauma model potentially lead to numerous Ph.D. theses and research publications. Only after a body of data has accumulated will the theory be either proven or rejected. The most likely *scientific* outcome is that a bit of both will occur; the theory will be proven, but modifications will be required.

The origins of the trauma model are in my work with comorbid patients over the last twenty-one years. They are my teachers. I thank them for presenting the problem in such poignant and compelling form. I thank also the many other professionals who have taken trauma seriously as a theme in psychiatry. The trauma model as I have constructed it draws on the work of many different people. If there is to be a paradigm shift in psychiatry, it will be due to the collective work of many individuals. My task here is to present a unified, testable summation of this collective effort.

I. THE PROBLEM OF COMORBIDITY

1

GENERAL CLINICAL EXPERIENCE

As a psychiatric resident at the University of Manitoba in Winnipeg, Canada from 1981 to 1985, I was taught that the genetic basis of schizophrenia was an established scientific fact. The evidence for this conclusion cited by my teachers was the Danish adoption studies. In fact, because of methodological limitations, the Danish adoption studies do not demonstrate that there is a genetic basis for schizophrenia (Ross and Pam, 1995). Subsequent research in the 1980's and 1990's has advanced the field and corrected many of the methodological problems of the Danish adoption studies (Cannon, Kaprio, Lonnqvist, Huttenen, and Koskenvuo, 1998). It is now established that the concordance rate for schizophrenia in monozygotic twins is about 45% compared to about 10% in dizygotic twins. Although serious problems such as the equal environments assumption have not been adequately controlled for in schizophrenia genetics research (Pam, Kemker, Ross, and Golden, 1996), the quality of the evidence supporting a genetic component to schizophrenia is much higher than it was during my residency.

Despite the lack of conclusive evidence at the time, the genetic basis of schizophrenia was regarded as a scientific fact during my residency. This conviction among my teachers was based on ideology, not science. A number of clinical myths followed from the belief that schizophrenia is a genetically-caused biomedical brain disease.

One of the clinical myths I was taught in my residency I call *the myth of young Johnny*. The myth of young Johnny followed from the theory that there is a genetic basis to schizophrenia. Johnny was a normal boy until his first year of college. In retrospect he may have had some odd thought patterns and been somewhat more withdrawn than usual for a year or two, but prior to that prodromal period he was a normal kid from a normal family. Then, all of a sudden, the tragedy of mental illness struck Johnny's brain. The demon had been lurking inside him all these years, waiting to attack. Johnny had an acute first-break psychosis. Although it might have been triggered by the stress of college, basically the illness was programmed by his genome. Johnny's uncle Ted was a very strange, reclusive man, but never received treatment.

The length of the prodrome was variable. In some cases it might be more than ten years, but in all cases, the unfolding of the clinical disease was driven from within the cell nucleus.

Johnny had schizophrenia, a brain disease caused primarily by the gene for schizophrenia. The "gene" might be polygenetic, it might be more a gene region than a single gene, and we might be talking about partial penetrance and multiple loci, but the causality was basically endogenous, biological and genetic. Environmental variables at most could have a minor influence on symptom content or might trigger the first psychotic break in a stress-diathesis model. The emphasis, in my residency training, was all on diathesis, however, with the stress being non-specific and general.

Treatment for Johnny was medication. The medical doctor, the psychiatrist, provided that. The psychosocial component of the treatment was simple-minded. It consisted of education about the illness for the patient and family, encouragement to stay on medication, and social work support. Everyone claimed to treat schizophrenia within a comprehensive biopsychosocial model, but the psychosocial elements were simple-minded and consigned to social workers and nurses. The diagnosis, medication and initial education were provided by the psychiatrist. The myth of young Johnny is summarized in Table 1.1

Table 1.1. The Myth of Young Johnny

	Present	Absent
Trauma	-	+
Normal Family	+	-
Genetic Cause	+	-
Environmental Cause	-	+
Brain Disease	+	-
Normal Before Illness	+	-
Needs Medication	+	-
Needs Psychotherapy	-	+

Why do I call this *the myth of young Johnny*? Because I rarely met Johnny in the academic Department of Psychiatry. Then there was Johnny's high school buddy, Greg, who was also a normal kid from a normal family. He had a different biomedical disease caused by a different abnormal gene. He got sick a year later, and his diagnosis was bipolar mood disorder. Lithium could help Greg but not Johnny. That's why it was important to make the correct diagnosis, which was the doctor's job. I met Greg more often than I met Johnny.

I did see many cases of schizophrenia and bipolar mood disorder during my residency. And I did prescribe neuroleptics, antidepressants and lithium. If I didn't see Johnny, who did I see then? I saw the typical major mental illness caseload of any university teaching hospital. I worked through the differential diagnosis of schizophrenia, schizoaffective disorder, and bipolar mood disorder many times as a resident, and from 1985 to 1990, did so many times as an attending physician covering six acute care university hospital teaching beds. I diagnosed and treated anticholinergic delirium and other organic conditions. It was the typical experience one would expect on any Emergency Department-driven university teaching ward.

Like the other residents, I learned to identify the patient's psychiatrist from the prescribed medications the patient was taking. There were a number of psychiatrists in the department who were polypharmacists. When one of their patients came to the Emergency Department and was seen by the psychiatry resident on call, it was easy to tell that the patient was being treated by one of three or four psychiatrists because of the long list of psychotropic medications. Often the doctor could be identified with certainty because of certain idiosyncratic prescribing patterns.

For instance, one physician often prescribed two milligrams a day of the neuroleptic, trifluoperazine. This low dose of trifluoperazine would be tucked inside a medication regime that included a tricyclic antidepressant, a higher dose of another neuroleptic, an anticholinergic agent, a benzodiazepine, a combined opiate-barbiturate medication, and perhaps one other psychotropic of some kind. Sometimes lithium would also be prescribed. In the nineties, an anticonvulsant would be added.

One might simply conclude that this was irrational polypharmacy, which it was. But that is not the whole story. Although the medication plan made no scientific sense, and was accompanied by high rates of non-compliance, side effects and drug-drug interactions, in a way it made clinical sense. Why? Because the myth of Johnny could not account for the bulk of the clinical caseload.

Although I didn't realize it at the time, the polypharmacy regimens I saw commonly as a resident were a tacit recognition of the trauma model.

They were based on a clinical recognition of *the problem of comorbidity*, which is accounted for by the trauma model. Such prescribing patterns are not a thing of the past. An article in the *Journal of Urology* (Hudson and Cain, 1998) describes an eleven year old boy who was being treated for severe behavioral problems, depression, attention deficit disorder with hyperactivity and oppositional defiant disorder.

This boy's regular psychiatric medications included fluoxetine, valproic acid, benztropine, haloperidol, clonidine, trazodone and nasal desmopressin. One week before he presented with hemorrhagic cystitis, risperidone had been substituted for the haloperidol. His symptoms abated one week after risperidone was stopped and haloperidol restarted, and were absent a month later. According to the trauma model, there is an alternative treatment plan for children, adolescents and adults who receive many different medications and diagnoses within conventional psychiatry. The odds that this boy is a trauma patient are very high within the trauma model, because the model states that extensive comorbidity is accompanied by high rates of chronic childhood trauma.

Another recent article in the *Journal of the American Medical Association* (March, Biderman, Wolkow, Safferman, Mardekian, Cook, Cutler, Dominguez, Ferguson, Muller, Riesenberg, Rosenhal, Sallee and Wagner, 1998) describes a multi-center trial of sertraline versus placebo in the treatment of obsessive-compulsive disorder in children and adolescents. There were 107 children age 6 to 12 years, and 80 adolescents age 13 to 17 years in the study, which was funded by the pharmaceutical company that manufactures sertraline, Pfizer Inc.

The results showed that 42% of subjects on sertraline were very much or much improved compared to 26% of the subjects on placebo. Since 26% of subjects will get better on placebo, this means that 26% of the subjects who responded to sertraline would have done as well if they had been randomized to placebo. This means that only (1.00 - 0.26 = 0.74) 74% of the subjects who responded to sertraline did so because of a unique pharmacological effect they could not have obtained with placebo. It follows that only (0.74 x 0.42 = 0.31) 31% of children and adolescents with obsessive-compulsive disorder get a good response to sertraline which can be attributed solely to the pharmacological effect of the drug. This unique pharmacological response rate is not significantly different from placebo response rate.

This is true for all psychiatric medications. Ballpark, all the different types of psychiatric medication are effective in 65% - 70% of cases, while placebo is effective in 35% - 40%. If we use 70% and 40% to illustrate the logic, the unique effect of the drug which requires the pharmacological properties of the drug is 0.70 x (1.0 − 0.4) = 0.42 or 42%, which is no better than the placebo response rate of 40%. This relationship is illustrated in Figure 1.1.

Figure 1.1. The World Literature on Psychiatric Drugs Proves that the Direct Chemical Effects of All Drugs is Equal to the Placebo Response Rate

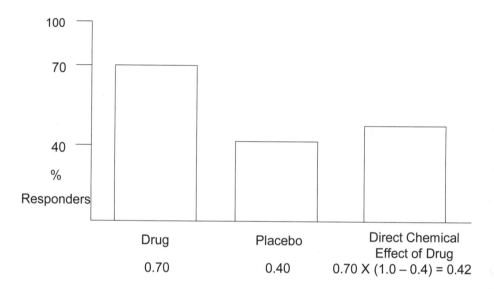

The reason it is better clinically to prescribe sertraline than placebo is not because the unique pharmacological effect of the drug is superior to placebo, but because the drug provides the combined effects of drug and placebo, which are superior to placebo alone. In any event, 58% of children and adolescents in the study received no appreciable benefit from taking sertraline, while 37% experienced insomnia, 17% nausea, 13% agitation and 7% tremor. Sertraline is a much safer drug with fewer side effects than many of the medications prescribed to the eleven year old boy with hemorrhagic cystitis reported in the *Journal of Urology*.

Psychiatric patients with many different diagnoses who receive many different psychotropic medications simultaneously are likely to suffer a number of negative consequences. There are many such people in the mental health system and they are very expensive from a managed care perspective. Besides conventional side effects and drug-drug interactions, such patients are also much more likely to be non-compliant simply because of the large number of pills involved. Forgetting doses, double-dosing, dropping drugs from the regime without consulting the psychiatrist, gastrointestinal side effects and interactions with street drugs all cause a roller coaster effect in terms of blood levels of the different medications. Countless interactions must occur between the different drugs due to their changing blood levels, competition for enzymes, activation of enzymes and other mechanisms.

There is another problem. There are no scientific drug studies for polypharmacy regimens in polydiagnostic patients. Drug studies funded by drug companies are virtually the sole source of data concerning the efficacy of psychiatric medications. Only the drug companies are financially motivated or have the resources to conduct the large, expensive studies required by the federal governments of the industrialized world. How are these drug studies conducted?

Take antidepressants as an example, a type of drug company study I have participated in personally. All such studies are designed by the drug companies in response to federal requirements. There must be inclusion and exclusion criteria, informed consent, adequate monitoring of physical health status, a randomized placebo-controlled prospective design, and so on. The inclusion criteria are straightforward. Basically, to participate in an antidepressant study, a subject must currently be clinically depressed and score above cutoff levels on depression scales. Usually the diagnosis must be major depressive disorder.

It is the exclusion criteria that are important. The subject cannot have a currently active substance abuse problem, cannot suffer from schizophrenia, schizoaffective disorder or any organic mental disorder, and *cannot be acutely suicidal*. The world's literature on the efficacy of antidepressants is based on physically healthy individuals with simple, clean psychiatric profiles who are not acutely suicidal. This is why meta-analytic reviews of drug studies involving thousands of clinically depressed subjects randomized to both drug and placebo include no subjects who committed suicide. You can't get into the studies if you are acutely suicidal.

There are no scientific data demonstrating the efficacy of psychotropic medications in acutely suicidal polydiagnostic patients. Why? Because these patients are too complicated and messy for the drug companies to fool around with. To get the new drug approved by the federal government, it isn't necessary to provide data on these patients. Clean, straightforward outpatients are all that is required. Johnny is a good drug study subject, but Johnny rarely gets admitted to a psychiatric ward.

Most patients admitted to inpatient psychiatric facilities are either actively addicted to substances, acutely suicidal, polydiagnostic, organically impaired, or so psychotic they could not give informed consent to participate in a drug study. This is the day in and day out workload of inpatient psychiatry. Yet the drug studies exclude such patients. This is true for all classes of psychiatric medication.

How are subjects recruited for drug studies? I learned as a resident that subjects for drug company-funded studies are not available in the University Department of Psychiatry. It is very difficult if not impossible to recruit subjects from inside the Department. Why? Because the subjects have to be so clean that they are too clean to be in hospital-based caseloads. When I completed a study of buspirone versus diazepam and placebo for treatment of generalized anxiety disorder for a drug company (Ross and Matas, 1987), I was unable to recruit a single subject from within the Departments of Psychiatry or Family Medicine. All subjects were recruited through a newspaper ad. I could not find a single case of generalized anxiety disorder in my teaching hospital.

Surprisingly, the same is true for drug studies of depression. Subjects are routinely recruited through newspaper ads because psychiatrists and Psychiatry Departments cannot provide subjects who meet the exclusion criteria. There was an unacknowledged paradox in my residency training. I was told that family physicians could handle the straightforward cases of anxiety and depression. The psychiatrist was required for the complex cases. That seemed to make sense. The psychiatrists, after all, are the experts in psychotropic medication.

I was told that psychiatrists have more extensive scientific training in mind-body interactions, side effects of psychotropic medication, and psychiatric differential diagnosis. This is in fact true. The paradox is that as soon as a patient meets threshold for referral to a psychiatrist, the scientific foundation of the psychopharmacology disappears. Family physicians see and treat the patients who could qualify as drug study subjects. The ones they refer to psychiatrists are the ones who fail to meet the exclusion criteria. These are the patients for whom there are no data. In fact, the family physician's psychopharmacology is scientific, the psychiatrist's is anecdotal.

Of course this is an oversimplification. But it is true for the bulk of the inpatient caseload in psychiatry, which consists of patients who would not be allowed to participate in drug studies. This means that the use of even *single* psychotropic medications in the acutely suicidal or polydiagnostic patient is without scientific foundation. The problem increases exponentially when we consider the subject on six, seven or eight psychotropic medications simultaneously. None of these medications has a proven, uniquely pharmacological effect that is superior to placebo, for the logical reasons outlined above.

To reiterate, although polypharmacy for psychiatric inpatients is without scientific foundation or rational explanation, it is nevertheless intuitively accurate in a sense. It is true that such patients do not get better on a single medication. It is true that they present difficult problems in differential diagnosis and have a great deal of comorbidity. Each drug prescribed can be prescribed properly for one of the comorbid diagnoses.

The problem is, there is no scientific literature concerning how to proceed psychopharmacologically when the different diagnoses are all made on the same patient. The drug literature tells you what to prescribe for depression, obsessive-compulsive disorder, bipolar mood disorder, panic disorder, schizophrenia, alcohol withdrawal, and attention deficit disorder. But what about the patient who meets criteria for five or six different Axis I disorders? For this patient, the modal patient on a psychiatric ward, the scientific literature is silent.

As I worked on the inpatient wards during my psychiatry residency, and for five years after completing my training, I frequently met another patient, Albert. Albert had been seeing psychiatrists for twenty years, since he was a teenager. His current diagnosis was bipolar mood disorder. He was taking lithium, amitriptyline, haloperidol, cogentin, methotrimeprazine, and flurazepam. He smoked marijuana regularly and may have been knocked unconscious in a car accident as a teenager.

Previous diagnoses in Albert's medical record, which was in three thick volumes, included schizophrenia, schizoaffective disorder, atypical psychosis, rapid-cycling bipolar mood disorder, alcohol abuse, antisocial personality disorder, amotivational syndrome secondary to chronic marijuana abuse, temporal lobe epilepsy and personality disorder not otherwise specified. It was not possible to reconstruct a picture of Albert's childhood from the medical record and there was no mention of childhood physical or sexual abuse.

Albert had two teenage children he had not seen for ten years. His wife left him because of his drinking and he lost touch with his children within a year of the divorce. His father was a heavy-drinking alcoholic who died in a car crash when Albert was seven. By description, the father could have had undiagnosed bipolar mood disorder. Albert's mother was treated in the Provincial Mental Hospital thirty years ago for an unknown diagnosis. She had a series of boyfriends after her divorce, two of whom abused Albert physically on a chronic basis. From age nine to eleven, Albert was molested by his male babysitter.

I was taught to ignore Albert's trauma history and to concentrate on making the correct diagnosis. That was my job as a doctor. From the diagnosis, I was taught, the treatment plan would follow automatically, with fine-tuning based on my clinical experience and judgment. Albert would attend a couple of group therapy sessions for assertiveness training and life skills per day. The rest of the day he would sit around waiting for his medication, or perhaps go on an outing.

The details of the trauma history varied, as did the names, ages and diagnoses of the patients. But this was not a random sample of the general population from a trauma perspective. The "clinical material" I worked with was a veritable tidal wave of trauma. Yet trauma was basically ignored as a theme, factor or cause of the patients' problems. If challenged, all treatment team members would pay lip service to the biopsychosocial model. But in operational reality, the trauma histories were simply irrelevant to the inpatient treatment plan. It took me longer to learn that the trauma was also irrelevant to the outpatient treatment plan.

It was as if 80% of the patients were Nazi concentration camp survivors. I was actively taught to ignore this fact, and to concentrate on my work as a doctor, which was to make diagnoses and prescribe medication. My training was typical then and would be typical today.

Another observation I made as a resident also surprised me. I noticed that the academic professors of psychiatry did not personally treat individuals with major mental illnesses, with very few exceptions. The professors saw only drug study-type patients or long-term psychoanalytical patients. Not a single professor was trying to treat serious mental illness with any form of psychotherapy. Therapy was for the light, neurotic cases only. Medications were for the serious cases. Few professors were directly, personally responsible for the ongoing medication management of serious cases.

Everyone claimed to be doing "therapy" with inpatients, but the therapy was simple-minded. Sometimes an expert in behavioral modification techniques would be called in on a difficult inpatient case, since psychotherapy was out of the question and medications weren't working well. The behavioral prescription was always a simple reward and punishment regime.

With serious cases, nothing of any complexity, cleverness, or elegance was ever done under the heading of psychotherapy or behavioral therapy. What were the psychiatrists doing, then? What activities were they carrying out which required four years of specialty training after medical school? I could not answer this question by the time I completed my residency training. Why? Because I never saw psychiatrists at work.

During four years of psychiatric training, I never watched a psychiatrist do a complete mental status examination. I never watched a psychiatrist do individual psychotherapy with a patient. I never watched a psychiatrist do a full diagnostic interview on a new patient. I simply never watched psychiatrists at work. The only exceptions were a few family therapy sessions and two short-term psychoanalytic psychotherapy assessments.

Compare this to the number of hours I spent watching and assisting surgeons in the operating room as a medical student. Or watching obstetricians deliver babies. Or internists do procedures. As a medical student I spent hundreds of hours watching doctors work. In four years of training as a psychiatrist I watched psychiatrists at work for less than ten hours. Yet I am a certified specialist in psychiatry, a Fellow of the Royal College of Physicians and Surgeons of Canada. I was a Chief Resident and Laughlin Fellow of the American College of Psychiatrists, and I conducted original research and drug company contract studies as a resident.

I was not a slouch, nor was I at a marginal medical school. I received the standard psychiatric training. In four years of medical school, four years of psychiatry residency, and fifteen years of practice, I have watched psychiatrists at work a total of less than twenty hours. Does this make any sense? Does this sound like *medical* training? Clearly not. But there is a good reason why it is not necessary to watch psychiatrists at work in order to learn how to treat major mental illness. Psychiatric treatment for major mental illness does not involve any skills which must be learned by direct observation. The rules for making diagnoses, prescribing medication, and providing straightforward psychoeducation can be learned in the hallway, in the seminar room, or at a desk.

Within the biomedical reductionist model that dominates academic psychiatry today, there is no compelling need for psychiatric residents to watch psychiatrists at work. The necessary skills can be acquired without such direct observation. Unfortunately, the myth of young Johnny and the biomedical model of separate genetic illnesses cannot account for the bulk of psychiatric inpatients, nor can they provide adequate treatment outcomes. This is because of the problem of comorbidity. Contemporary psychiatric treatment for major mental illness is inadequate not because of deficiencies in individual psychiatrists, but because of deficiencies in the dominant biomedical model of mental illness. The individual psychiatrists are adhering to the rules of the biomedical model and its diagnostic and therapeutic systems. They are taught to do so at medical school.

I learned during my residency that extensive comorbidity and polypharmacy are common. I concluded that the biomedical model could not account for the clinical data or the prescribing patterns of my teachers. Something else had to be going on. Psychiatrists were effective at treating Greg, and other patients with relatively clean, clear diagnoses, but not Albert.

The trauma model is my effort to bring scientific order to these years of experience.

2

A TRAUMA VIGNETTE

In this section the experiential, clinical background for the trauma model is presented. No effort is made to formalize the model, explain in any detail how it can solve the problem of comorbidity, or define its testable predictions. The trauma model's roots in common sense and shared experience can best be illustrated with a clinical vignette.

A biologically and genetically normal woman has had an uneventful childhood and life course. She has not experienced any significant trauma outside the normal range of experience, would score in the normal range on psychological testing, and is considered by all who know her to be well adjusted. At age twenty-six this woman is the victim of a rape by a stranger. The rape occurs in a public park during the daytime, and the woman has done nothing careless to place herself at risk. She does not experience any physical trauma to her head and does not lose consciousness. The rapist is observed getting up off the woman, pulling up his pants and running away by another person who comes on the scene by chance. This person calls the police on a cellular phone. Semen is recovered from the woman's vagina and later genetically matched to the perpetrator, who is arrested for another rape.

During the rape itself the woman experiences peritraumatic dissociation. She feels depersonalized; during the most violent part of the rape and during the period of penetration, she watches the event from outside her body. Suddenly she finds herself back in her body and the perpetrator is gone. While describing the rape to police, she is unable to account for significant portions of the experience or reconstruct a continuous narrative of it. She has no memory of the assailant's face.

The woman immediately develops symptoms of posttraumatic stress disorder. She has nightmares of being chased and murdered, which she never had before. She has repeated intrusive recollections of the rape, sometimes including details she could not previously recall. She is tense, keyed up, anxious and fearful much of the time. She scans the environment for detail and has an extreme startle response to stimuli that previously would not have affected her. She will not go near the park, and drives several miles out of her way in the morning to avoid going near it on the way to work. Although she walked in public parks almost daily for years up to the rape, she now will not walk alone anywhere in public.

Because of the nightmares, she loses a lot of sleep. As well, she avoids the nightmares by staying up late. The resulting fatigue begins to affect her concentration and performance at work. She will not let her boyfriend, with whom she previously had frequent, mutually satisfying sexual relations, touch her. When he tries to touch her, she experiences fearful hyperarousal and has to take a shower. She takes at least three showers a day in order to get rid of the dirt on her body and she can still feel the rapist's semen on her. She develops other psychosomatic symptoms including vaginal pain, painful periods, muscle and joint pains, and diarrhea and nausea.

Because of her declining performance at work, the woman comes into conflict with her controlling, chauvinistic male boss. They have several angry confrontations at the office. Nothing like this has ever occurred in her work environment before. Demoralized by her difficulties with her boss and boyfriend, exhausted from lack of sleep, and overwhelmed with traumatic anxiety, she begins to drink in the evenings and uses alcohol to go to sleep. She becomes tired, drained of energy, overwhelmed and despondent. She has many negative cognitions about herself, men and life in general.

Within a few weeks, this previously psychiatrically normal woman has become polysymptomatic. She approaches or exceeds diagnostic threshold for many different DSM-IV-TR diagnoses. These include posttraumatic stress disorder; major depressive episode; dissociative amnesia; alcohol abuse; obsessive-compulsive disorder; specific phobia; panic disorder with agoraphobia; primary insomnia; nightmare disorder; adjustment disorder with mixed disturbance of emotions and conduct; and somatoform disorder not otherwise specified. If her belief that she was dirty and still had the rapist's semen on her skin became fixed, one might consider a diagnosis of body dysmorphic disorder or delusional disorder, somatic type.

The normal response to a stranger rape is to develop the twelve independent psychiatric disorders listed in Table 2.1.

DSM-IV-TR exclusion rules and clinical judgment might reduce the diagnoses to posttraumatic stress disorder and major depressive episode, but it is clear that the woman has developed symptoms from all across Axis I. If her behavioral conflicts with her boss and boyfriend and her unstable moods had been a longstanding pattern, she might receive a diagnosis of borderline personality disorder. A selective serotoin reuptake inhibitor (SSRI) would likely provide some benefit and relief, but would not return this woman to her baseline state.

Table 2.1 The Normal Response to a Stranger Rape

Symptoms of	Present Beforehand	Arising After the Rape
Peritraumatic Dissociation	-	+
Posttraumatic Stress	-	+
Dissociative Disorder	-	+
Phobia	-	+
Somatization Disorder	-	+
Sleep Disorder	-	+
Sexual Dysfunction	-	+
Depression	-	+
Obsessive Compulsive Disorder	-	+
'Personality Disorder'	-	+
Substance Abuse	-	+
Delusional Disorder	-	+

For the purposes of this vignette, the assumption is that this woman had a normal genetic endowment. She was not at elevated genetic risk for any psychiatric disorder. Her risk for developing any of the disorders listed above, in the absence of the rape, was either at or below the baseline risk for the general population, corrected for age.

Consider the expected psychiatric profile for this woman if, instead of a single-episode adult-onset rape, she had been sexually molested by her father, uncle and brother from age five to thirteen. What would we expect the psychiatric profile of this woman to look like in this second scenario? Surely it would be the same as for the single rape in adulthood, but more so. Here we have the basic postulate of the trauma model in vignette form.

Consider additionally a victim of purely physical trauma who arrives by ambulance at a hospital emergency department. This person has been in a serious motor vehicle accident and is in hypovolemic shock. Her fractured shin bone is protruding through her skin. She is bleeding, sweating and moaning. Her pulse is elevated, her blood pressure is low, her tissues are swelling in multiple locations, and many chemical reactions are occurring throughout her body that would not have occurred in the absence of the car accident. She has a "chemical imbalance."

Does the physician called to see this woman begin to speculate about the gene for her chemical imbalance? Does he decide to submit a research grant to find out which chromosome is responsible for this abnormal condition? Such a response would be unscientific. It wouldn't make medical sense. The emergency physician treats what he assumes to be the genetically and biologically normal response to severe physical trauma. This is his *medical* analysis of the situation.

In the next stretcher bay, another emergency medical officer is attending to a 65-year old man with a myocardial infarction. The man is obese and hypertensive. His blood lipid profile is highly elevated. He has smoked two packs of cigarettes a day for forty years and has done virtually no aerobic exercise since he was an adolescent. The man's father and paternal grandfather both died of heart attacks in their fifties.

Does the physician wonder which chromosome is causing his patient's heart attack? Does he consider the possibility of gene therapy directed at the gene for heart attacks? No. Again, such thinking makes no medical sense, even though family history is part of the risk profile of the patient. The idea that the cause of the myocardial infarction could be localized on a single chromosome, let alone in a single gene, except perhaps in a tiny minority of cases, is untenable from scientific and medical perspectives. The cause of the myocardial infarction is far too multi-factorial ever to be reduced to a single gene, or even a definable set of genes. Even the endogenous biological components of the causation of the heart attack are not controlled by a single chromosome.

Similarly, the complex clinical picture of the car crash victim is "caused" by countless different genes. Countless genes participate in countless bodily functions involved in the trauma response; no molecular biologist would ever consider searching for a gene for hypovolemic shock. The concept of a gene for hypovolemic shock makes no biological sense. Even to speak of a single gene for blood vessels, a gene for blood pressure regulation, or a gene for skin or bone is scientifically untenable, though all these bodily structures and functions are elements of the trauma response.

The same logic applies to the rape victim. To consider a search for the gene controlling her trauma response makes no biological sense. There cannot be a single gene for this complex set of symptoms that span most of DSM-IV-TR, or even a definable and finite set of genes or gene regions. Nevertheless, without genes the woman would not exist and could not respond to the environment in any way. To say that the trauma response has nothing to do with genes would be biologically absurd, and simply the reciprocal error of logic.

The vignette of the twenty-six year old rape victim provides the clinical foundation of the trauma model. How can one best understand her extensive comorbidity from a medical and scientific perspective? From a trauma model perspective, her polydiagnostic syndrome is due to environmental activation of countless regions of her normal genome.

3

CLINICAL EXPERIENCE IN A TRAUMA PROGRAM

I arrived in Texas from Canada in early November, 1991 and have been running a hospital-based Trauma Program here ever since. During this period of time, over 2000 individuals have been admitted to the Program for a total of over 4000 admissions. The average number of admissions per patient over this time period is about two; the average daily census is about 13; 90% of patients are female; 50% of patients are on medicare and 50% are managed care cases; 50% are from outside Texas; the average length of stay is in the range of 14 days; and there has been no single admission that lasted 100 days. Eighty per cent of the patients meet structured interview criteria for posttraumatic stress disorder.

In addition, I have been running a second Trauma Program in Grand Rapids, Michigan since February 1, 1998 and a third Program in Torrance, California since December 1, 1999. During the first quarter of 2000, there were about 40 inpatients in the three programs at any given time. This is the clinical experience base of the trauma model.

Patients must meet inpatient acuity criteria for general adult psychiatry in order to be admitted to the Trauma Programs. Most are acutely suicidal, and the remainder are homicidal or acutely disorganized and unable to function. Many patients have long histories of involvement in the mental health system prior to their trauma being addressed in treatment. Some would be regarded as low-functioning borderlines within conventional psychiatry, while others have included practicing physicians, lawyers, nationally funded research scientists, and corporate managers. Some patients present complex behavioral management problems, while others can be managed with ease from a behavioral perspective.

A sample of 103 of these patients, all of whom met DSM-IV-TR and Dissociative Disorders Interview Schedule (Ross, 1997) criteria for dissociative identity disorder, had the comorbidity profile on the Structured Clinical Interview for DSM-III-R (SCID) (Ellason, Ross, and Fuchs, 1996) illustrated in Table 3.1. Overall, of the 107 patients, 98.1% met lifetime criteria for a mood disorder, 89.7% an anxiety disorder,

19

74.3% a psychotic disorder, 65.4% a substance abuse disorder, 43.9% a somatoform disorder, and 38.3% an eating disorder.

Table 3.1. Frequencies of Selected Diagnoses in 103 Trauma Program Inpatients On the Structured Clinical Interview for DSM-III-R (SCID)

Disorder	Percentage Positive
Major Depressive Episode	97.2
Posttraumatic Stress Disorder	79.2
Panic Disorder	69.2
Substance Abuse	65.4
Obsessive Compulsive Disorder	63.6
Borderline Personality Disorder	56.3
Schizoaffective Disorder	49.5
Social Phobia	45.8
Somatization Disorder	41.1

On the SCID the average number of Axis I disorders per patient was 7.3 (S.D. 2.5), which did not include the dissociative disorder, or sleep disorders and psychosexual disorders, both of which are pervasive in the population. The modal number of Axis I disorders was 8. The average number of diagnoses on Axis II was 3.6 (S.D. 2.5), and the modal number was 3. The overall average number of lifetime psychiatric disorders on the SCID was 10.9, to which we can add the dissociative disorder, which is not diagnosed by the SCID, and probably a sleep and psychosexual disorder. This means that the average patient in our program has met criteria for 14 different psychiatric disorders lifetime.

The average patient in our program would be the most difficult client in most outpatient psychotherapy caseloads. This is true in terms of quantity and complexity of comorbidity and in terms of behavioral management. In other large series of dissociative identity disorder cases (Ross, 1997), 25% - 50% of subjects have received prior diagnoses of schizophrenia from a psychiatrist, half have received neuroleptics, 12% - 16% have received electro-convulsive therapy, 75% have been hospitalized, and 75% have attempted suicide prior to the dissociative disorder being diagnosed. The modal patient has received many different diagnoses and psychotropic medications.

Setting aside any disputes about the validity of dissociative identity disorder, it is clear that prior clinicians have regarded many of these patients as suffering from severe mental disorders requiring inpatient treatment with neuroleptics and electro-convulsive therapy. At the level of clinical impression, the sample of 103 patients who received the SCID appears to be representative of the more than 2000 individuals admitted to my Dallas Trauma Program in terms of complexity and chronicity of comorbidity.

In terms of trauma histories, inpatients with dissociative identity disorder virtually without exception report severe, chronic childhood trauma (Ross, 1997). In large series, 68% - 90% report childhood sexual abuse, while 60% - 82% report childhood physical abuse. It is therefore evident that sexual abuse and physical abuse alone are neither necessary nor sufficient conditions for the development of dissociative identity disorder. However, in three large series, the number of subjects who reported either or both childhood physical and sexual abuse ranged from 88.5% - 96.0%. This is consistent with clinical experience in our inpatient program.

For all Axis I disorders, one expects to see the most severe cases on inpatient wards. One expects to encounter milder clinical and subclinical variants in the general population, a pattern which appears to hold for dissociative identity disorder. From the perspective of the problem of comorbidity, it is the inpatients who are of interest. In terms of the logic of the trauma model, debates about the validity of dissociative identity disorder are irrelevant, since the problem of comorbidity remains even if the dissociative disorder is deleted from the belief system of the diagnostician.

The purpose of this chapter has been to establish the clinical experiential base for the trauma model and the clinical foundation of my interest in the problem of comorbidity.

4

THE PROBLEM OF COMORBIDITY

A more formal statement of the problem of comorbidity is required before the trauma model can be proposed as its solution. The biomedical model dominates psychiatry today. In its current form, the biomedical model in psychiatry is bioreductionist and assumes that major mental illness is driven predominantly by the genome. The biomedical model is always couched as a biopsychosocial model, but this is not an accurate description of how it actually functions.

For instance, a recent Finnish study found concordance rates for schizophrenia to be 46% in monozygotic twins and 9% in dizygotic twins (Cannon et al, 1998). One might conclude from such data that the etiology of schizophrenia is half genetic and half environmental. The authors, however, applied a statistical model to their data and concluded that 83% of the cause of schizophrenia is genetic. If one accepts this conclusion, it follows that the psychosocial contributions to the etiology of schizophrenia are minimal, and limited to triggering otherwise inevitable gene expression or modifying symptom content.

The basic goal of biomedical psychiatry is to identify separate genes for separate diseases. The diseases must have distinct pathophysiologies driven by their distinct genetic abnormalities, and the DSM-IV-TR diagnostic system must be able to differentiate them from each other. Although the DSM-IV-TR system is atheoretical and phenomenological in its diagnostic criteria sets, at a structural level it is the product of the dominant paradigm in psychiatry. The rules and structure of the DSM-IV-TR system, which were first codified in DSM-III in 1980 (American Psychiatric Association, 1980), are designed to separate disorders from each other. The inclusion and exclusion rules of the system cannot deal with the problem of comorbidity.

Similarly, the single gene-single disease model of biomedical psychiatry cannot deal with the problem of comorbidity. According to the biomedical model, schizophrenia, major depressive disorder, panic disorder, alcoholism and obsessive compulsive disorder are distinct diseases. They are caused by distinct genetic abnormalities. It is irrelevant to the analysis whether these abnormalities are housed in single genes, gene regions, or clusters of genes.

A problem arises when we consider the prevalence of these disorders in the general population. In order to keep the arithmetic simple, let's assume that the lifetime prevalence of schizophrenia in the general population is 1%, of major depressive disorder 10%, panic disorder 3%, alcoholism 10%, and obsessive compulsive disorder 2%. This means that these five disorders should co-occur in (.01 x .10 x .03 x .10 x .02 = .00000006) 6 in 100 million individuals. This means that fifteen people in the United States should have all five of these disorders sometime in their lives.

Data from the National Comorbidity Survey (Kessler, McGonagle, Zhao, Nelson, Hughes, Eshleman, Wittchen, and Kendler, 1994; Kessler, Zhao, Katz, Kouzis, Frank, Edlund, and Leaf, 1999) illustrate the problem of comorbidity. The lifetime prevalence of the disorders inquired about in the National Comorbidity Survey is shown in Table 4.1.

Table 4.1   Lifetime Prevalence of Psychiatric Disorders in the National Comorbidity Survey (N=8,098)

Disorder	%
Any psychiatric disorder	48.7
Any type of substance abuse disorder	26.6
Major depressive episode	17.1
Alcohol dependence	14.1
Simple phobia	13.3
Social phobia	11.3
Alcohol abuse without dependence	9.4
Drug dependence	7.5
Dysthymia	6.4
Agoraphobia without panic disorder	5.3
Generalized anxiety disorder	5.1
Drug abuse without dependence	4.4
Panic disorder	3.5
Manic episode	1.6
Nonaffective psychosis*	0.7

*Schizophrenia, schizophreniform disorder, delusional disorder, atypical psychosis

Based on the National Comorbidity Survey data, the number of respondents who should have major depressive disorder, panic disorder and substance abuse is (0.103 x 0.023 x 0.113 = 0.00027) about 3 individuals out of 10,000. In the entire Survey there should have been (8,098 x 0.00027 = 2.2) only two or three individuals with these three disorders. What were the actual data?

The lifetime prevalence for any psychiatric disorder was found to be 48.0%. However, only 21% of respondents had a single psychiatric disorder, while 1134 (14%) had three or more. Of the 2389 individuals who had a psychiatric disorder of some kind in the previous year, 58.9% had three or more disorders.

This means that in the general population, over half of people with recent psychiatric problems suffer from the problem of comorbidity. Finally, of these individuals with a severe disorder in the previous year, 89.5% had three or more psychiatric disorders. Severe problems were defined as active mania, nonaffective psychosis, or problems causing hospitalization or severe role impairment. Only a tiny minority of individuals with major mental illness do not suffer from the problem of comorbidity. Only fourteen diagnoses were inquired about in the National Comorbidity Survey, so the data underestimate the prevalence of extensive comorbidity by a large margin.

Now consider the prevalence of undiagnosed dissociative identity disorder among psychiatric inpatients. Eight studies including six in North America, one in Turkey and one in Norway indicate that 5% of general adult inpatients have undiagnosed dissociative identity disorder which can be detected with structured diagnostic interviews, either the Dissociative Disorders Interview Schedule (Ross, 1997) or the Structured Clinical Interview for DSM-IV-TR Dissociative Disorders (Steinberg, 1995). These are individuals who are not claiming that they have dissociative identity disorder, and who have never been told by a clinician that they have the disorder. Other research (Ross, 1997) indicates that at the time of initial diagnosis with the Dissociative Disorders Interview Schedule, subjects with dissociative identity disorder report the extensive childhood physical and sexual abuse typical of cases in treatment.

One private for-profit psychiatric hospital chain in the United States, Charter Medical Corporation, admitted 120,000 individuals to its adult inpatient facilities in a single year, according to its 1996 annual report. This would mean that 6,000 individuals with undiagnosed dissociative identity disorder were admitted to the Charter system in that year. This is only a fraction of the inpatient treatment provided in the country, however. If we consider the Charter caseload alone, and cancel the dissociative identity disorder diagnoses, we are still left with 6,000 patients who meet criteria for an average of thirteen Axis I and II disorders lifetime. If we consider the fact that the undiagnosed dissociative identity disorder group are only a subset of the inpatients with chronic, complex comorbidity, we encounter a serious arithmetical problem.

If psychiatric disorders are separate biomedical conditions, then, given their prevalence rates in the general population, less than one person on the planet should have the degree of comorbidity characteristic of dissociative identity disorder. In violation of the biomedical model, we can extrapolate from the existing data to the conservative conclusion that 6,000 individuals of this type are admitted to one hospital system in one country each year. It is clear that no matter how conservatively we make our assumptions, the arithmetic refutes the biomedical model.

An unavoidable conclusion follows: we require a paradigm shift in psychiatry. Although there may be separate genes or gene regions for some cases of some psychiatric disorders, from a public health perspective comorbidity which consumes major amounts of health care resources per year cannot be accounted for by the single gene-single disease model. This is true no matter how much the single gene model is modified in terms of multiple loci, partial penetrance and other postulates.

It is always instructive to look at psychiatric problems from a medical perspective. Let's assume that inflammation of the conjunctiva, arthritis of the knee and painful urination (dysuria) are separate biomedical problems. If that is true, they should co-occur at the product of their baseline rates in the general population. Why, then, do some specialists see many more cases per year than should occur in their catchment area?

The answer is simple from a medical perspective. Although all three of these conditions can occur as separate disorders, they can all be symptoms of gonorrhea. The basic treatment for all three when they co-occur due to gonorrhea is penicillin. In medical terminology, penicillin is *rational* treatment because it is based on a scientific understanding of the cause of the clinical syndrome and the mechanism of action of the treatment.

Similarly, when I was in medical school, I never saw a single case of either Kaposi's sarcoma, pneumocystis pneumonia or acquired immunodeficiency. All three disorders, I was taught, were extremely rare.

A family physician might not see a single case of either three diseases in an entire career. Now, all medical students, interns and residents see all three of these disorders, and in AIDS clinics they co-occur in the same patient. Based on the epidemiology of these disorders up until 1981, when I graduated from medical school, not a single doctor in North America should see all three conditions in the same patient.

What is the solution for the problem of comorbidity in medicine? When conditions that can occur as separate disorders co-occur in the same patients at levels high above chance, it is evident that a common etiology accounts for their co-occurrence in the affected individuals. The causes of isolated arthritis of the knee are myriad. When arthritis of the knee co-occurs with conjunctivitis and dysuria, the medical student is taught to suspect a common etiological agent, namely the gonococcus. Similarly in the AIDS patient, the common theme is the HIV virus.

When we see extensive comorbidity in medicine, we look for a common environmental agent driving the symptomatology. Most often the identified etiological agent is an infectious organism or a toxin. For instance, patients I saw with lead encepalopathy from sniffing gasoline presented with neurological and psychological problems involving many different areas of the brain. The treatment for all these symptoms was chelation therapy. From a medical perspective, our initial assumption should be that the solution to the problem of comorbidity in psychiatry lies in environmental input, not in the genome. Lead encephalopathy is the genetically normal response of the organism to high blood lead levels.

In psychiatry there is no model to account for the problem of comorbidity, yet extensive comorbidity is a pressing fact of daily life in psychiatric hospitals and academic Departments of Psychiatry. Several other facts further undermine the single gene theory of psychiatric disorders, and make the need for a solution to the problem of comorbidity more urgent. This is because, absent the gene theory, there is no model of any kind under serious consideration in mainstream academic psychiatry to account for major mental illness.

Take schizophrenia as an example. It is accepted as scientific fact in psychiatry that schizophrenia is a biomedical disorder with a genetic basis. In round figures, it is also accepted that only 10% of schizophrenics have an affected relative, only 45% of affected monozygotic twins have an affected co-twin, and only 10% of children and siblings of an affected individual have the disorder. These figures tell us immediately that schizophrenia is not a classical Mendelian disorder. If it was caused by either a recessive or a dominant gene, concordance in monozygotic twins would be 100%.

If schizophrenia was caused by a dominant gene, half the children of an affected individual would have the disorder, and if by a recessive gene, one quarter. Everyone is agreed that if it exists, the genetic cause of schizophrenia must be polygenetic, modified by partial penetrance, or be in some other ways variable and complex.

It is important to consider the fertility rate of schizophrenics. Again in rounded, ballpark figures, we can agree that schizophrenics reproduce at 20% the rate of the general population. If schizophrenia is inherited, there is a problem. Consider the number of schizophrenia genes present among a population of great-great grandparents. In the great grandparental generation these genes should have been diluted by 80% due to differential reproduction rates. In the grand parents, the prevalence of the genes should be 4% and in the parents it should be under 1%. The prevalence of schizophrenia in the general population should drop by 99% within four generations.

Yet, the epidemiology tells us, the lifetime prevalence of schizophrenia is stable worldwide at about 1%. If we run the numbers in reverse, they become even more absurd. If the lifetime expectancy for schizophrenia is 1% in people currently under 18 years of age, then it must be 4% in their parents, 20% in their grandparents, 100% in their great grandparents, and in one more generations going backwards it must be over 100%.

When psychiatrists and molecular biologists do studies of large samples in order to find high density pedigrees for gene mapping, they have great difficulty finding pedigrees with more than two affected members. This follows logically from the fact that only 10% of siblings of an affected individual are themselves affected. Only 1% of schizophrenics should have two affected siblings, and only one in a thousand should have three affected siblings. Since the rates for other relatives are lower than for siblings, it is very difficult to find high density pedigrees.

In medical school I spent several hours in a cystic fibrosis clinic one afternoon. I remember one mother telling me that she did not consider herself unfortunate because another mother in her support group had two children with cystic fibrosis. Common sense tells us that the ease of finding high density pedigrees for cystic fibrosis, compared to the great time, energy and expense required to find high density pedigrees for schizophrenia is evidence against the preponderance of the genetic component to the etiology of the schizophrenia.

Another problem arises from the patterns of comorbidity in the first degree relatives of schizophrenics, individuals with mood disorders, and controls (Taylor, Berenbaum, Jampala, and Cloninger, 1993). Studies consistently find that the rates of mood disorder and schizophrenia are equally elevated in the relatives of both clinical groups, and higher in the relatives of both clinical groups than among relatives of controls. What seems to breed true, if anything, is not individual DSM-IV-TR disorders, but a general predisposition to major mental illness. The symptom profile of the major mental illness is highly polymorphous.

Another consistent finding in psychiatric research is relevant to the problem of comorbidity, and cannot be accounted for by the biomedical model in its current form. When the index disorder is borderline personality disorder (Zanarini, Frankenburg, Dubo, Sickel, Trikha, Levin, and Reynolds, 1998), posttraumatic stress disorder (Engdahl, Dikel, Eberly, and Blank, 1998), or dissociative identity disorder, the *norm* is high levels of comorbidity. A tiny minority of affected individuals have the disorder in pure form, with no diagnosable comorbidity. For instance, among 379 patients with borderline personality disorder, and 107 individuals with dissociative identity disorder, comorbidity rates were as shown in Table 4.2.

Table 4.2 Lifetime Comorbidity in Borderline Personality Disorder (BPD) and Dissociative Identity Disorder (DID)

Disorder	BPD %	DID %
	(N=379)	(N=107)
Mood	96.3	97.2
Anxiety	88.4	89.7
Posttraumatic Stress	55.9	80.0
Substance Abuse	64.1	65.4
Borderline Personality	100.0	56.3
Eating	53.0	38.3
Somatoform	10.3	43.9
Dissociative	-	100.0

The only missing data from Table 4.2 is the prevalence of dissociative disorders in the borderline group. In both studies, the SCID was used to assess comorbidity, and the SCID does not make dissociative diagnoses.

One would have to postulate from the data, however, that the rate of comorbid dissociative disorders in borderline personality disorder is not less than 65%. Given the highly similar patterns of comorbidity in these two populations, attempts at differentiation of etiological models for the two disorders are unlikely to be productive.

Within the dominant conceptual system of late twentieth century psychiatry, there is only one way to account for the problem of comorbidity. One of the disorders is arbitrarily assigned the status of primary disorder and the other disorders are defined as secondary and comorbid. Thus, Zanarini et al (1998) write that, "the number of multiple and shifting comorbid axis I disorders commonly experienced by borderline patients made it difficult for clinicians to accurately diagnose and ultimately treat the underlying personality pathology. In contrast, our data indicate that the pattern of complex lifetime axis I comorbidity evidenced by borderline patients is a useful marker for their borderline diagnosis."

This way of looking at the problem defines borderline personality as the underlying problem, and defines the Axis I disorders as "markers." The question left unanswered is, "What is borderline personality disorder a marker of?"

An alternative viewpoint is that borderline personality disorder is an epiphenomenon of untreated mood disorders. In the extensively comorbid patient, if depression is assumed to be the primary problem, the question becomes, what is the depression a marker of? Within the biomedical model, the answer is, "A gene for depression."

The genetic solution to the problem of comorbidity is untenable, for the reasons given above. Since the problem of comorbidity is so pressing clinically, economically, and scientifically, and since no alternative model is under serious consideration within academic psychiatry, the trauma model becomes the potential driver of a paradigm shift in psychiatry.

II.   ASSUMPTIONS OF THE TRAUMA MODEL

5

NATURE VERSUS NURTURE

In biological terms, human life consists of an interaction between the genome and the environment. Within contemporary biology, it is assumed that the genome is the fundamental driver of the organism. This biological reductionism has been accepted in the popular culture and in psychiatry. Newspapers carry announcements that a gene has been found for obesity, attention deficit disorder, schizophrenia, anxiety, breast cancer and countless other ills of human kind. Psychiatry draws its biomedical model from the general genetic-reductionist model in biology. Your genes cause you to have two hands, one head, two legs and schizophrenia. The fortunate thing is that not everyone has the gene for schizophrenia.

From a public health point of view, specific genes for specific diseases account for a minute fraction of the morbidity and mortality in the general population. I remember being amazed in medical school when I actually went on the wards and saw real patients. I had been taught a great deal about rare diseases and their differential diagnosis, but that is not what I saw on the wards. The wards were full of the long-term complications of cigarette smoking, alcoholism and failure to take insulin regularly. If we eliminated cigarettes, alcohol and the HIV virus from the general population, there would be a lot of empty beds in the teaching hospitals today. If, in addition, we eliminated obesity and everyone with diabetes and hypertension was compliant with their medication, doctors would face an employment crisis.

The bioreductionist might object that there is a gene or genes for obesity. This theory can be disproven by taking an airplane from Dallas to Amsterdam. Why would the gene for obesity be present at a higher frequency in the Caucasian population of Dallas than in the capitals of Europe? The higher rate of obesity in Dallas than in Amsterdam is obvious from a few minutes observation of both populations. Let's not forget that the rates of obesity have sky-rocketed in the United States over the last thirty years, although there has been no significant change in the genome in North America.

Well, the bioreductionist might argue, there is a gene for obesity, but it isn't expressed in environments that lack excessive money and fast food. If one accepted this argument, it would follow that the gene for obesity has no biological meaning in the absence of its environmental promoter.

The biology of obesity is very different from the biology of cystic fibrosis or Huntington's chorea. The individual who is genetically doomed to get either of those diseases is 100% doomed independently of experience or environment. The problem with the biomedical model in psychiatry is that it is trying to force psychiatric disorders into the biology of cystic fibrosis and Huntington's chorea. A similar problem applies to the gene for obesity. Even if such a gene exists, the emergence of the phenotype depends absolutely on an environmental promoter. Even the most die-hard genetic reductionist would presumably concede that the obese phenotype can exist in the absence of a specific gene for obesity. The gene for obesity, it follows from this concession and the above logic, is neither a necessary nor a sufficient cause of the obese phenotype.

Compare this to the situation with cystic fibrosis, the genetics of which are scientifically understood. Cystic fibrosis is a genetically determined autosomal recessive disease. There are no arguments or disputes about this point in medicine. What about lung cancer? I was taught in medical school that smoking markedly increases one's risk for lung cancer. Not all smokers get lung cancer and not all people with lung cancer are smokers. It is a matter of increased risk. In one lecture I was taught that a heavy smoker who works in a uranium mine has a risk of lung cancer 800 times the rate in the general population. In a physics of the environment course, I learned that less than one millionth of a gram of plutonium is sufficient to cause lung cancer in virtually everyone, if the plutonium is inhaled as dust.

Why are molecular biologists not searching for the genes for lung cancer or heart attacks in the way psychiatrists are searching for the gene for schizophrenia? Because that is not how the *biology* works in lung cancer or myocardial infarction. There is no gene for lung cancer causing the disease of the heavy-smoking uranium mine worker. It is obvious to everyone that the uranium worker's lung cancer is caused by an interaction between his normal genome and the environment. It would be biologically absurd to postulate the existence of a lung cancer genotype in heavy-smoking uranium miners with the lung cancer phenotype.

Imagine that we eliminated carcinogens, allergens, bacteria, viruses, moulds, fungi, street drugs, alcohol, cigarettes, unhealthy food and physical trauma from the environment. In addition, the population exercised regularly and was compliant with all prescriptions. Who would be coming into the emergency department? There wouldn't be enough people with single diseases caused by single genes to keep the emergency department open. The people with single gene diseases would still need doctors, but how often do people come to the emergency department with a *genetic* emergency?

The biomedical model in psychiatry regards human beings as genetically programmed machines. As far as major mental illness is concerned, the environment is allowed to modify gene expression only to a minor degree. From a public health perspective, this doesn't make any medical sense. Why? Because, if we coined the term *major medical illness*, the overwhelming role of the environment in major medical illness is obvious.

There is a problem with the fundamental genetic model in biology. The genome is assumed to be the primary controller reading out a predetermined outcome. But this cannot be how the biology actually works. In the absence of environmental instructions, the genome would be meaningless and inert. The genome is absolutely dependent on the environment for its purpose. Without an environment to adapt to, there wouldn't be anything for the genome to do. The AT, GC base pairs would be biologically inert without environmental input.

It is as if we have become culturally mesmerized by the mantra of *genes*. Without an environment, genes could not activate themselves. We think of the genes as little human beings sitting in small racecars. We think that the genes make decisions, control themselves and their vehicle, and are the drivers of the system. The genes have become God. But they are not. Genes are just sequences of AT, GC base pairs. They are no more in control of life than the atoms in a crystal are in control of the crystalline structure. The crystalline structure is absolutely dependent on environmental conditions for its actualization. Similarly with the DNA.

What does this reasoning have to do with the problem of comorbidity and the trauma model? Consider panic disorder. Imagine that there is a gene for panic disorder. How could such a gene evolve in the absence of environmental danger? How would the gene ever be selected for or activated?

The answer, from the bioreductionist perspective, is that panic attacks are caused by an abnormal gene. The evidence that panic disorder is genetic, the bioreductionist might argue, is in part the existence of spontaneous panic attacks which are not environmentally cued. The whole point is that the panic attacks have no realistic environmental meaning. That is why they are pathological. If one accepts the postulates of the bioreductionist model, this appears to be a compelling argument. However, it is refuted by the relationship between panic attacks and panic disorder.

Consider the epidemiology of panic attacks in the general population (Walker, Norton, and Ross, 1991). In surveys, about one quarter of college students report having had a panic attack in the last month, and one third a panic attack in the last year. The distribution of panic attacks is continuous, not bimodal. Many people have a few panic attacks, some have quite a few, and fewer have many. It is not true that there are two distinct groups of people in nature, occasional and frequent spontaneous panickers.

The bioreductionist argument from spontaneous panic attacks hinges on a distinction between spontaneous and cued panic attacks. For spontaneous panic attacks to be clinical evidence of a causative single gene, or region or cluster of genes, the cued panic attacks must be epiphenomena of the spontaneous ones, explicable by behavioral and learning principles. If the distinction between cued and spontaneous panic attacks is retracted, there is no longer a phenomenological reason to postulate the existence of a specific causative gene. Why? Because, absent the distinction, all panic attacks have been conceded to be explicable by behavioral learning principles.

Let us retain the distinction and see where it leads. If spontaneous panic attacks are caused by an abnormal gene, the gene is present in at least half of the population, since this is a conservative estimate of the lifetime prevalence of spontaneous panic attacks. The question then arises, why do some people experience more spontaneous panic attacks than others? This can easily be accounted for by variable gene penetrance. From this explanation, another problem arises.

We have already been logically compelled to retain the spontaneous-cued distinction and concede that cued panic attacks are epiphenomena explicable by behavioral learning principles. We are now stuck with the conclusion that the DSM-IV-TR disease of panic disorder is defined by a biologically arbitrary degree of gene penetrance. This arbitrary degree of penetrance has no scientific or numerical properties because all that is required by DSM-IV-TR rules is "recurrent unexpected Panic Attacks." What is the threshold for "recurrent," once a decade, once a year, once a month, or once a week?

By DSM-IV-TR rules, panic disorder cannot exist without secondary cognitive-behavioral epiphenomena such as anticipatory anxiety and behavioral change. From a genetic point of view, these diagnostic criteria are biologically unrelated to the postulated gene for panic disorder. They would also occur in panic disorder caused by hyperthyroidism and in iatrogenic drug-induced panic disorder; in both those conditions, there is no reason to assume the existence of a genotype for panic attacks.

The analysis becomes even more compelling when we consider the fact that agoraphobia is entirely epiphenomenal from the perspective of the single gene for panic attacks. What makes one person with a given frequency of spontaneous panic attacks develop panic disorder, then agoraphobia, when another person with the same frequency of attacks develops none of the secondary cognitive-behavioral phenomena required to make the DSM-IV-TR diagnosis? The explanation must lie outside the postulated gene for panic attacks.

The bioreductionist is now compelled to postulate the existence of one gene for spontaneous panic attacks and a second gene for the phobic response to panic attacks. The second gene must also have varying degrees of penetrance. It is biologically absurd to suggest that a phenomenon as complex as the cognitive-behavioral response to panic attacks of the individual meeting DSM-IV-TR criteria for panic disorder with agoraphobia is controlled by anything less than dozens of genes. We have just destroyed the single gene theory of panic disorder.

Another problem must be solved by anyone who wishes to rehabilitate the genetic theory of panic disorder. If panic disorder is caused by a gene, why is it treatable with cognitive-behavioral therapy? This fact is absolutely incompatible with the theory that panic disorder is driven inexorably by an abnormal gene. If we assume a single specific gene with a fully activated phenotype, the expression of the gene can be turned off by talking. It follows that psychotherapy can directly modify gene expression.

Here we have a cosmic joke on the bioreductionists. The assumption of a specific gene for panic attacks has forced us to the conclusion that psychotherapy can turn off genes which have previously been activated by endogenous biological mechanisms. The assumption that the panic attack gene has been turned on by endogenous biological variables controlled by the genome is essential to the bioeductionist model, for panic disorder, depression, schizophrenia, and all other mental disorders.

I am perfectly happy to accept the conclusion that psychotherapy directly regulates gene expression. One can assume that this conclusion is distasteful to bioreductionists, who must now counter the above logic and arguments.

From a trauma model perspective, there is really no problem with the theory that psychiatric disorders can be caused by single genes. If one assumes the existence of such genes, they can be activated by endogenous biological mechanisms. This could be the case in disorders which occur by themselves without serious comorbidity. However, the argument concerning panic disorder leads to the conclusion that the genotype can be rendered phenotypically silent by psychotherapy. One is forced to conclude that other environmental inputs besides psychotherapy could have the same effect. These might include self-help, falling in love, and having a good marriage.

Once one assumes that the phenotype can be turned off by the environment, it follows that it can also be turned on by the environment. This is the assumption of the trauma model. The trauma model does not require the existence of single genes for single disorders, but can accommodate them if they exist in nature. As we saw in earlier chapters, however, the problem of comorbidity cannot be solved by the biomedical model in its current form. Therefore the biomedical model is a subset of the trauma model.

Rather than nature *versus* nurture, the trauma model is based on a postulate of nature *with* nurture. Our culture is based on a reductionist solution to Cartesian dualism (Ross, 1995). Modern science has divided the universe into dissociated body and mind, then defined mind as a trivial epiphenomenon of the brain. We have repeated this logic with the genome and made it the ghost driving the machine: mind is controlled by brain in a unidirectional, reductionist causality; genome controls biology in a similar fashion. That is why biologists talk about discovering the "secret of life" through mapping the genome.

The Human Genome Project cannot provide an explanation of the genetics of major mental illness, because the genome has biological meaning only in the genome-environment interaction. The environment controls the genome as much as the genome controls the environment; the two polar realities speak distinct languages and depend on translators in the cell membrane and in the intracellular space to communicate.

The problem with the bioreductionism in contemporary psychiatry is not philosophical, it is biological. That is not how the *biology* works. Forcing the genetics of major mental illness into the cystic fibrosis model will never work scientifically. The trauma model assumes an infinitely complex set of multidirectional feedback loops in the conversation between genome and environment. The following two statements are equally incorrect: trauma causes posttraumatic stress disorder; the genome causes posttraumatic stress disorder. Neither the genome nor the environment are sufficient alone, though both are necessary.

A statistical model which converts concordance rates for schizophrenia of 46% for monozygotic twins and 9% for dizygotic twins into an 83% genetic causation of schizophrenia is biologically mistaken. That simply isn't the way the biology works. It is not a matter of a trauma model *versus* a biological model. The trauma model is itself a biological model. It must be, because mind and brain are a unified field in nature. According to the trauma model, experience has a profound effect on the structure and function of the brain. This effect is modulated in part through the genome. W.B. Yeats asked how we can tell the dancer from the dance. The trauma model answer is, we can't. The dance is the interaction between genome and environment, and we are the dancers.

Consider the situation with smallpox. How did the antibody for smallpox evolve? There is a high degree of redundancy in the immune system. There was never a pre-existing specific gene for smallpox antibody production waiting for the smallpox virus to come along. There was a gene for antibody production that happened to manufacture an antibody capable of binding the smallpox virus. This gene was selected for by the environment in two ways: individuals who had the gene survived better; and individuals who produced a better-binding antibody survived better. There was a genetic drift in favor of a more and more specific smallpox antibody.

Now that there is no smallpox virus in the environment, the gene has no function. It is biologically inert and meaningless. People who have not been vaccinated for smallpox do not have circulating smallpox antibodies. The gene has been turned off. Through evolution it will either remain as a biologically silent section of the genome, or drift into production of a different antibody. The control of whether the gene exists, and whether it is activated and has a biological function, is absolutely in the hands of the environment. Similar logic applies in psychiatry.

6

THE SCIENTIFIC STATUS OF DISSOCIATION

The status of anxiety, mood, substance abuse, and psychotic disorders within psychiatry is not in doubt. These categories of mental disorder are accepted as legitimate without question, and each is the subject of single gene-single disease theories. The same is not true for the dissociative disorders. Since dissociation is a core feature of the trauma response, the scientific status of dissociation must be clarified in order to provide a firm foundation for the trauma model.

The word *dissociation* has many usages within psychiatry, some of them quite vague. At times, dissociation and repression are regarded as synonyms, at other times they are separate concepts. The word *repression* does not appear anywhere in DSM-IV-TR. Dissociation is a category of disorder and a symptom descriptor in DSM-IV-TR, while repression is a core concept in psychoanalytical theory. The different meanings of the words dissociation and repression are summarized in Table 6.1

Table 6.1. Different Meanings of Dissociation and Repression

Repression	An ego defense against impulses and wishes
Repression	An ego defense against conflict and trauma involving horizontal splitting
Dissociation	An ego defense against conflict and trauma involving vertical splitting
Dissociation	An operational definition embedded in valid and reliable measures of dissociation
Dissociation	A technical term in cognitive psychology
Dissociation	A general term in many sciences, used to describe dissociation between variables, eg. A dissociative constant.
Dissociation	A descriptive, phenomenological term in DSM-IV

Repression is a postulated intrapsychic defense mechanism within Freudian theory. As formulated, it is not scientifically testable. Confusion arises because, within psychoanalytic theory, repression has two separate meanings. Historically, Freud subscribed to a trauma model early in his career, as exemplified by *Studies on Hysteria* (Breuer and Freud, 1986/1895). Freud held that the cause of his patient's dissociative, mood, anxiety and other symptoms was childhood sexual abuse. Subsequent to *Studies on Hysteria*, he decided that the abuse histories were false memories. He repudiated the seduction theory.

Freud was now faced with a problem. Why did so many female patients present with a complex array of symptoms and false memories of childhood sexual abuse? His answer? Repression. It is when repression theory is correct that the memories are false. Repression is an ego defense against unacceptable id drives. The defense is only partially effective, and the unacceptable id drives break through as false memories of incest. The false memories are an expression of oedipal desires to have intercourse with the father.

Repression theory, in this sense, is an ego defense against internal drives, wishes and conflicts. It has little or nothing to do with sensory input or external experience. Repression in this sense is an unnecessary postulate for the trauma model.

However, there is the second meaning of repression. Repression is also a defense against traumatic events. Memory, affect and cognition about the event are repressed into the unconscious, where they are inaccessible to conscious recollection. In this meaning, repression is a defense for coping with trauma and the events are assumed to be real. This second meaning of repression is incompatible with the repudiation of the seduction theory.

Dissociation, as the term is used in the dissociative disorders field in the late twentieth century, is not a synonym for the first meaning of repression. What about the second meaning of repression? Like repression, the word dissociation has several meanings. In one meaning, dissociation is a postulated intrapsychic defense mechanism harnessed to cope with trauma. In this meaning, dissociation could potentially be a synonym for repression. However, even here, dissociation is a distinct concept from repression (Hilgard, 1977).

In one of its two psychoanalytical meanings, repression is a postulated unconscious intrapsychic defense mechanism in which material unacceptable to the ego is pushed down into the id, or unconscious mind. The material is pushed down across a horizontal split in the psyche between ego and id. This defensive action is called *horizontal splitting*.

As a postulated intrapsychic defense mechanism, dissociation involves *vertical splitting*. Material unacceptable to the ego is pushed laterally across a vertical barrier into a dissociated compartment of the ego. It is never lost to the ego as a whole, and is never repressed into the unconscious (Hilgard, 1977). Dissociation is not a synonym of repression even in psychoanalytical theory.

What, then, are the scientific meanings of the word dissociation? These are several. First, dissociation is a descriptive and phenomenological term in DSM-IV-TR. The dissociative disorders section is not based on a theoretical defense mechanism. The DSM-IV-TR meaning of dissociation is as scientific, observable and testable as any other term in the DSM system. Dissociation is an *observed phenomenon* and a *reported symptom*. It is not a theory or personal belief.

Consider the wording of the amnesia criterion for dissociative amnesia in DSM-IV-TR: "inability to recall important personal information, usually of a traumatic or stressful nature, that is too extensive to be explained by ordinary forgetfulness." Exclusion criteria stipulate that this cannot be organic amnesia. DSM-IV-TR dissociative amnesia is a reported symptom with two major possible explanations ruled out: organic brain damage and ordinary forgetfulness. There is no statement of any preferred or necessary mechanism.

The logic of dissociative amnesia in DSM-IV-TR is exactly parallel to the logic of conversion disorder. In a conversion disorder, the patient reports anesthesia. An organic cause is ruled out and, "Psychological factors are judged to be associated with the symptom or deficit because the situation or exacerbation of the symptom or deficit is preceded by conflicts or other stressors."

A conversion paralysis makes the point more clearly. The patient is unable to move his arm. The clinician observes this to be the case. The arm is not moving. Why? The clinician rules out organic causes and makes a judgment that the symptom is causally related to antecedent stress. In DSM-IV-TR, trauma is severe stress, and stress is mild trauma. The clinician does not make a diagnosis of conversion disorder based on a personal belief or a theory that the patient's arm cannot move. The conversion paralysis is a clinical observation made with 100% inter-rater reliability.

In more subtle cases, where there is a symptom but no sign, as in dissociative amnesia and conversion anesthesia, the same logic prevails. Almost all DSM-IV-TR diagnoses depend on symptoms. In medicine, symptoms are subjective reports by the patient, while signs are objective and observed by the physician. There are more symptoms than signs in psychiatry. How do we know our patients are really hearing voices, experiencing obsessive thoughts, having delusions, or feeling sad? Because they tell us so. A patient may look sad, anxious, or insane, but this is not required for the diagnosis. How many diagnosticians have actually watched a patient with bulimia throw up, an alcoholic drink, or a compulsive hand washer washing hands? Direct observation of the behavior is not required by the rules of DSM-IV-TR or accepted standards of clinical care.

Decisions to start, stop and change medications are routinely made solely on the basis of patient report. The diagnosis of bipolar mood disorder, for instance, and the decision to start lithium, are routinely made in cases where prior manic episodes have never been observed directly by a psychiatrist or collateral historian. Of course, it is always desirable to obtain collateral history, but such external corroboration is not required in routine practice. Nor is it required by the rules of the DSM system. Within the trauma model, dissociative symptoms are held to this common standard. They are reported symptoms. That is what psychiatrists work with.

In science, one starts with an observation. One then develops a hypothesis. The next step is to design and conduct a test of the hypothesis. The test of the hypothesis is called an experiment. Data are gathered and analyzed, and the hypothesis is confirmed or disconfirmed. The hypothesis may be rejected, accepted or modified as a result of the experiment.

Dissociation, in its DSM-IV-TR meaning, is not a theory or hypothesis, it is an observation. The observation is made by the same rules that apply to anxiety, mood, substance abuse and psychotic disorders. Pathological dissociation is a field of scientific study in the same way and to the same degree as any other symptom cluster in psychiatry.

The second meaning of dissociation is the operationalized definition of dissociation imbedded in self-report measures such as the Dissociative Experiences Scale, and structured interviews such as the Dissociative Disorders Interview Schedule and the Structured Clinical Interview for DSM-IV-TR Dissociative Disorders (Ross, 1997). These measures have been the subject of federal research grants, hundreds of peer-reviewed professional papers, and much statistical analysis. The clinical measurement of pathological dissociation is carried out by the same scientific rules and standards as the scientific measurement of anxiety, depression, psychosis, and substance abuse.

The third meaning of dissociation is a technical term in cognitive psychology. Dissociation in this sense is one of the most robust, proven and rigorously demonstrated phenomena in cognitive psychology. The phenomenon has been called *dissociation* in cognitive psychology for decades (Cohen and Eichenbaum, 1993). Again, it is a phenomenon, not a theory, belief or postulate.

The form of dissociation most relevant to DSM-IV-TR is dissociation between procedural and declarative memory. For this to take place, procedural and declarative memory must be separate subsystems, a fact proven by an enormous literature in many different species, and within many different experimental paradigms. In a biologically trivial example, a complete dissociation between procedural and declarative memory is observed after surgical removal of the hippocampus.

If procedural and declarative memory are regarded as modules, in general two modules can be dissociated from each other for an infinite number of reasons. A known mechanism for dissociation between modules is inactivation of one module. The inactivation can be due to surgical destruction of brain tissue, but need not be. A module could in principle be inactivated by medication, the action of some other module, simple error, motivated forgetting, or countless other mechanisms. Genes are chromosomal modules, and may be dissociated from each other due to inactivation of one module.

Dissociation between procedural and declarative memory has also been demonstrated experimentally in the normal brain. *Repetition priming* is the classical proof of dissociation between intact procedural and declarative memory. In a typical repetition priming experiment, subjects are presented with lists of homophonic word pairs such as *read-read* and *bare-bear*. Subjects memorize the list but are later unable to remember *read-reed* in a free recall trial. In clinical terminology, they have amnesia for that word pair. The mechanism of the amnesia is irrelevant to a demonstration of the reality of the phenomenon.

Subjects are then asked to write down the name of a tall, thin, tubular aquatic plant that grows in marshes. Subjects who have been primed with the *read-reed* word pair more often spell *reed* incorrectly as *read* than do control subjects who have memorized word lists that do not include that word pair. Although this is a small phenomenon, its size is irrelevant. It is an absolute scientific fact that dissociation between procedural and declarative memory takes place in the normal human brain. This is proven within many different experimental paradigms which tap many different tasks and areas of the brain. Information can be registered and stored accurately in procedural memory, and can be having a measurable effect on behavior and verbal output in the complete absence of declarative memory of that information.

The experimental evidence for the reality of dissociation between procedural and declarative memory is conclusive. Of course, numerous questions remain about the quantity of memory that can be dissociated, the degree to which it can influence behavior, the limits on accurate retrieval of the memory, and the mechanisms involved.

The best general definition of dissociation is the least technical one. Dissociation is the opposite of association. When two things are in association, they are connected with each other, interacting, or in relationship with each other. When two things are dissociated from each other, they are compartmentalized, disconnected, or out of relationship with each other. Both association and dissociation can be normal or pathological. Both can be caused by myriad different mechanisms. Both are pervasive aspects of normal and pathological brain function.

Dissociation in the general sense is an accepted fact in the scientific community. It occurs in the genome, in physical chemistry, and everywhere in nature. Dissociation is a phenomenological term in DSM-IV-TR, an operationalized term in the clinical measurement literature, and a proven fact in cognitive psychology. That is why dissociation can be admitted to the trauma model.

Confusion may arise when a clear distinction is not made between the phenomenon of dissociation and the postulated intrapsychic defense mechanism of dissociation. The defense mechanism of dissociation is only one of many possible causes of the phenomenon of dissociation.

In summary, dissociation and repression are not synonyms. Repression, and with it the entire edifice of psychoanalytical theory, could be rejected completely, and this would have no effect on the established scientific validity of dissociation. Likewise, the dissociative disorders do not require repression theory for their diagnosis or treatment. Repression theory can be evoked by psychoanalysts to explain the dissociative disorders, but this is true for virtually all disorders in the DSM system.

Dissociation is a proven phenomenon in cognitive psychology, and measures of pathological dissociation have well established reliability and validity, based on the same rules and criteria applied to the measurement of anxiety, depression, psychosis, and substance abuse.

7

THE PROBLEM OF FALSE MEMORIES

The problem of comorbidity is a pressing clinical fact. It is part of the day in and day out workload of the inpatient psychiatrist. How do we know that the problem of comorbidity exists? Because we observe it in the clinic. In addition, there is a clinical research literature which confirms the existence of the problem.

In order for the trauma model to solve the problem of comorbidity, there must be evidence that the trauma actually occurred. Since memory is error-prone, inexact and reconstructive in nature, the accuracy of an uncorroborated memory is always in doubt. Normal memory is influenced by myriad biological and social-psychological variables (Bremner and Marmer, 1998; Brown, Scheflin, and Hammond, 1998; Lynn and McKonkey, 1998; Pezdek and Banks, 1996; Spanos, 1996; Spiegel, 1997). There is no reason to assume that traumatic memory is more accurate than memory of mundane events, in fact the reverse. The trauma model assumes that traumatic memory is more error-prone, fragmented, distorted and damaged than normal memory (van der Kolk, McFarlane, and Weisaeth, 1996). Therefore the problem of false memories must be addressed in trauma model research.

Traumatic memory can be artificially divided into two separate categories for the purposes of discussion. A trauma memory may be continuously present or hidden behind an amnesia barrier. "Amnesia barrier" is a clinical metaphor and does not necessarily imply any special mechanism beyond those of normal psychology, for instance the mechanisms operating in repetition priming. There is no scientific evidence that continuously held trauma memories are more or less accurate than memories which have been recovered. Nor is there any scientific evidence concerning the relative accuracy of spontaneously recovered memories versus those recovered due to therapeutic procedures.

A confabulated memory may be mistaken clinically for a recovered memory. There is no procedure to differentiate confabulation from accurate memory recovery at the clinical level. Recovered memories of extensive trauma can be corroborated and proven to be accurate (Kluft, 1998), and yet there is no limit to the amount of trauma memory that can be confabulated (Ross, 1994). The reversed amnesia for trauma reported by Kluft (1998) is too extensive to be explained by ordinary forgetting.

In reality, there is no such thing as a continuously held memory. Normal memory involves the repeated loss and recovery of information. The term *amnesia* is used when ordinary recall effort cannot retrieve a memory that would ordinarily be retrievable, such as a rape the previous week. By definition, for dissociative amnesia to be present the memory must be stored accurately but be inaccessible to ordinary recall effort. But what is ordinary recall effort? And what are flashbacks? It is a paradox of traumatic memory that events cannot be recalled by conscious effort but at the same time intrude involuntarily. How is it that a memory cannot be recalled by conscious effort yet intrudes involuntarily? We have a very crude scientific understanding of how traumatic memory works, and how it does not work.

If a memory is not potentially recoverable, dissociative amnesia is not present. One would speak of organic amnesia or normal forgetting. But how unrecoverable is unrecoverable? How much recall effort must be expended before we reach the limits of ordinary recall effort? The situation only becomes clear when we consider the clear clinical case. In the absence of physical or drug-induced causes, amnesia for a rape the previous week is clearly an example of dissociative amnesia, using *dissociative* in its phenomenological sense. Such amnesia cannot be explained by ordinary forgetting.

Through spontaneous processes, in response to the general processes of therapy, or in response to specific therapeutic procedures, the memory of the rape may be recovered. This recovered memory could be mostly accurate, partly accurate, or completely confabulated. In the latter case it is technically a confabulation not a recovered memory, but this distinction is moot without external corroborative or disconfirming evidence. The phenomenon could be called memory recovery, cued retrieval, amnesia reversal, de-repression, or cognitive avoidance reversal. Although the terms chosen have different connotations and ideological loadings, the phenomenon under study is reversal of dissociative amnesia. Dissociative amnesia is defined phenomenologically in DSM-IV-TR.

There is no way to tell clinically whether a given recovered memory is true or false. The scientific facts cut both ways. Except for impossible memories, such as a memory of being decapitated, there is no way to tell on clinical grounds whether a memory is true or false. One cannot conclude that a memory is false anymore than one can conclude it is true. There are no clinical criteria which can make the differentiation in either direction. This is also true of so-called continuously held memories.

Clinical criteria which cannot make the differentiation include: plausibility or implausibility; amount of detail; degree of narrative coherence; subjective conviction or disbelief in therapist or patient of the reality of the memory; similarity or dissimilarity of the memory to externally confirmed or disconfirmed events; accompanying affect or physiological arousal; consistency or inconsistency from session to session; honesty or dishonesty of the patient; improvement or deterioration of the patient in any time frame; accompanying body language; similarity or dissimilarity to other patient reports; and presence or absence of secondary gain. This list of criteria is repeated in Table 7.1.

Table 7.1 Clinical Variables Which Cannot Differentiate Accurate From Inaccurate Memories

Plausible	Vs	Implausible
Detailed	Vs	Vague
Coherent	Vs	Fragmented
Convincing	Vs	Unconvincing
Consistent	Vs	Inconsistent
Similar to Client's Other Confirmed Events	Vs	Not Similar to Client's Other Confirmed Events
Similar to Other Clients' Reports	Vs	Not Similar to Other Clients' Reports
Congruent Accompanying Affect	Vs	Incongruent Accompanying Affect
General Honesty of Client	Vs	General Dishonesty of Client
Improvement with Therapy	Vs	Deterioration with Therapy
Presence of Secondary Gain	Vs	Absence of Secondary Gain

The trauma model must be confirmed by study of events that are proven to have taken place. This might include natural disasters, air and train crashes, military combat, epidemics, violent crime and sexual assault. It could also include incest and child pornography when objective evidence or reliable corroboration of the events is available.

The problem is that a great deal of incest and childhood sexual and physical abuse was never witnessed, is denied by the perpetrator, and generates no physical evidence. This is true shortly after the events and even more true in therapy twenty years later. The reality of reports of childhood sexual abuse is a methodological problem from a scientific perspective. There are research methods and designs available to deal with the problem.

One could study corroborated cases and compare them to uncorroborated cases on variables of interest. One could interview victims first and alleged perpetrators second, then compare cases with and without perpetrator corroboration. One could compare childhood sexual trauma to verified adult sexual trauma on variables of interest, and one could compare sexual to non-sexual trauma. The point is that these are methodological problems. All scientific models and theories pose such problems, and all scientific research involves solutions to methodological and technical problems.

What evidence exists that accurate recovery of memories previously inaccessible with ordinary recall effort is possible? This is an interesting question, even though such accurate memory recovery is not a necessary postulate of the trauma model.

Erdelyi (1996) provides conclusive evidence that *reminiscence* is a pervasive and fully documented phenomenon in cognitive psychology and the experimental memory literature. Reminiscence is the recall of items that were not recalled on previous recall trials. *Oblivescence* is the failure to recall items that were recalled in previous trials. *Hypermnesia* occurs when reminiscence exceeds oblivescence and amnesia occurs when oblivescence exceeds reminiscence. Amnesia and hypermnesia are net outcomes of the ratios of reminiscence and oblivescence. Normal forgetting includes reminiscence for some items.

The literature demonstrates conclusively that repeated recall effort increases reminiscence. Variables that can affect reminiscence include: the type of stimulus; duration of stimulus presentation; the subjective valence or meaning of the stimulus; age, arousal, intoxication, fatigue and other state variables of the subject; presence of recall cues; and time lapse since presentation of the stimulus.

In a typical experiment, subjects are presented with word lists. Repeated recall trials demonstrate both reminiscence and oblivescence at the item level, with neither amnesia nor hypermnesia. The curve of number of items recalled accurately over a series of recall trials is flat. However, if the stimulus was a set of pictures, the curve slopes upwards dramatically with repeated recall trials; there is a large excess of reminiscence.

In other experiments, stimuli are presented in high and low arousal conditions. Reminiscence increases dramatically with repeated recall trials when items presented in the high arousal condition are recalled in the high arousal condition. Inversely, oblivescence prevails when items presented in the low arousal condition are recalled in the low arousal condition.

There is no doubt about the scientific status of reminiscence. Like dissociation, it is one of the most replicated and rigorously demonstrated phenomena in cognitive psychology. Although the memory literature is directly relevant to the clinic, by and large severely traumatized subjects have not been included in the studies, which are primarily conducted on normal college students. That is good because it demonstrates that reminiscence is a fact of normal psychology. It is unfortunate because trauma warrants much more thorough study as an experimental variable.

The purpose of this chapter is to establish that the problem of false memories is taken seriously within the trauma model. The scientific way to state the relationship between childhood trauma and adult psychopathology is in terms of *risk*. One speaks of *risk factors*, *correlates*, and *predictor variables* within most research designs. More definitive research designs which allow for causal attributions are described in the next section. In most retrospective research on the long-term consequences of childhood trauma, one must speak of *reported childhood trauma*.

8

TESTABILITY OF THE MODEL

In order for a model to be scientific, it must be testable. The model must be formulated in such a way that it leads to specific research predictions. The research and experiments may confirm or disconfirm the model, but it must in principle be falsifiable. Otherwise it is not scientific. It has taken me two decades to transform the trauma model from a clinical intuition into a formal scientific theory.

I propose that chronic childhood trauma is to psychiatry as germs are to general medicine. Family physicians, internists, surgeons and pathologists must all deal with the medical consequences of infection on a daily basis. Germs are everywhere in their practices. All doctors must be knowledgeable about the types of infectious organisms, their effects, and their sensitivity to antibiotics and other medications. The medical generalist knows a great deal about germs.

Some diseases are non-infectious in nature. An example would be a fracture of the radius. Treatment of the uncomplicated fracture of the radius requires no knowledge of infectious diseases. However, it is a different story with a compound fracture. In a complicated fracture, the risk of infection is high and the appropriate antibiotics must be prescribed. Sterile operating technique is observed. In this situation, uncontrolled infection with staphylococcus aureus can cause more trouble than the original injury. Germs can complicate the course, treatment and outcome of non-infectious medical problems.

Other medical problems are classified as infectious diseases. Subspecialists in infectious diseases may be called in on such cases, or the infection may be handled successfully by a generalist. Infectious diseases can be trivial, such as the common cold, or catastrophic, such as gas gangrene. Certain medical conditions increase the risk of infectious complications, the leading example today being AIDS. In AIDS, the disease itself is not as lethal as the secondary opportunistic infections.

According to the trauma model, the various forms of serious chronic childhood trauma are psychiatry's bacteria, viruses, moulds and fungi.

These psychiatric noxious agents are endemic in the environment. Serious childhood trauma causes some psychiatric disorders; these are the pure infectious diseases of psychiatry. Trauma complicates all aspects of the clinical picture in disorders which are not in themselves intrinsically trauma-related.

Trauma affects the onset, symptomatology, comorbidity, course, response to psychotherapy and psychopharmacology, and outcome of all disorders in DSM-IV-TR. The way in which trauma influences these variables is predictable and testable. The sequence of steps in the exposition of the trauma model are: define the problem of comorbidity as the core problem to be solved; create the trauma model at the level of clinical intuition; and transform the model into a formal scientific theory.

The trauma model provides a reorganization of the conceptual foundation of psychiatry. According to the trauma model, what is today called general adult psychiatry is in fact a small sub-specialty. This small sub-specialty deals with single diseases having primarily endogenous etiologies. The proper diagnostic procedure in this sub-specialty results in a single primary diagnosis which then determines the primary treatment plan. Trauma psychiatry, on the other hand, is actually general adult psychiatry. Within trauma psychiatry, differential diagnosis results in tabulation of a complex field of comorbidity. The treatment plan takes diagnosis into account, but is not driven by any single diagnosis.

Within biological psychiatry in its current form, psychopharmacology is the primary treatment and drugs are differentiated by diagnosis. We have antidepressants, antipsychotics, anxiolytics, and mood stabilizers. These are the psychiatric equivalents of anticonvulsants, antibiotics, and antihypertensives. Within trauma psychiatry, the treatment plan is not differentiated by diagnosis to anywhere near the same degree. Individual diagnoses are still made, but their place in the clinical universe is more humble than it is in current biological psychiatry.

In the next section, the testable predictions of the trauma model will be defined in detail. Some predictions lead to crucial experiments on which the model either stands or falls, others lead to experiments the results of which will either support the model or generate revisions of it. In order to be scientific, a model need not be correct, it need only be testable. The trauma model is a comprehensive, testable model of mental illness.

III. THE TRAUMA MODEL

9

GENERAL PRINCIPLES OF THE TRAUMA MODEL

The trauma model is based on a number of general principles. Additional assumptions are made within trauma therapy; these will be dealt with in the next section. Here I will explain the principles inherent in the scientific, experimental and research elements of the model. The principles are summarized in Table 9.1.

Table 9.1 General Principles of the Trauma Model

- Definition of Trauma
- Measurement of Trauma
- Trauma Dose-Response Curves
- Developmental Susceptibility
- The Threshold Principle
- Priming
- The Noxious Effect of Active Disease
- Heterogeneity Within Diagnostic Categories
- Selection Bias
- Treatment Failures Tend to Be Trauma Model Cases
- Treatment Intervention at Different System Levels
- Animal Models of Trauma
- Diagnostic Non-Specifity of Selective Serotonin Reuptake Inhibitors (SSRI's)
- When the Perpetrator is a Primary Attachment Figure

Definition of Trauma

Trauma is defined operationally by the measures available in the field (Pincus, Rush, First, and McQueen, 2000). Conventionally, trauma is the impact on the organism of a traumatic event. This approach to trauma is imbedded in the DSM-IV-TR criteria for posttraumatic stress disorder, which require the presence of a traumatic event. The traumatic event is defined in DSM-IV-TR (page 467) as including two features:

-        the person experienced, witnessed, or was confronted with an event or events that involved actual or threatened death or serious injury, or a threat to the physical integrity of the self or others.

- The person's response involved intense fear, helplessness, or horror. Note: In children, this may be expressed instead by disorganized or agitated behavior.

DSM-IV-TR recognizes that, for the definition of trauma, events cannot be disentangled from the response to those events; by DSM-IV-TR rules, there is no pure "traumatic event" in nature, independent of the trauma response of the individual. This makes sense and doesn't make sense. Witnessing all your family members die in a major car wreck, when you were a passenger in the same car, is surely a traumatic event for everyone, but, in theory, if there is no trauma response, the event does not meet criterion A for PTSD.

By DSM-IV-TR rules, two people can experience the same event. For one person it was a traumatic event, for the other it was not. The DSM-IV-TR definition makes sense, despite this apparent incongruity, because it is the trauma response that is of interest in psychiatry. If an event takes place and there is no trauma response, there is no psychiatric problem. What is it that makes trauma traumatic, then, and what is a traumatic event?

I can't answer these questions in any scientifically complete fashion, nor can anyone else. However, looking at the event, there are numerous events which everyone would agree qualify as traumatic. These include witnessing the violent death of loved ones, major natural and transportation disasters, rape, violent assault, combat, and being in a major fire. The threshold for inclusion in the list of traumatic events is a measurement and definitional problem, not a conceptual problem.

Looking at the trauma response, intense fear, helplessness, or horror certainly qualify as trauma responses, but they do not exhaust the list of possibilities. In the DSM-IV-TR criteria for acute stress disorder (page 471), it states that while experiencing the criterion A event, the person may experience numbing, detachment, absence of emotional responsiveness, a reduction in awareness of his or her surroundings, derealization, depersonalization, or dissociative amnesia.

If these responses are present to an extreme degree throughout the event, then there will be no fear, helplessness, or horror. Therefore all these Criterion B items from acute stress disorder should be added to the second item in Criterion A, which is the immediate response to the traumatic event. I would add depression and psychotic symptoms to the list.

The basic idea is that there is an extreme event and an extreme response. The extreme response is statistically normal if the event is extreme enough, but looks like an "over-reaction" if the event is minor. The over-reaction is likely due to priming, as discussed below.

The conventional definition of trauma is incomplete because it focuses too much on traumatic events, on bad things that should not have happened. For complex, highly comorbid patients, the bad things that happened in childhood are probably less important, less damaging, and less traumatic than the events which did not happen. It is the errors of omission by the parents, not the errors of commission, which are the fundamental problem. The deeper trauma is the absence of normal love, affection, attention, care, and protection. The trauma is not being special to mom and dad. But this deeper trauma does not meet criterion A for PTSD.

From the perspective of trauma therapy, it is trauma to the person's attachment systems during childhood which really counts. The betrayal of trust is often more hurtful than the abusive event itself. DSM-IV-TR definitions of trauma are influenced by the fact that many specialists in PTSD became interested in trauma while working in the VA system, and while treating Vietnam combat trauma, which resulted in a focus on abnormal events in adulthood. Childhood incest and emotional neglect, for instance, are surely traumatic, but do they really meet criterion A for PTSD if they are not accompanied by threats or violence, or if there is no threat of malnourishment?

In the end, no summary definition of trauma has much utility. Trauma is a complex interaction of external events and the organism's response to them. There are numerous causal arrows and feedback loops going in a variety of directions. There are risk and protective factors in the past, present and future at biological, psychological and social levels. I have included this definitional section mainly to demonstrate that the trauma model is not based on a simplistic, reductionist, linear, or unidirectional definition of trauma.

Measurement of Trauma

Measurement of trauma is a technical problem within the model, not a conceptual one. I will make no effort to review the numerous measures available in the field, nor will I discuss the technical problems in any detail. The standard principles of psychometrics must be brought to bear on the measurement of trauma, and the usual rules of statistical analysis apply. As in all areas of science, advances in our understanding of trauma often depend on the development of new tools and procedures. A good example of a new tool is the Dissociative Experiences Scale (DES) (Bernstein and Putnam, 1986; Ross, 1997).

Publication of the DES and its initial reliability and validity data opened up fertile research possibilities which have resulted in hundreds of publications. The DES is useful because of its ease of administration and scoring combined with its robust psychometric properties. The trauma model depends on the existence of reliable, valid measures for its verification. A comprehensive source of information about measures of psychopathology, including trauma measures, is the *Handbook of Psychiatric Measures* (Pincus, Rush, First, and McQueen, 2000).

Trauma Dose-Response Curves

In pharmacology, dose response curves are of great interest. I remember constructing dose-response curves of the responses of sections of rabbit gut to various medications during medical school. Dose-response curves can have different shapes, depending on the physiology involved. The basic idea is that the response of the receptor, tissue, or organism varies with dosage. The dose-response relationship may be linear or non-linear.

Consider acetaminophen as a treatment for childhood fever. Imagine that the acetaminophen is being administered in liquid form a drop at a time. Initially, there will be no reduction in fever. The first fifty drops will have no effect. As dosage increases, the response remains at zero. Then the shape of the curve changes. From fifty to two hundred drops, fever is reduced as dosage increases. Over two hundred drops there is no further reduction in fever. This results in the typical dose-response curve shown in Figure 9.1. If the figure was specific to the acetaminophen treatment of fever, the x axis would be labeled *dosage of acetaminophen in milligrams* and the y axis would be labeled *reduction in fever in degrees centigrade*.

The trauma model assumes that there is a dose-response curve for trauma. A typical graph having the shape of Figure 9.1 would plot trauma dose against symptom score. An example of such a graph could be constructed from general population data using the Dissociative

Disorders Interview Schedule (DDIS) and the Dissociative Experiences Scale (DES).

Figure 9.1. A Typical Dose – Response Curve

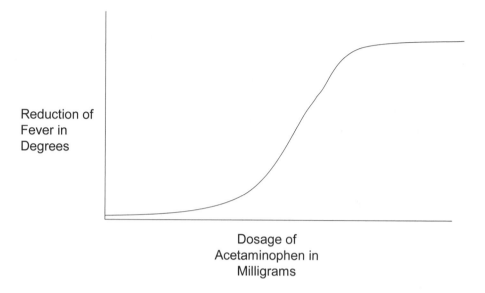

Reduction of
Fever in
Degrees

Dosage of
Acetaminophen in
Milligrams

In the relevant study, the DES and DDIS would be administered to a random sample of five thousand people in the general population. The childhood sexual abuse trauma dosage would be plotted on the x axis and the DES score on the y axis. How would trauma dosage be calculated from the DDIS? This could be done quite simply. For childhood sexual abuse, the trauma dosage would be the sum of the sexual abuse items in the DDIS (Ross, 1997).

On the DDIS, childhood sexual abuse trauma dose = number of perpetrators of sexual abuse + number of types of sexual abuse perpetrated + years of sexual abuse + age at onset of sexual abuse. Age at onset would be scored as 18 if onset was at age 1 or less, 17 if at age 2, and so on down to zero. Although this is a crude measure and a simple methodology, the prediction is that the correlation between the DDIS trauma score and the DES score would be very high, probably above 0.60.

Research designs in which sexual abuse is treated as a dichotomous variable cannot generate a dose-response curve, nor can they yield full insight into the trauma-symptom relationship. For instance, childhood sexual abuse cannot function effectively as a variable in correlation analyses or regression analyses if it is reduced to a simple presence or absence of abuse. One could have experienced childhood sexual abuse but be in the initial flat sector of the dose-response curve. In this situation, there would appear to be no relationship between childhood sexual abuse and the symptom cluster under consideration.

Similarly, simple rates of reported childhood sexual abuse in various psychiatric disorders may not reveal differential trauma-relatedness across disorders. If the baseline rate of childhood sexual abuse in the general population is 10%, in bulimia 30% and in borderline personality disorder 60%, this does not tell us much. The trauma-symptom relationship may be present in some people with bulimia and childhood sexual abuse and absent in others due to dose-response considerations. It may be present to the same degree in 10% of people with bulimia and 40% of people with borderline personality disorder. The rates by themselves give us only the most preliminary information.

Definitive trauma model research must consider the trauma dose-response relationship, the overall rates of abuse in different disorders and populations, and the role of trauma in sub-groups within each diagnostic category. The rate of childhood sexual abuse in bipolar mood disorder might be the same as the baseline rate in the general population, for instance. From this one could correctly conclude that bipolar mood disorder is not an intrinsically trauma-related disorder. That is not the end of the story, however. Bipolar subjects at the high end of the trauma dose distribution might display a profound interaction between their trauma and their disorder. For that subgroup of bipolar patients, the trauma model might apply as fully as it does in borderline personality disorder. At the same time, the trauma model could be irrelevant for most bipolar patients.

In general, the components of childhood sexual abuse relevant to calculating trauma dosage are: age at onset; duration; number of acts; severity of acts; number of perpetrators; degree of intimidation, threats and violence; bizarreness of acts; how closely related the perpetrator is to the victim; whether the victim is dependent on the perpetrator for basic care and survival; secrecy of the acts; and combination of the sexual abuse with other forms of trauma.

Much the same criteria would apply for physical and emotional abuse. For emotional abuse key factors might include: inconsistency and variability in parental rules; presence of double binds; extreme differences in intrafamilial and extrafamilial behavior of parents; enforcement of impossible performance standards; and deviant parental belief systems.

The cognitive errors and symptom profile of trauma could be present in a person who grew up in a "normal" family. There could be a complete absence of physical abuse, sexual abuse, and physical neglect. The trauma could be extreme, but not observable to child protection agencies. For instance, a mother who sets impossible performance standards, then withdraws love and activates highly affectively charged negative characterological attributions about her child in response to inevitable performance failure, could generate a trauma profile in her child.

Combine this maternal behavior with inconsistent, changing and arbitrarily applied rules for earning maternal love and approval, and the stage is set for learned helplessness. Diagnostically the grown child might suffer from depression; panic disorder driven by hypervigilant efforts to predict withdrawal of maternal affection and obsessive-compulsive disorder driven by desperate attempts to control the universe and make it safe and predictable. Danger, catastrophic abandonment, and proof of inadequacy would be lurking everywhere in this adult's world.

Such trauma presents formidable measurement problems. It may, however, be as traumatic as sexual abuse and physical abuse. If so, failure to measure these components of childhood trauma could result in misattribution of the trauma response to co-existing physical and sexual abuse, or obscuring the specificity of the trauma response by mis-categorizing subjects as non-traumatized.

A methodological problem arises from the fact that the various forms of chronic childhood trauma tend to overlap and co-occur. One would not expect to find many families with serious neglect and sexual abuse in which there was no physical or emotional abuse. Attempts to control for and disentangle all these components of the trauma may prove to be extremely difficult or futile.

Developmental Susceptibility

The trauma model assumes that there is a window of developmental susceptibility for causation of the full problem of comorbidity. The window opens at conception and never closes fully. It is a matter of a decreasing degree of vulnerability with increasing age, not of dichotomous open and shut conditions of the window. The window gradually becomes more closed over the life cycle, but extreme adult-onset trauma can perhaps reopen it.

There is a confounding variable. Severe, chronic childhood trauma rarely starts *de novo* at age fourteen. What appears to be a developmental issue could be an artifact of the distribution of chronic trauma across the life cycle. The distribution could be controlled for experimentally by including people first traumatized in nursing homes, as battered spouses, as prisoners of war, and as victims of serious socioeconomic upheaval and war. Does child abuse hurt people because they are children? Or have we mistakenly reached this conclusion because social conditions expose more children than adults to severe chronic trauma in our culture?

Common sense and several branches of science tell us that children have unique susceptibilities. Their brains are more adaptable. This provides a survival advantage in severe head injury cases. A child can adapt to and recover from much more brain damage than an adult. The inverse must also be true. The child's brain must be more capable of wiring in the biological effects of trauma. This is the down side to plasticity.

There is a large body of research proving that the brain depends on environmental input for its development and function. The experimental kitten has its eyes sewn shut for a period of time; it becomes permanently blind. Blindness does not occur if the eyes are sewn shut for the same period of time outside the window of developmental susceptibility. The human child with a "lazy eye" becomes blind in the lazy eye if the good eye is not patched. The child's brain can be damaged in a physically measurable fashion by poverty of environmental input. This fact is true of all mammals. Psychosocial dwarfism is a recognized diagnosis in pediatrics, and is caused by inadequate environmental input in the presence of an adequate diet.

Outside the brain, an example of developmental susceptibility is premature closure of the growth plate in the femur in children treated with methylphenidate (Ritalin). This complication does not occur in the treatment of adult attention deficit disorder. Similarly, in terms of physical trauma, damage to the growth plate due to fracture is not a problem for adults because they have finished growing. The acne and pimples of adolescence, and the osteoporosis of post-menopausal women are examples of disorders driven by endocrine changes across the life cycle. One would assume that the changing internal endocrine environment across the life cycle must interact with trauma in some way.

Children are developing cognitively as well. Trauma therapy takes this into account in terms of *the locus of control shift*. The child in concrete operations and the sensorimotor stage of development will react to trauma differently than the adolescent who has mastered formal operations. The differences will be especially relevant to cognitive therapy for trauma.

Related to the principle of developmental susceptibility is the concept of developmental fixation. Clinically, adult survivors with extensive comorbidity are locked in the cognitive and behavioral patterns of childhood. Experimental paradigms from developmental psychology should be able to demonstrate this fixation. The severe childhood trauma survivor should perform differently on tests of moral judgment, and cognitive development. Tests in which the performance of the normal child is counter-intuitive would meet the methodological criticism that performance expectations are self-evident to the subjects.

The Threshold Principle

Thresholds are relevant throughout medicine. Consider seizures. Some individuals have low seizure thresholds. Neuro-electrical processes in their brains exceed the threshold intermittently and they have spontaneous seizures. They receive a diagnosis of epilepsy. In some cases, seizures can be provoked with strobe lights or other stimuli used as diagnostic tests. The stimuli do not cause seizures in control subjects.

On the other hand, an adequate dose of electricity to the brain will cause a seizure in everyone. This is the foundation of electroconvulsive therapy. Certain medications lower the seizure threshold and cause seizures as side effects in a percentage of normal subjects. Other medications raise the seizure threshold, are called anticonvulsants, and are prescribed for epilepsy.

Thresholds of countless kinds are found throughout physics, chemistry, and biology, from precipitation of crystals out of solution to post-synaptic activation of a neuron. The trauma model assumes that people are born with varying endogenously set trauma thresholds. They may be susceptible or resistant. Some individuals may develop extensive comorbidity in response to a given trauma dose, while others will not.

If the trauma dose is set high enough, virtually everyone will develop serious psychiatric comorbidity. As interrogators know, every man has his breaking point. Both for individuals and for populations, intervening variables may shift the trauma dose-response curve left or right. A biological example of this phenomenon is the oxygen uptake curve of normal hemoglobin, which takes the form shown in Figure 9.1. In this instance, the x axis plots the partial pressure of oxygen in the atmosphere and the y axis the degree of saturation of hemoglobin oxygen binding sites. The higher you climb up a mountain, the less oxygen is bound to your hemoglobin.

The oxygen saturation curve is shifted left when the body synthesizes a compound that promotes oxygen binding. It takes about three weeks for this process of acclimatization to altitude to occur. That is why athletes who are going to compete at high altitude spend three weeks adapting prior to competition. With their oxygen binding curves shifted left, they are able to bind more oxygen than they could when adapted to sea level. This is also the reason why climbers spend weeks at base camp before trying to climb Mount Everest.

In terms of psychological trauma, the dose response curve is shifted right by many variables. These can be summarized as healing, soothing, stabilizing and normalizing variables. For a given amount of sexual abuse, the outcome will be better if there was a kind, loving grandmother, neighbor or school teacher; if the child could excel at sports, school or hobbies outside the home; if a non-offending parent taught and modeled healthy self-soothing skills; and so on.

Inversely, for a given amount of sexual abuse, the curve will be shifted left and the outcome will be worse if these variables are absent and other forms of trauma are present. In principle, all of these variables can be quantified.

Priming

Priming occurs throughout nature and the human world. It is easier to open a lock that has been opened before because it is not as stiff. A car starts more easily in the Canadian arctic in January if the engine has been "primed" by pumping the accelerator before turning the key in the ignition. Similarly with trauma. A core postulate of the trauma model is that a trauma response to any given traumatic event will be primed by prior trauma. Among Vietnam combat veterans, a specific prediction follows. Holding combat exposure dose constant, individuals are at higher risk for developing posttraumatic stress disorder if they experienced chronic childhood trauma.

Another methodological approach would be to vary the combat exposure dose and do an analysis of covariance. The basic idea is the same.

Priming cannot be reduced to simple leftward shifts of the trauma dose response curve. There are probably specific changes in the brain. For instance, chronic childhood trauma will cause elevated circulating cortisol levels, which in turn will affect neuronal gating functions in hippocampal neurons. More toxic metabolites, elements and compounds than normal will enter the neurons, resulting in damage of some cells and death of others. The result will be hippocampal atrophy on MRI scan, hippocampal hypoactivity on PET scan and impairment of hippocampal function.

The effect would be more than a leftward shift of the curve if new phenomena emerged due to the hippocampal damage. The woman in chapter two who was the victim of a stranger rape in adulthood might experience not simply more severe symptoms because of childhood sexual abuse, but clusters of symptoms not seen in a control woman without childhood sexual abuse who was subjected to the same trauma.

The Noxious Effect Of Active Disease

In many areas of medicine, the disease itself is damaging. The longer one has high lipid levels, the more plaque accumulates in arteries. As a result, blood pressure increases, and destructive feedback loops are set in place. Similarly, in rheumatoid arthritis, an acute flare-up results in more damage to the joint if it is not brought under control quickly with anti-inflammatory medication. In arterial embolus, it is vital to do an embolectomy as quickly as possible to prevent tissue death.

The same may be true in psychiatry. Early intervention in first break psychosis may improve prognosis by interrupting the noxious effects of the disease state itself. This could be true at both sociological and biological levels. Clearly, untreated psychosis can cause social alienation and occupational deterioration. Perhaps there is a toxic biological effect too. Perhaps neuroleptics work not just by acute suppression of symptoms, but by a kind of neuropsychological anti-inflammatory action. Perhaps the inflammatory process itself has a toxic effect on the brain, increasing the damage with increasing duration of untreated acute disease.

From a trauma model perspective, the complications of trauma can be exacerbated by closed feedback loops set up within the psyche and brain. An example is flashbacks. Whatever the brain is trying to do with flashbacks, untreated recurrent flashbacks are themselves traumatic. Ongoing active posttraumatic stress disorder can result in complications such as alcoholism, unemployment, alienation, and subsequent drift into a marginalized life style which carries a high risk of further traumatization. This could occur through car accidents, bar fights, angry encounters with friends and employers, rejection by spouses, and countless other feedback loops. The unresolved trauma causes more trauma.

The trauma model predicts that feedback loops in the social environment, in the trauma victim's cognitions, and in brain regulation follow the same logical patterns. When a victim of childhood trauma with borderline personality disorder puts herself and everyone around her in double binds, her neurotransmitter systems are probably in trauma-driven double binds too. For instance, it might be that danger increases noradrenalin-driven hypervigilance, which triggers soothing neuroregulation by serotonin. This could set up a double bind in which the only way to experience soothing is through self-infliction of danger. One feels better when a noradrenalin fear response is activated because then serotonin is activated. Conversely one feels unsafe when there is no fear response because serotonin activation is low.

Endless oscillation in this double bound neurotransmitter system would be expected to lead to serotonin exhaustion and clinical depression. The depression would follow logically from both the psychological experience of childhood neglect and abuse, and from the neurotransmitter double bind.

Heterogeneity Within Diagnostic Categories

The trauma model cannot account for all mental illness because not all individuals with DSM-IV-TR diagnoses have experienced serious trauma. Additionally, the model assumes etiological heterogeneity within diagnostic categories. For any given diagnosis, there are many possible causal pathways. This is true in medicine generally. A patient can present to the emergency department in congestive heart failure due to primary cardiac problems. The next day another patient can present with an identical clinical picture, but the cause of the congestive heart failure is in the lungs.

In psychiatry, the negative symptoms of schizophrenia may be caused by the disease process of schizophrenia, concurrent depression, side effects of medication, or chronic institutionalization. Simply looking at an individual symptom in isolation, or even a cluster of symptoms, does not allow one to determine etiological pathway. An educated guess about etiology requires consideration of the context of the symptom, which may include other symptoms, course, family history and associated life experience.

None of the major symptoms in psychiatry have any diagnostic specificity. If one assumes that the different disorders in which these symptoms occur are separate biomedical diseases, one is committed to the concept of etiological heterogeneity for any given symptom.

Any given symptom can have different etiologies in different patients with the same disorder, or the same etiology in different patients with different disorders. There are only so many ways the brain can react to external trauma or endogenous disease; sadness, anxiety, thought disorder, dementia, dissociation, addictive craving, and so on are part of a limited collection of psychiatric symptoms generated by the brain. Similarly with any other organ; heart, lungs, liver and kidneys can only generate a limited range of symptoms. There is no reason to expect that the brain should generate discrete sets of symptoms for discrete etiologies. Rather, one should expect permutations and combinations of symptom patterns and etiologies in different DSM-IV-TR disorders.

Patients with complex comorbidity are experiencing symptom production from numerous areas of the brain. This could be due to one unified etiology or the interaction of many etiological factors. Any given theory, including the trauma model, can apply only to a subgroup of patients with depression, schizophrenia, panic disorder, or alcoholism. This is also the case in the patient with extensive comorbidity. The question is, how large is the subgroup to whom the theory applies? The trauma model is based on the assumption that trauma is the major etiological contributor in the polydiagnostic patient. However, the model not only allows but predicts the existence of an atraumatic subgroup within the category of polydiagnostic patient.

Selection Bias

Selection bias is usually considered a methodological limitation of a research project. In the case of the trauma model, selection bias is the whole point. The problem of comorbidity arises from a biased sample of all individuals meeting criteria for one or more DSM-IV-TR disorders. The trauma model assumes its own limitations by definition. It cannot apply to individuals who have not experienced significant trauma beyond the usual hardships of life. It is the biased sample that proves the model, and the model by definition cannot be generalized to the entire population.

From a practical perspective, the trauma model predicts that trauma patients generate a highly disproportionate share of psychiatric health care costs.

Treatment Failures Tend to Be Trauma Model Cases

A core prediction is that treatment failures include an over-representation of trauma model cases. This is true throughout DSM-IV-TR, in all sectors of the health care system, and for all treatment modalities. The treatment could be cognitive-behavioral group therapy for bulimia, neuroleptic medication for schizophrenia, AA groups for alcoholism, antidepressant medication for depression, or behavioral treatment for a germ phobia.

Irrespective of diagnosis and treatment modality, patients can be divided into two treatment outcome categories: successes and failures. Patients who respond well to trials of standard therapy tend to have little or no comorbidity and less trauma. Treatment failures have more comorbidity and more severe trauma. In terms of research design, outcome could be classified as a success-failure dichotomous category or in terms of symptom reduction on continuous measures. This approach is used in all drug company-funded studies of new psychiatric medications.

The basic trauma model research design is to take a group of treatment failures and randomize them to another course of standard therapy versus a course of trauma therapy. The standard therapy is a subset of the trauma therapy. If standard treatment is an antidepressant for depression, this will be continued in trauma therapy. If it is AA groups for alcoholism, that will be continued. The model predicts that trauma therapy will provide a superior outcome. If the standard therapy was dropped from the trauma therapy protocol, outcome would probably deteriorate. Stated another way, the unique component of trauma therapy and the standard treatment component are synergistic.

Treatment Intervention at Different System Levels

The trauma model postulates that etiology cannot be inferred from treatment response. In general medicine, response to placebo does not differentiate organic from psychogenic pain. Within psychiatry, panic disorder provides the best example of the logic.

Panic attacks can be spontaneous or cued. Cued panic attacks can be triggered by exposure to a psychosocial stimulus (an elevator or other phobic stimulus) or a chemical challenge (caffeine or other compounds). The phenomenology of biologically and psychologically cued panic attacks is the same. Panic disorder can be treated with medication or cognitive-behavioral therapy.

The idea is that brain-mind is a unified field. Interventions at one level in the field can have effects at other levels. That is how medication relieves symptoms. The trauma model predicts that psychotherapy changes brain function and structure in a measurable way. Until recently, our measures have been too coarse to detect such effects. Within the trauma model, normalization in biological measures of brain function should correlate with symptom reduction and positive treatment outcome. Brain scans should function as psychotherapy outcome measures.

Causal attribution of change to the therapy depends on controlling the relevant variables through standard methodological manipulations. This is no more complex a problem than attributing change to active medication in a randomized placebo-controlled prospective drug study.

At the level of etiology, the model predicts that biological dysregulations can be caused by trauma, or psychological symptoms by endogenous biological dysregulations. The presence of a "chemical imbalance" and response to medication does not weigh in favor of either an environmental or an endogenous etiology. Nor does the presence of a psychological conflict or cognitive error weigh in favor of either form of causality. All logical combinations of etiology and treatment response are assumed to occur. The modal case with complex comorbidity involves numerous co-occurring examples of all logical categories.

Animal Models of Trauma

In medicine, it is desirable to have an animal model of a disorder. The animal model allows for experimental manipulation of variables and procedures that are not ethical in humans. This fact came to my attention when I decapitated and performed post mortem splenectomies on one hundred mice one morning in medical school.

The trauma model predicts that animal models of severe, chronic childhood trauma can be developed quite readily. A considerable literature of this sort already exists. The Harlow monkey experiments can be thought of as abuse research, for instance (van der Kolk, 1987).

Assume that neglect is the trauma variable under study. The mothers of infant mice, monkeys, rats or rabbits can be forced to neglect them through a number of different manipulations. The trauma model predicts that the neglect will cause characteristic biological dysregulations and abnormal behaviors. The behaviors will be the animal model for a DSM-IV-TR diagnosis, say depression. Since psychotherapy cannot be done with lab animals, treatment for them will be limited to medications. As "depressed" adults, the lab animals will respond to antidepressants with normalization of their relevant behavior. The biological dysregulation induced by the neglect will also normalize in response to the antidepressant. Stopping the antidepressant will result in re-emergence of the abnormal biology and behavior.

Human experimental subjects in this research will be clinically depressed adults with histories of childhood neglect. They will exhibit the same biological dysregulation seen in the lab animals. Again, both clinical state and biology will normalize on antidepressants and relapse on discontinuation of antidepressants. The experiment must take into account spontaneous normalization of the biological dysregulation as part of the natural history of the active clinical disorder.

What about psychotherapy? The trauma model predicts that effective psychotherapy will also normalize the biological dysregulation. If this occurs, no subjects with a full response should relapse when psychotherapy is discontinued.

With this kind of data at hand, psychiatry would be approaching what is called *rational* treatment in medicine. We would have a psychiatry anchored securely in animal models, known biological dyregulations in functionally relevant brain areas, and good correlation of remissions in the biology and the symptoms. This would leave many questions about mechanistic detail unanswered, but would take us far beyond the current state of psychiatry.

Diagnostic Non-Specificity of Selective Serotonin Reuptake Inhibitors (SSRIs)

A key observation of relevance to the trauma model is the fact that SSRIs work for many different DSM-IV-TR disorders. These include depression, bulimia, obsessive compulsive disorder and panic disorder, four disorders assumed to be distinct biomedical diseases within contemporary biological psychiatry. The diagnostic non-specificity of the SSRIs keeps increasing with more research. However, the mechanism of action of the medications is always assumed to be selective serotonin reuptake inhibition. This poses a problem.

If the SSRIs have only one mechanism of action, then only two explanations for their diagnostic non-specificity of action are possible: 1) the separate disorders are not biologically distinct, and therefore are not separate diseases or 2) the biological etiologies of no more than one of the disorders are in the serotonin system.

The trauma model predicts that individual DSM-IV-TR disorders cannot be linked to separate individual neurotransmitter systems at the level of etiology. The brain is far too complex and there is far too much talk between neurotransmitter systems and brain regions for etiology to be localized in a single neurotransmitter system. The SSRIs illustrate this fact by the range of DSM-IV-TR disorders for which they are effective.

The SSRIs probably resemble acetominophen more than penicillin. Rather than having a specific mechanism of action directly related to the etiology of the disorders they treat, they treat brain "fever" of many types. Whether the "fever" is occurring in the part of the brain causing anxiety, psychosis, sadness, obsessions, or cravings, serotonin soothes the afflicted system. This postulate will be expanded on in the next chapter.

When the Perpetrator is a Primary Attachment Figure

The problem of attachment to the perpetrator is the core target of trauma therapy, as explained in the fourth section. The postulate is that dependence for biological survival on the perpetrator creates unique conflicts at psychological and biological levels not seen in other forms of trauma. The problem of comorbidity and the problem of attachment to the perpetrator are intertwined with each other. From a psychotherapy perspective, attachment conflicts are the core problem to be addressed in the patient with complex comorbidity. The primary text supporting this postulate is *Betrayal Trauma* by Jennifer Freyd (1996).

Dependence for biological survival is seen in certain forms of adult-onset trauma. These include prisoner of war camps, abductions by serial killers and extreme sexual offenders, hostage situations, and certain interrogation situations. It is under these conditions that one observes *transmarginal inhibition* (Sargant, 1957), identification with the aggressor or Stockholm Syndrome.

The adult-onset forms of trauma which create a dependency for biological survival provide models for the conditions typical for children in chronic trauma households. The specifics of the attachment elements of the model will be clarified in the fourth section.

These general principles of the trauma model will be refined and expanded on in subsequent chapters.

10

MOOD DISORDERS

Depression is the major symptom in psychiatry. It is the most common, disabling and treatable of the serious psychiatric symptoms. The big five in psychiatry are depression, anxiety, psychosis, dissociation and substance abuse. If we consider substance abuse to be, strictly speaking, a behavior rather than a symptom, depression is the most common serious psychiatric symptom in the general population. It is also the psychiatric problem most commonly treated by psychiatrists.

In a survey of 454 individuals in the general population in Winnipeg, Canada using the Dissociative Disorders Interview Schedule (DDIS) (Ross, 1991), the lifetime prevalence of major depressive disorder was 21.1%. This compares to a rate of 17.1% among 8,098 respondents in the National Comorbidity Survey (Blazer, Kessler, McGonagle, and Swartz, 1998). When the Winnipeg sample, which was demographically representative of the entire city of 650,000 people, was divided into respondents who reported childhood physical and/or sexual abuse (N=57) and those who did not (N=397), the lifetime prevalence of depression in the abused respondents was 57.9% compared to 15.9% in the non-abused. This is a signal-to-noise ratio of 4:1.

Looked at the other way around, the overall rate of reported childhood physical and/or sexual abuse in the sample was 12.6%. Among the 96 respondents positive for depression, however, the reported rate of childhood abuse was 34.4%. If the sample is divided into the 96 respondents with depression and the 358 without depression, rates of childhood abuse in these two groups are 34.4% and 6.7%. Now the signal-to-noise ratio is 5:1. The rates of trauma in the two groups differ by one order of magnitude. We can conclude from these data that childhood trauma is a risk factor for depression.

A limitation of the DDIS is that it inquires only about physical and sexual abuse. The data might be even more striking if a more complete inventory of childhood trauma had been administered. With higher precision tools, the signal-to-noise ratio might exceed 10:1. Trauma research of this sort could result in differences between groups of two orders of magnitude.

The role of depression in the trauma model is based on a very simple observation. It is depressing to be abused. Beyond that, depressed people often describe sad events in their lives. I was taught as a resident that loss of a parent before the age of ten is a risk factor for depression. I remember treating a depressed man in his sixties as an attending physician in Winnipeg. He became clinically depressed after receiving news that his nursing home was being closed. The relationship between sad and stressful events and depression is self-evident.

I was involved in one drug study for depression while working as an academic psychiatrist in Winnipeg. As part of the study, I had to present the study to a special meeting of the Faculty of Medicine's ethics committee. The inclusion of a placebo in such studies is mandated by the Health Protectorate Branch in Canada. However, a psychiatrist in the Department of Psychiatry was challenging approval of the study on the grounds that it is unethical to include a placebo in drug studies. He said that randomizing someone to placebo deprives them of a known more effective treatment, which is unethical. My counter-arguments prevailed and the study was approved.

My arguments were: inclusion of placebo is mandated by the government; we don't know *a priori* that placebo is inferior to this particular drug in this particular patient sample; acute suicidal ideation is an exclusion criterion; informed consent is given; the duration of the study is only six weeks; subjects can drop out at any time; the study had already been approved at all the other study centers in Canada; and, the ethics of such studies have been approved by all journals and editorial boards which have published results.

In the course of thinking about drug treatment of depression, organizing my arguments for the ethics committee meeting, and reviewing my training experience, I realized that my teachers failed to recognize a contradiction in the prevailing doctrine. I was taught that depression is a biomedical brain disease with a genetic basis. I was taught that it can be triggered by life events, but can occur without environmental triggers.

I was taught that depression tends to last a long time. A single major depressive episode tends to last at least six months and may last twenty-four months. In some people it lasts even longer. That is why it is important to make the diagnosis and prescribe medication early. The wait for spontaneous remission can be a long one. When I took these accepted facts and looked at the drug study literature, I realized that something didn't make sense.

In drug studies, about 35% of subjects respond to placebo. If you look at the weekly depression scale scores in these studies, most of the antidepressant response has occurred by the end of the first two weeks. Let's assume that the rate of natural remission of a major depressive episode is such that 90% of subjects are well by 24 months. Let's assume, for sake of illustration, that the percentage of subjects going into remission is 6% per month for the first six months, and 3% per month for the last eighteen months. These figures result in 90% remission over two years.

How is it that 35% of subjects get better in two weeks on placebo? The above assumptions predict a placebo response rate of less than 9% over six weeks. No plausible assumptions about spontaneous remission rates in nature even remotely approach a 35% placebo response rate in two weeks. Subjects are recruited into the drug studies at varying points in the natural history of their major depressive episodes. Why do the placebo responses either occur or not occur in the first two weeks of the study? There are very few subjects who fail to respond to placebo for the first two weeks, then suddenly develop a full placebo response in the last four weeks. Yet this is the pattern predicted by spontaneous remission.

It is clear that the placebo response rates are far above the spontaneous remission rates in studies with several dozen antidepressants involving hundreds of thousands of subjects around the world. This relationship is summarized in Figure 10.1.

Figure 10.1. Drug Response, Placebo Response and Spontaneous Symptom Decay Curves in An Antidepressant Study

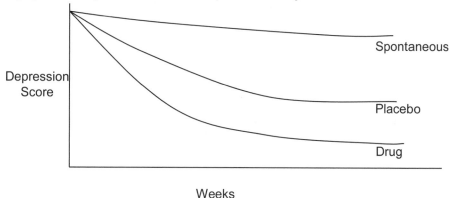

Placebo is an active intervention with an active antidepressant effect

that cannot be explained by spontaneous remission. If the phenotype of depression is assumed to be turned on by a gene, it is a fact that it is turned off by a placebo. If it is assumed that gene expression cannot be turned off by a placebo, then depression is not caused by a gene in at least 27% of cases of depression (the placebo response rate minus the maximum plausible spontaneous remission rate). Since there is no phenomenological difference between the 27% of depressions responding to placebo and those requiring an antidepressant, there is no need to assume the existence of a genotype for the individuals who require active medication to obtain an antidepressant effect.

Overall, about 70% of subjects respond to medication in antidepressant drug trials compared to 35% who respond to placebo. Logic reviewed in a previous chapter tells us that of the subjects who respond to medication, 35% would have responded as well if randomized to placebo. This means that of all subjects randomized to active medication, only (0.70 x 0.65 = 0.45) 45% experienced an antidepressant effect based on a pharmacological requirement for active medication. If we increase the placebo response rate to 41%, then the placebo response rate and the unique pharmacological response rate are equal at (0.70 x 0.59 = 0.41) 41%. We already know that cognitive therapy for major depression is as effective as antidepressant medication, so amplification of the placebo response rate to 41% is not a far-fetched idea.

The natural history of major depressive episode, the pharmacological data on antidepressants, and the assumption of an endogenous genetically-driven biomedical disease are incompatible with each other, unless we assume that gene expression can be turned off by human interaction. The trauma model makes that assumption. Once one assumes that gene expression can be turned off by human interaction, it is difficult to disallow the conclusion that abnormal psychiatric genes can be turned on by human interaction.

We are back to the basic postulate of the trauma model: the depressed phenotype can occur with and without a depressed genotype; the depressed phenotype can be turned on and off by both biological and psychological variables; and this is true in both the presence and the absence of the depressed genotype. The specific gene for depression is now nervously looking upward at Occam's Razor poised above it.

I will now examine the specific predictions of the trauma model concerning depression.

Phenomenology

The one existing study that looks at the relationship between childhood physical and sexual abuse and the features of adult depression found several significant effects (Levitan, Parikh, Leage, Hegadoren, Adams, Kennedy, and Goering, 1998). One was an association between mania and childhood physical abuse. The trauma model makes a number of specific predictions about the relationship between the phenomenology of mood disorders and childhood trauma.

If patients with bipolar mood disorder were divided into those with extravagant hypersexuality during the manic phase, and those without, the former subgroup would report higher rates of childhood sexual abuse. I am thinking of women I saw in Canada who would masturbate naked on the front lawn when manic, be wildly promiscuous, or walk down major streets naked during the daytime. Such patients should have higher scores on the Dissociative Experiences Scale and have the rest of the trauma comorbidity pattern to a greater degree.

Cyclothymic disorder can be very difficult to differentiate from dissociative instability of mood and identity. I predict that rates of childhood trauma and comorbidity are higher in cyclothymia than in bipolar mood disorder. There may be a spectrum from bipolar mood disorder at the left hand end to cyclothymic disorder at the right hand end. As one moves right on the spectrum, there is more trauma and comorbidity, more rapid cycling of mood, less structure to the mood disorder in terms of clear onset and offset of mood states, more mixed states, and an increasing likelihood of a previous clinical diagnosis of borderline personality disorder. The bipolar-cyclothymia continuum is shown in Figure 10.2.

Figure 10.2 The Trauma – Mood Disorder Continuum

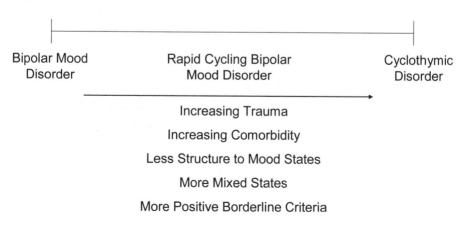

| Bipolar Mood | Rapid Cycling Bipolar | Cyclothymic |
| Disorder | Mood Disorder | Disorder |

Increasing Trauma

Increasing Comorbidity

Less Structure to Mood States

More Mixed States

More Positive Borderline Criteria

In terms of unipolar depression, depressed subjects could be divided into those with uncomplicated depression versus those with psychotic features. The DSM-IV-TR psychotic features are either exaggerations of the locus of control shift (see chapter on the locus on control shift), in which case they are called mood-congruent, or typical Schneiderian symptoms of trauma, in which case they are called mood-incongruent. Psychotic depression should be accompanied by much higher rates of childhood physical and sexual abuse.

From a trauma model perspective, the distinction between major depressive disorder, recurrent, severe with psychotic features (DSM-IV-TR 296.24) and schizoaffective disorder (DSM-IV-TR 295.70) is arbitrary. Whether the Schneiderian symptoms are manifest during major depressive episodes only, or also outside major depressive episodes is not of fundamental interest. When the psychotic symptoms arise from the trauma pathway to positive symptoms of schizophrenia, their temporal overlap or independence from periods of depression does not affect the conceptualization or treatment plan. Patients with psychotic depression should score higher on the Dissociative Experiences Scale than non-psychotic controls, and should score higher when depressed than when euthymic.

The melancholic features of depression could be no more than severity criteria, in which case they would occur in both severe atraumatic depression and severe trauma depression, or they could be more frequent in trauma depression. From a trauma perspective, the distinction between dysthymic disorder and major depressive disorder is of little utility because the complex comorbid patient is almost always positive for both. Trying to differentiate borderline personality disorder, cyclothymic disorder, schizoaffective disorder, and dysthymic disorder with intermittent psychotic major depressive episodes, is a Herculean task with unclear treatment implications.

If depressed subjects were divided into those with less than three comorbid diagnoses lifetime and those with six or more, the comorbid group would have much higher rates of trauma and psychotic features. The basic idea is that a great deal of the DSM-IV-TR phenomenology of depression is actually the phenomenology of trauma. It can occur in conjunction with or independently from active abnormal mood.

Natural History

In general, the trauma model predicts an earlier age at onset and more complicated course for any DSM-IV-TR disorder occurring in the context of complex, chronic comorbidity. Consider two groups of ten year old children, both with major depressive disorder; even in these early onset patients, onset will be earlier the more severe the trauma. The distinction becomes more clear when we divide adult subjects with major depressive disorder into two groups; those with first episode before age ten and those with first episode after age twenty. Rates of trauma and comorbidity will be far higher in the earlier onset group, as will rates of psychotic features.

Independently of trauma, one would expect more major depressive episodes to occur in subjects with earlier onset simply because they have had more time to accumulate episodes. However, when age at onset is controlled for, the traumatized patients will have more major depressive episodes per decade than the non-traumatized. The trauma subgroup will also show more increase in the number of episodes per decade and higher rates of conversion to bipolar mood disorder. The trauma subgroup will have more readily discernible psychosocial triggers to their major depressive episodes, and the episodes will tend to be longer.

Finally, rates of attempted and completed suicide will be higher in the traumatized depressed patients. Parceling out the role of childhood trauma in suicide and parasuicide will be complex because much of the effect of the trauma is mediated through comorbidity and the negative psychosocial feedback loops set up by unresolved trauma. The idea is that the trauma, comorbidity, more severe depression, more malignant natural history, greater psychosocial dysfunction and increased suicide all go together as a package.

Epidemiology

I was taught in my residency that depressed women have more depressed female relatives and more male relatives with antisocial personality disorder and alcoholism than do non-depressed control women. The interpretation of this finding was that the gene for affective spectrum disorders expressed itself as depression in the women and antisocial personality and alcoholism in the men. The trauma model hypothesis is that it is depressing to be a woman in an extended family of alcoholic antisocial males.

Family studies of depression need to control for trauma. There may be pedigrees in nature with relatively clean major depressive disorder disease, little trauma, and little comorbidity. Endogenous biological causes including genetic ones are likely easier to find in these pedigrees. Any gene or genes for depression are going to be harder to find if trauma-driven depression is not excluded from the genetic studies. As designed to date, endogenous-biological research on depression has failed to exclude large amounts of environmental noise.

In trauma pedigrees, the rates of depression in abused women will be higher than in non-abused women. The rates of alcoholism and anti-social personality will be higher in perpetrator men than among non-perpetrators. Perpetrator males might appear to be passing on a gene for depression to their daughters, however they likely do not practice assortive mating. Perpetrator males with depressed daughters probably marry women from trauma pedigrees more often than non-perpetrator males. There is a confound because perpetrator males practice non-assortive mating with respect to depression in females; they seek out victims as wives and create victims in their daughters. Simultaneously, they seek out antisocial alcoholics for friends and create them in their sons.

Rates of depression should be higher in certain target populations. These include people who were: children in Romanian orphanages; children in Vietnam in the 1960's; street children in Rio de Janeiro; children in Bosnia in the 1990's; sexually abused children in North America; children in Ethiopia who went on long marches to Red Cross stations; children of famine in Nigeria; and children who survived multiple hurricanes in Bangladesh. Rates of depression should be lower in people who grew up in intact nuclear families without abuse or severe environmental trauma.

Looking at depressed women with children: rates of depression should be higher among the children if the mother was abused as a child; rates of abuse should be higher in depressed than non-depressed children; rates of abuse should be higher in children whose mothers were abused; depressed children should have more abusive fathers; and children whose mothers were abused should have more abusive fathers. This is how the cycle of depression and abuse works. Predictions of the trauma model concerning mothers, child abuse and depression are shown in Table 10.1.

In the most comorbid adult patients, the picture should be one of extreme trauma in the childhoods of both the parents. The trauma will include physical, sexual, and emotional abuse, neglect, family violence, death and loss of primary caretakers, general family chaos and dysfunction, and all other imaginable forms of trauma. Looked at epidemiologically, the effect of trauma will be everywhere in the patterns of familial transmission of depression.

Table 10.1. Mothers, Abuse, and Depression

| Mother | | Children | |
Abused	Depressed	Rates of Depression	Rates of Abuse
+	+	++++	++++
+	-	+++	+++
-	+	++	++
-	-	+	+

Similarly, wherever cultural and economic trauma is high, depression will be present at higher rates, accompanied by higher comorbidity. Cultural trauma provides an opportunity for controlling the trauma variable because in the presence of rapid destruction of a culture, rates of depression should increase dramatically in a few generations, a time period far too small for any meaningful change in the genome.

From a predictive standpoint, the trauma experienced by an individual by age ten should be a powerful predictor of the risk for future major depressive episode. All such effects should be particularly predominant in major depressive disorder and dysthymic disorder. The trauma model assumes that bipolar mood disorder without significant comorbidity has a primarily endogenous biological cause. The effects of trauma in bipolar mood disorder are more pathoplastic than etiological. This effect can nevertheless by clinically significant.

Twin and Adoption Studies

The problems to be addressed in twin and adoption studies of depression follow from trauma model predictions about the epidemiology. Studies of the concordance rates for depression in monozygotic and dizygotic twins are incomplete when trauma is not taken into account as a variable.

When both dizygotic twins have been severely abused, concordance rates for depression will be higher than in non-abused monozygotic twins. When abuse rates are set high enough, a ceiling effect occurs such that concordance rates for monozygotic twins cannot be significantly higher than those for dizygotic twins. Concordance rates for abuse will be higher in monozygotic than dizygotic twins.

In adoption studies, rates hinge on whether the subjects are adopted into or out of trauma pedigrees. If the biological child of an abused depressed mother is adopted into a non-abusive family, risk for depression will drop to the baseline in the general population. In the absence of an environmental promoter, the gene for depression does not express itself. Inversely, when the child of a non-abused, non-depressed mother is adopted into an abusive family, risk for depression will be much higher than for other children retained in the biological mother's extended family. The depressed phenotype is expressed in the absence of the genotype. Such data lead directly to Occam's Razor. Why postulate the existence of a gene?

A gene for depression only becomes a necessary postulate when studies are done in non-trauma pedigrees. When children are adopted in and out of non-trauma pedigrees and the predictions of the genetic model are confirmed, then environmental causation has been controlled for adequately. The principle of the necessary environmental promoter is best demonstrated in the extreme cases. The methodological question then becomes where to set the threshold for trauma. When do we stop talking of trauma and instead focus on stress? The precision of tools measuring trauma becomes increasingly important as the threshold for trauma is lowered. In extreme trauma cases, the crudest tools suffice to generate statistically significant confirmations of trauma model predictions

Biology

The trauma model states that the supposed biology of depression is often actually the biology of trauma. An example is the dexamethasone depression test (DST). The DST was hailed as a laboratory test for depression during my residency training and DSTs were ordered on a non-research, clinical basis by psychiatrists. I was instructed to order DSTs by my teachers. The DST had disappeared completely from clinical practice by 1990. Why? There had been no change in the basic data that 66% of patients with depression will show a non-suppressor response on the DST compared to 5% of patients with other psychiatric disorders, once medical causes of non-suppression are excluded.

The DST disappeared because it has no utility as a clinical diagnostic measure (Ross, 1986; Ross and Pam, 1995). There are three relevant groups of patients; clinically depressed, intermediate, and clinically not depressed. In each group there may be a positive or negative DST. This results in six cells. If the patient is clinically depressed, the diagnosis will be made and treatment instituted irrespective of DST result. Positive results are defined as true positives and negative results as false negatives.

If the patient is not clinically depressed, the diagnosis will not be made and treatment will not be instituted irrespective of DST result. Positive results are defined as false positives and negative results as true negatives. This leaves only the intermediate, clinically ambiguous group. For this group, negative results are meaningless since there is no way to determine if they are true or false negatives. This leaves only the intermediate group with a positive DST. However, the DST cannot be used in this group because there is no way to determine whether the result is a true or false positive.

If the assumption is made that the DST result is a true positive, there is now no way to determine the rate of true and false positive DSTs, and the test has no scientific validity. Using the DST as a diagnostic tool in the one group for which it has potential utility destroys the scientific status of the test as a diagnostic tool. There was never any clear recognition of this logical dilemma in psychiatry; the DST quietly disappeared from clinical psychiatry without comment.

Enthusiasm has moved on to PET scans and other technology. However, the logical problem persists no matter what the diagnosis and what the biological measure. The ceiling for the reliability of a biological diagnostic test is the reliability of the clinical diagnosis. No biological test can ever increase the reliability of a DSM-IV-TR diagnosis, and therefore no biological test can validate a DSM-IV-TR diagnosis. The only way we know that a test has provided a positive test for depression is because we have already decided that the patient is depressed. If we run the logic in reverse we set up a tautology in which the diagnosis depends on the test and can be made in the absence of the phenotype. We now have no possibility of meaningful treatment outcomes measures. Our chief theorist has become Dr. Franz Kafka.

I was taught in my residency, from 1981 to 1985, that the DST tapped into the etiological abnormality in depression, namely noradrenalin dysregulation, noradrenalin being a key neurotransmitter in hypothalamic-pituitary communication. Psychiatry has gotten quiet about noradrenalin theories of depression in the 1990s since the SSRIs have taken over the market. However, during my residency I was taught that there are noradrenergic and serotonergic depressions. I was taught to memorize which antidepressants were predominantly noradrenergic and which predominantly serotonergic. Visiting professors quizzed me on this knowledge. The exceptional resident had the list well memorized.

The problem was that there was no way to differentiate noradrenergic from serotonergic depressions. Patients could be low, normal or high on metabolites of both neurotransmitters and respond or not respond to both classes of antidepressant in a random fashion. The DST did not help sort things out. The DST was reduced to a research tool, or at most a marker that would support the decision to stop an antidepressant. The idea was that if the DST had normalized, the risk of relapse on discontinuation of the antidepressant was lower because the underlying biology of the major depressive episode had normalized. Even this predictor function of the DST has been too weak to be approved by managed care.

The trauma model predicts that the DST has a great deal to teach us about the psychobiology of trauma. Since cortisol is the major mammalian stress response hormone, one would expect dysregulation of the hypothalamic-pituitary-adrenal (HPA) axis in the chronically traumatized mammal. In the relevant experiment, two groups of human subjects are matched for current depression scores and demographic characteristics. There are one hundred subjects in each group, all currently clinically depressed.

The first group has severe childhood trauma and extensive comorbidity, the second has no trauma and mild comorbidity. The rate of DST non-suppression will be 95% in the first group and 10% in the second group. This is because the DST is tapping into the psychobiology of trauma rather than the intrinsic and unique psychobiology of depression. If the trauma subjects were removed from the pool of 5% of subjects with other psychiatric disorders who have a positive DST, the rate of non-suppressor responses in psychiatric controls would fall to 1%. This would compare to 95% non-suppression in traumatized depressed subjects. Now we have a differentiation of two groups on a biological measure approaching two orders of magnitude. The differentiation is predicted by our knowledge of mammalian physiology. The same logic applies to many other biological measures studied in depression. The trauma model predicts that DST suppressor and DST non-suppressor subtypes of unipolar depression should differ on the variables listed in Table 10.2

Table 10.2. DST Supressor and Non-Suppressor Subtypes of Depression

	Suppressor	Non-Suppressor
Trauma	+	++++
Adrenal Hypertrophy	+	++++
Comorbidity	+	++++
Early Age of Onset	+	++++
Antidepressant Response	++++	+

Consider reduced REM latency. Depressed subjects with and without reduced REM latency could be compared on relevant variables. The group with reduced REM latency would have more trauma, comorbidity, posttraumatic stress disorder, trauma nightmares and nightmare-induced awakenings.

Returning to the DST, the trauma model predicts that the chronically traumatized adrenal glands of the abused child undergo hypertrophy. Over-stimulation of the HPA axis results in a measurable increase in adrenal size on MRI scan and a significant correlation between adrenal volume and trauma dose. This effect is present by age ten because most of the trauma dose has been accumulated by then. The relevant study will include normal controls, children with depression and trauma, and children with depression but no trauma. There will be a low correlation between number of months clinically depressed and adrenal size because depressed ten-year olds without trauma histories will not have adrenal hypertrophy. They will not look any different on their HPA axes than non-abused, non-depressed controls.

The trauma model gives rise to a *serotonin tolerance theory*. The serotonin tolerance theory arises from the observation that SSRIs are effective in many different disorders including depression, panic disorder, posttraumatic stress disorder, bulimia and obsessive compulsive disorder. If one assumes that serotonin reuptake blockade is the mechanism of action of SSRIs in all these disorders, then a problem occurs. A hypofunction in the serotonin system cannot be the cause of all these different disorders if they are supposed to be biomedically distinct diseases. The psychopharmacological data provide strong evidence against the biomedical specificity of DSM-IV-TR disorders.

I propose that the etiologies of these different DSM-IV-TR disorders lie outside the serotonin system. Serotonin is a soothing, healing, dampening or modulating neurotransmitter. If we assume for purposes of illustration, that depression is caused by an abnormality in the noradrenalin system, bulimia by a dysregulation in gamma-amino-butyric acid, and obsessive-compulsive disorder by an abnormality in glutamate transmission, serotonin can modulate and normalize all these other systems. It follows from this model that SSRIs should be beneficial in all disorders arising in brain systems modulated by serotonin. The action of the SSRIs has nothing to do with the etiologies of the disorders.

Assume for a moment that depression can be caused by a primary deficiency of either noradrenalin or serotonin. One would predict that depression could occur in individuals with normal noradrenalin and low serotonin. But one could also have normal noradrenalin and high serotonin in a depressed individual whose serotonin was working overtime to compensate for low noradrenalin. This would be equivalent to someone with compensated hypothyroidism, in which T3 is normal but TSH is high. In some cases, the compensation would cause the depression to remit, but in others there might also be an elevated threshold for remission and persistent depression. Using such logic, one can predict the occurrence of depression in all possible combinations of serotonin and noradrenalin levels. In all scenarios, boosting serotonin will be helpful.

The role of serotonergic presynaptic blockade might be similar to the role of amphetamines in attention deficit disorder. The SSRIs might simply boost a modulatory system which is itself normal, thereby correcting a problem elsewhere in the brain which requires more than the usual degree of modulation.

If serotonin modulates, soothes, or dampens hyperarousal, fear, excess dissociation, depressed mood and other affects associated with childhood trauma, two things should occur. The serotonin system should be hyper-stimulated in the chronically traumatized child, and this should result in synthesis of a high number of post-synaptic serotonin receptors. From the perspective of the abnormally numerous serotonergic post-synaptic receptors, a normal concentration of serotonin in the synapse will look like a deficiency. The post-synaptic receptors will therefore experience withdrawal in the presence of normal levels of serotonin. The person will have serotonergic tolerance. Behaviorally, the individual with post-synaptic serotonergic tolerance will have to generate chaos, danger and self-abuse in order to boost serotonergic transmission, reverse withdrawal, and overcome the serotonin tolerance created by the childhood abuse.

The behavioral paradox takes the same form as the neurotransmitter paradox. The system experiences soothing and safety only in the presence of fear and danger, because fear and danger are required to activate the serotonin system sufficiently to overcome the trauma-induced tolerance.

In this model, SSRI prescriptions are an analog of methadone maintenance for opiate addiction and tolerance. In fact, the same logic applies to the trauma model of endorphin or GABA tolerance and therefore to the increased liability in trauma survivors for addiction to exogenous opiates or benzodiazepines, which are GABA agonists.

Treatment Outcome

The basic postulate of the trauma model is that treatment failures include an over-representation of comorbid trauma patients. This is true irrespective of DSM-IV-TR diagnosis and treatment modality. There are two possible impacts on the pharmaceutical industry: 1) trauma patients who are not excluded from drug trials are reducing the drug response rate and narrowing the gap between drug and placebo, or 2) drug trial exclusion criteria are excluding a huge market from systematic research.

The drug company which first took the problem of comorbidity seriously could generate a significant marketing edge if it invested in the relevant investigational new drug applications and clinical trials, particularly for SSRIs and novel neuroleptics. The more unrecognized trauma patients are currently being included in Phase III drug studies, the narrower the gap between drug and placebo, the larger the N required for significance, and the greater the developmental cost of the drug.

The same logical structure would apply to trials of pharmacotherapy and psychotherapy for depression. Subjects would be entered in phase I of the study, in which all subjects would receive standard active treatment.

There is no need for a placebo control in phase I. At the end of Phase I, treatment non-responders would be entered into Phase II. In Phase II, they would be randomized to ongoing standard treatment versus trauma therapy. The prediction of the trauma model is two-fold; 1) in phase II, trauma therapy would improve outcome, and 2) treatment non-responders in Phase I could be predicted by baseline trauma measures and degree of comorbidity.

Revisions to DSM-IV-TR

The mood disorders are one of the cleanest sections of DSM-IV-TR. All disorders included in the section belong there, and the criteria sets for depression and mania fit with clinical experience, discriminate the two states well, and are easy enough to memorize to be practical. The main problem with the mood disorders section overall is that it contains too many sub-categories and modifiers for anyone to be able to use the scheme clinically. Table 1 on page 376 of DSM-IV-TR includes twelve categories of mood disorder with six episode modifiers for each. There is no way that the average clinician can memorize and use an algorithm of this complexity to make reliable diagnoses.

From a trauma model perspective, the main problems with the mood disorders section have been shunted over into the schizophrenia and other psychotic disorders section, and will be discussed in the next chapter. As proposed in this chapter, the major problem is with the psychotic features occurring in depression and mania and their relationship to trauma.

In general, DSM-IV-TR rules are set up to separate disorders into distinct categories. This may make sense for the single gene-single disease model, and may apply to the bipolar patient with modest levels of comorbidity. The DSM-IV-TR system simply cannot handle the patient with extensive trauma-driven comorbidity. It doesn't make sense to think of the symptoms as being due to ten or fifteen different diseases. This is like diagnosing tachycardia, hypovolemia, hypotension, disrupted epidermal integrity, and histamine activation as separate diseases in the car accident victim. The DSM-IV-TR inclusion and exclusion rules for mood disorders cannot make sense of the patient with extensive comorbidity. This is true of the rules in the mood disorder section and in other sections.

For instance, according to criterion B for major depressive disorder on page 344 of DSM-IV-TR, the major depressive episode cannot be "superimposed on schizophrenia." This makes no sense. If 17.1% of respondents in the general population have experienced a major depressive episode, major depressive episodes should occur as truly independent, comorbid conditions in at least 17.1% of schizophrenics. The idea that depression is "superimposed" on schizophrenia is the reciprocal of the assumption that schizophrenia "underlies" depression. This is a scientifically arbitrary assumption driven by ideology.

Inversely, schizophrenia cannot be diagnosed when the "schizophrenia" occurs only during major depressive episodes. By DSM-IV-TR rules, this is called major depressive disorder with psychotic features. The depression "underlies" the "schizophrenia" in psychotic depression and an independent diagnosis of schizophrenia is not made. In one situation, depression underlies schizophrenia, and in the other schizophrenia underlies depression. How do we know that these rules are based on true distinctions in nature?

From a trauma model perspective, these distinctions are meaningless in the patient with extensive comorbidity. All the various symptom clusters are elements of an inclusive trauma response. Psychiatry will never have a rational diagnostic system until the problem of comorbidity is solved and incorporated into the DSM-V, DSM-VI, or DSM-VII rules.

11

SCHIZOPHRENIA AND OTHER PSYCHOTIC DISORDERS

Schizophrenia is of particular interest for several reasons. It is a terrible psychiatric disorder; it generates the greatest financial burden of any psychiatric disorder, in terms of lost productivity and incurred health care and other social system costs; and, it is the core turf of psychiatry, politically and ideologically. Bipolar mood disorder is a close second, but schizophrenia is the core biomedical brain disease in psychiatry, according to mainstream academia at the beginning of the third millennium A.D.

Within the trauma model, both schizophrenia itself and psychotic symptoms in general are highly trauma-driven. The logic of the discussion parallels that for the mood disorders.

Phenomenology

There is a major problem with the DSM-IV-TR definition of schizophrenia. According to the dominant ideology in psychiatry, schizophrenia is actually *the group of schizophrenias*. Schizophrenia is a complex, variable group of disorders with more than one cause, all of which are lumped together under the DSM-IV-TR criteria for the disorder. Not even psychiatrists who believe in the single disease model of mental illness believe that schizophrenia is a single disease.

But that is not the main problem. According to DSM-IV-TR, schizophrenia requires only one symptom, auditory hallucinations: "Only one criterion A symptom is required if delusions are bizarre or hallucinations consist of a voice keeping up a running commentary on the person's behavior or thoughts, or two or more voices conversing with each other" (page 285).

Unfortunately, the DSM-IV-TR definition of schizophrenia makes no sense medically. By DSM-IV-TR logic, schizophrenia could be renamed *command hallucination disorder*.

Command hallucination disorder is equivalent to *cough disorder* or *fever disorder*. In no other branch of medicine is a complex, heterogeneous, severe disorder defined by a single symptom. This problem in the DSM-IV-TR definition of schizophrenia makes it impossible to narrow the schizophrenia subject group sufficiently to obtain consistent findings in any area of research. Since the DSM-IV-TR criteria for schizophrenia are so problematic, I will talk mostly about the phenomenology of psychotic symptoms in general; the logic can also be applied to the single disease of schizophrenia.

There is a profound problem with the mental status examination of psychotic symptoms in contemporary psychiatry. Current psychiatric practice is equivalent to a cardiology in which physicians examine the pulse, but never use a stethoscope. Worse than that, the only information gathered about the pulse is its rate. In fact, in internal medicine, there are many types of pulse: regular, irregular, regularly irregular, irregularly irregular, water hammer, and others I forget. In ancient systems of medicine, complicated subsystems of pulse were catalogued.

Numerous types of heart sounds can be detected by the stethoscope, including clicks, rubs, and murmurs. The stethoscope can be placed in different locations, the patient can be made to sit or lie in different positions, and sounds heard through the stethoscope can be correlated with many other observations about neck veins, enlargement of the liver, absence of pulses in the foot, calf pain on walking, and so on.

The mental status examination of auditory hallucinations in psychiatry has become extremely narrow and limited. Study of the phenomenology of psychosis requires a reversal of this one hundred-year old historical trend towards increasingly perfunctory mental status exam.

For instance, auditory hallucinations can vary in many different ways: by origin, internal versus external; by volume, loud versus quiet; in number, single, several or numerous; in age, child versus adolescent or adult; and in gender, male versus female. Voices can be punitive or kind. They can be interactive or fixed. Voices can talk to the person or about the person. They can comment on the person's thoughts, feelings or actions. They can give advice, or produce only gibberish.

Voices can be understood by the person as being symptoms of brain disease, spirit guides, demons, God talking, alter personalities, normal phenomena, or evidence that their brains are controlled by aliens from another dimension. People close to the person hearing the voice can view them as ill, interesting, possessed, divinely inspired, epileptic, normal, or stoned. All of these considerations are aspects of the phenomenology of auditory hallucinations.

Voices can take control of the person's body. These periods of executive control may or may not be accompanied by amnesia. The voices may remember things which the "person" cannot recall, and these experiences can sometimes be corroborated by other documents or people.

The phenomenology of psychosis is infinitely more complex than allowed by the mental status examination procedures of contemporary psychiatry. Within contemporary biomedical psychiatry, the richness of the phenomenology is irrelevant. Auditory hallucinations are symptoms of psychosis. Psychosis is caused by brain disease. The treatment is antipsychotic medication.

Within the conceptual system of contemporary psychiatry, there is no need to inquire about or document the phenomenology of psychosis in any detail. The details are irrelevant to the treatment plan and to research on the biology of psychosis. Within the trauma model, the opposite is true. This aspect of the trauma model was learned from the study of dissociative identity disorder (Ross, 1997).

Within contemporary biological psychiatry, voices are symptoms with which the patient is afflicted. The doctor works with the patient to get rid of the symptoms, which in psychiatry means prescribing medications. But within the trauma model, voices may be the patient too, in some but not all cases. The doctor may work with the voices to negotiate a new relationship between them and the part of the self in executive control. This approach need not be limited to voices occurring in dissociative disorders.

In general, according to the trauma model, psychotic symptoms are more common in individuals with trauma histories than those without. Psychotic symptoms are accompanied by more comorbidity the more trauma there has been. Overall, for conceptual purposes, one can assume the existence of two pathways to positive symptoms of schizophrenia, an endogenous disease pathway and a trauma pathway. The two pathways are interactive, not mutually exclusive.

The more predominant the trauma pathway in a given case, the more rich and complex will be the phenomenology of the psychotic symptoms. In trauma pathway cases, for instance, it is much more likely that the voices can be engaged in a rational conversation. In trauma cases, when the examiner asks the voice a question, the voice can answer inside the person's head, and the person can restate the answer out loud. This technique is called *talking through* in the dissociative identity disorder literature.

In conjunction with other variables, attempts to talk through to the voices allow the examiner to triage the individual to trauma or endogenous biological treatment. Engagement of the voices in a rational interchange functions as an indicator of etiology, a predictor of level of comorbidity, and a triaging decision for treatment. In trauma therapy, it can also be a treatment technique.

Other aspects of auditory hallucinations described by the comprehensive mental status examination can potentially serve the same functions. There is at present no agreed-upon method for differentiating psychotic from dissociative symptoms, particularly auditory hallucinations. This is a phenomenological problem which requires sustained, careful study. A great deal of research and treatment for psychosis has been confounded by the unrecognized presence of dissociation in the domain of psychosis.

Table 11.1. Psychotic Symptoms in Multiple Personality Disorder and Schizophrenia

	Multiple Personality	Schizophrenia
	(N=368)	(N=1739)
Average Number of Psychotic Features	4.9	1.3
	(N=368)	(N=2576
	%	%
Prevalence of One or More Psychotic Symptoms	87.0	55.5

Positive symptoms of schizophrenia, including auditory hallucinations, are actually more common in dissociative identity disorder than schizophrenia. In a paper summarizing large series of multiple personality cases and large series of schizophrenia cases taken from the literature, I showed that a higher percentage of multiple personality cases than schizophrenia cases report one or more Schneiderian first rank symptoms of schizophrenia. As well, the average number of

Schneiderian symptoms per patient is higher in multiple personality disorder than in schizophrenia (Ross, Miller, Reagor, Bjornson, Fraser, and Anderson, 1990). These findings are shown in Table 11.1.

In another study of the general population in Winnipeg, Canada (Ross and Joshi, 1992) I divided respondents into those who reported no Schneiderian first rank symptoms (N=397) and those who reported experiencing three or more lifetime (N=35): 45.7% of the respondents with three or more symptoms reported a history of childhood physical and/or sexual abuse compared to 8.1% of those with no psychotic symptoms.

There is a powerful relationship between trauma and psychosis in the general population and in clinical populations. The data I have published suggest that the trauma pathway may account for a larger percentage of the positive symptoms of psychosis overall than the endogenous disease pathway. Whether this is generally true can only be determined with further research.

What about the negative symptoms of schizophrenia? The trauma model predicts that there is a neglect pathway to negative symptoms of schizophrenia. The negative symptoms include loss of drive, emptiness, social withdrawal, and lack of emotions. They are what is missing in the person with schizophrenia.

Positive symptoms, on the other hand, are those which are present in people with schizophrenia but absent in normal people. They include hallucinations, delusions, agitation, and disorganized thinking.

Traumatic events are usually defined as events outside the range of normal experience, such as incest, rape, combat, natural disasters, and transportation disasters. Neglect, however, is the absence of good events which would happen in the normal course of life. The good events include consistent love, nurturance, guidance, protection, and limit setting by parents. According to the trauma model, neglect can be at least as traumatic as events like incest, physical abuse, combat and natural disasters. Neglect is the absence of something good, rather than the presence of something bad, but it is still traumatic.

A measure of neglect should predict negative symptoms of schizophrenia independently of the ability of a measure of active trauma to predict positive symptoms. The relationship between neglect and negative symptoms of schizophrenia is in fact already recognized in conventional psychiatry. My teachers and the textbooks told me that negative symptoms can be caused by chronic institutionalization. The other pathways to negative symptoms I was taught in my residency were medication side effects, comorbid depression, and the endogenous disease process of schizophrenia. Of the four pathways to negative symptoms recognized during my residency, only the endogenous disease pathway could not be inferred directly from clinical observation and patient histories.

There should be a purely or predominantly negative symptom form of schizophrenia which borders on pervasive developmental disorders and autism. Just as there are endogenous and trauma pathways to the positive symptoms of schizophrenia, there should be neglect and endogenous pathways to the negative symptoms. One might say that the negative symptoms of schizophrenia are the positive symptoms of neglect. The effects of institutionalization provide the best evidence for the neglect pathway to negative symptoms in adults.

These considerations have led me to postulate the existence of a dissociative subtype of schizophrenia, occurring on a spectrum shown in Figure 11.1.

Figure 11.1. The Dissociative Subtype of Schizophrenia

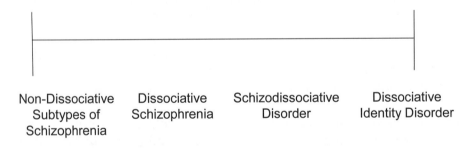

| Non-Dissociative Subtypes of Schizophrenia | Dissociative Schizophrenia | Schizodissociative Disorder | Dissociative Identity Disorder |

At the left hand end of the spectrum are the non-dissociative subtypes of schizophrenia, including paranoid, catatonic and undifferentiated. Moving right, one encounters the dissociative subtype of schizophrenia. These are individuals who have schizophrenia, but with prominent dissociative symptoms. Next there is an intermediate disorder I call schizodissociative disorder, then at the far right is dissociative identity disorder.

Symptoms vary by position on the continuum. Towards the left hand end one encounters more negative symptoms of psychosis, fewer positive symptoms, less psychological trauma, less comorbidity, and less responsiveness to psychotherapy. The voices become less interactive the further left you go, and there is more biology of endogenous psychotic disease.

Towards the right hand end of the continuum, there are more clearly structured and distinct ego states, the voices are more interactive, there is more comorbidity, and there is less formal thought disorder. There is more biology of trauma and less biology of endogenous psychotic disease. Overall, there are more positive and fewer negative symptoms of psychosis.

Schizodissociative disorder is an intermediate entity in which there is severe trauma, lots of comorbidity, an interactive quality to the voices, and ego states distinct enough to qualify for dissociative disorder not otherwise specified. The states are not as structured, personified or stable as those in dissociative identity disorder, however. In addition there is a difficult-to-define thought disorder.

The thought disorder is not as florid as one finds further left on the continuum, but it is definitely present. The person cannot process information in the usual way, cannot retain information in a stable fashion, and cannot learn from experience or psychotherapy as effectively as someone further right. Trying to attribute these problems to a psychotic thought disorder is difficult, because one must consider the confounding effects of dissociation, depression, attention deficit disorder, specific learning difficulties, substance abuse, and simple resistance to change.

An example of the biology of trauma which varies across the continuum is the non-suppressor response to the dexamethasone suppression test (DST) (Ross, 1992). There should be more abnormal DST results the further right you move on the continuum.

The continuum is a good example of a set of testable hypotheses which would never arise within the conceptual system of late twentieth century academic psychiatry.

Natural History

The natural history of psychotic symptoms varies depending on whether the etiological pathway is trauma or endogenous disease. In pure endogenous pathway cases, the onset of positive symptoms will better match *the myth of young Johnny*. There will be less prodrome, a more rapid rise in the psychotic symptom curve, less comorbidity, clearer periods of remission, and less deterioration from baseline over time.

In pure trauma pathway cases, there will be a more complex prodrome, a more gradual rise in the psychotic symptom curve, more comorbidity, and less clear periods of remission. In some cases there will be deterioration from baseline and in others not. This will depend on a host of factors including current social support, presence of healing and corrective persons and experiences in childhood, and innate hardiness.

Since so many permutations of abuse, neglect and endogenous disease are possible, clean predictions will be difficult to substantiate. Endogenous biological variables can include genetic predisposition, intrauterine insult, birth complications, and injuries, infections and other disease processes occurring after birth. Add to this the effect of substances of abuse, and the fact that psychotic symptoms can occur in Cluster A and B personality disorders and in many diagnostic categories on Axis I, and you have a hyper-complex etiological soup.

Generally, the most severe psychotic illnesses will involve high doses of both the endogenous disease and the trauma pathways.

Epidemiology

The epidemiological predictions for psychosis parallel those for depression. In the general population, psychotic symptoms are highly correlated with psychological trauma, and therefore in turn with extensive comorbidity. The first-degree relatives of pedophiles will have more psychotic symptoms than relatives of non-offender males.

The highest density of psychotic symptoms will occur in the relatives of men who are psychotic pedophiles, the least in relatives of men who are not psychotic and do not commit sexual offenses. Psychotic men who do not commit sexual offenses will have first-degree relatives with an intermediate density of psychotic symptoms, as will offenders without psychosis. However, symptom density will be greater in the pedigrees of non-psychotic offenders than in the pedigrees of non-offender psychotics. These relationships are illustrated in Table 11.3.

These effects will not breed true. For instance, the relatives of both non-psychotic offenders and non-offender psychotics will have more mood disorders than relatives of normal men, when depression in the index males is controlled for, or varied systematically in analyses.

The less child abuse and neglect there is in a culture, the lower the

Table 11.3. Psychotic Symptoms and Comorbidity in the First-Degree Relatives of Four Types of Men

Index Male		First Degree Relatives		
Pedophile	Psychotic	Psychotic Symptoms	Comorbidity	Incest
+	+	++++	++++	++++
+	-	+++	+++	+++
-	+	++	++	++
-	-	+	+	+

density of psychotic symptoms. Density of psychotic symptoms could be measured in three ways: percentage of the population with a DSM-IV-TR psychotic disorder; average number of psychotic symptoms per person, or average scores on measures of psychosis; and, prevalence of having one or more psychotic symptoms. The threshold in the latter analysis could be set at one, two, three or more psychotic symptoms lifetime.

Twin And Adoption Studies

An assumption of the trauma model is that DSM-IV-TR disorders do not breed true, even in predominant or pure genetic pathway pedigrees. What runs in families, both genetically and environmentally, is a predisposition to psychopathology in general. The genetic causes of psychiatric disorders, assuming they exist at all, simply do not result in clean DSM-IV-TR categories, except in perhaps a small minority of cases. In general, one can talk about a diagnostically nonspecific polygenetic predisposition for psychopathology, but not a gene for schizophrenia.

True genetic diseases breed true. For instance, relatives of people with cystic fibrosis have elevated rates of cystic fibrosis, but not Huntington's Chorea. Inversely, relatives of people with Huntington's Chorea have elevated rates of Huntington's Chorea, but not cystic fibrosis. In psychiatry, this is not the case. Having one psychiatric disorder increases the risk for having others in yourself and your relatives.

Twin studies already show that the genetic component of schizophrenia is not very strong. Overall, averaging all the studies together, the concordance rate for schizophrenia in monozygotic twins is only about 40%, perhaps 45%. In cystic fibrosis the concordance rate for monozygotic twins is 100%. This one piece of information proves that the environment is a major contributor to the emergence of the schizophrenic phenotype.

Restated in common English, if one identical twin has schizophrenia, the other twin gets it only 40% - 45% of the time. This is the concordance rate. The twins are genetically identical, setting aside any spontaneous mutations in their DNA. Therefore the environment is making a major contribution to whether a twin does or does not have schizophrenia.

In principle, simplifying the concordance problem to its basic logic, there are two possibilities: both twins have a gene for schizophrenia, but it is expressed in only one; or, neither twin has a gene for schizophrenia, and it is caused environmentally in neither, one, or both. The gene for schizophrenia is the genotype, while the actual clinical picture of schizophrenia is the phenotype.

The twin concordance data prove that one of two things is going on: 1) there is no gene for schizophrenia, or 2) the gene is either turned on by the environment in the identical twin who has schizophrenia, or turned off by the environment in the twin who does not have it.

These possibilities can be tested by adoption data that already exist in nature. The trauma model predicts that the risk for schizophrenia drops from 10% towards 1% if you are adopted away from a schizophrenic parent at birth into a healthy, normal family. How far the risk drops towards 1% depends on the percentage of the etiology that is due to the intrauterine environment. In principle, this variable could be controlled for by in vitro fertilization and implantation in surrogate mothers, an experiment which is unethical, but which has been carried out on a small scale naturalistically by fertility specialists.

The trauma model also predicts that the risk for schizophrenia, and psychotic symptoms in general, rises if you are adopted at birth out of a non-schizophrenic pedigree into a home with a schizophrenic parent. If these findings are not obtained with narrowly defined schizophrenia, they will hold for psychotic symptoms in general, as measured by existing structured interviews, standardized questionnaires, and self-report measures.

The twin data will show, once enough studies have been completed, that identical twins discordant for schizophrenia are also discordant biologically on relevant etiological variables, whatever those might prove to be. These findings will provide further evidence in favor of environmental etiology.

Twin studies can also demonstrate the interaction between genes, trauma and the psychotic phenotype. The psychotic phenotype can be defined narrowly by the presence of DSM-IV-TR schizophrenia; more broadly by the presence of any Axis I psychotic disorder or paranoid or schizotypal personality disorders; or by scores on measures of psychosis. The full machinery of psychometric analysis can be brought to bear on such scores including correlation, regression, receiver operating, and taxometric analyses.

The trauma model predicts the hierarchy of twin concordance rates shown in Table 11.4.

Table 11.4. Concordance Rates for Psychosis in Twin Pairs

Monozygotic	Dizygotic	Trauma in Both	Trauma in Neither	Concordance
+	-	+	-	++++
-	+	+	-	+++
+	-	-	+	++
-	+	-	+	+

Dizygotic twins concordant for extreme, chronic childhood trauma will have higher concordance for psychosis than monozygotic twins with no trauma. This finding will prove that the trauma pathway to psychosis is stronger than the genetic pathway.

Biology

As is true for depression, anxiety, and substance abuse, attempts to identify the endogenous biology of psychosis have been confounded by the unrecognized presence of trauma pathway symptoms. The existing research on the biology of psychosis needs to be redone or at the least re-analyzed. The presumption that psychosis means endogenous biological etiology is not questioned within contemporary academic psychiatry, not at the level of serious investment in research money, resources, time and energy.

Like the culture in general, contemporary psychiatry is focused on molecular biology. A simple unidirectional causal model dominates. The idea is that genes for mental illness are like genes for cystic fibrosis. They relentlessly cause psychiatric diseases from the cell nucleus out, and the fundamental biological processes are unaffected by culture, sociology or psychology. Sure, environmental interventions like antibiotics and chest physiotherapy can make a difference in cystic fibrosis, but they only affect the end state of the disease.

The fundamental cure of cystic fibrosis has to involve splicing out or shutting off the gene.

This is the dream of contemporary academic psychiatry, to treat psychiatric disorders by direct manipulation of specific causative genes or gene regions. The problem with the dream is simple: that is not how the biology works. According to the trauma model, the interaction between the genome and the environment that results in psychiatric disorders is subtle, variable, complex, and involves numerous bi-directional feedback lops between genome and environment. Except perhaps in a tiny minority of cases, the genetic component has limited or no diagnostic specificity.

There is no gene for schizophrenia in nature. Just like there is no gene for lung cancer. Some cases of lung cancer may be caused by specific genes which do not require an environmental promoter to produce the disease state. But it is certain that many people would not get lung cancer if they never smoked cigarettes. The same thing applies to schizophrenia, only more so, so much more so that a specific gene or set of genes for schizophrenia is a minor contributor to the overall rate of psychotic symptoms in the general population, if it exists at all.

Treatment Outcome

The general treatment outcome prediction of the trauma model applies to schizophrenia and to psychotic symptoms in general. There is no accepted, serious psychotherapy of schizophrenia in academic psychiatry, only because the trauma model has not yet been accepted.

The trauma model predicts that antipsychotic medication non-responders tend to be trauma pathway cases. The addition of trauma psychotherapy, including talking with the voices, to the treatment plan for medication non-responders will improve the outcome, as measured by standard measures used in the field.

It is possible that the trauma and endogenous disease pathways to psychosis can be differentiated by receptor subtype. For instance, the conventional neuroleptics, or antipsychotics, are post-synaptic dopamine receptor blockers at the D2 receptor subtype. D2 receptor blocker responders tend to have the non-dissociative subtypes of schizophrenia. D2 non-responders who then respond to D4 receptor blockers tend to have the dissociative subtype of schizophrenia or schizodissociative disorder. The overlap between schizodissociative and schizoaffective disorders is almost 100%.

As mentioned above, a specific property of the auditory hallucinations will predict D2 blocker non-responsiveness and improved outcome when trauma psychotherapy is added: the ability of the voices to engage in rational conversation with the therapist, either through talking through or by a switch of executive control.

About two thirds of inpatients with dissociative identity disorder meet structured interview criteria for schizophrenia or schizoaffective disorder. When treated with psychotherapy, these people experience a profound reduction of their psychotic symptomatology. If one rejects the validity of the dissociative identity disorder, and agrees to classify these people as psychotic, I have already provided evidence that trauma therapy is effective for psychosis (Ellason and Ross, 1997). This study is posted on my web page at www.rossinst.com.

Revisions To DSM-IV-TR

There are numerous problems with the DSM-IV-TR criteria for schizophrenia and other psychotic disorders. I will point out a few of them. The DSM-IV-TR requires only one symptom to make the diagnosis of schizophrenia. The positive symptoms of schizophrenia are far too non-specific to be diagnostic by themselves, no matter how many are counted. In fact, the more positive symptoms are present, the less likely the correct diagnosis is schizophrenia and the more likely it is dissociative identity disorder.

There need to be rules in both the schizophrenia and dissociative identity disorder sections telling the psychiatrist how to differentiate the two disorders. Guidelines should be drawn from the continuum for the dissociative subtype of schizophrenia, and then subjected to field trials. There should be more diagnostic emphasis on the negative symptoms of schizophrenia.

The comorbidity of schizoaffective disorder with posttraumatic stress disorder and the dissociative disorders needs to be brought into the DSM system.

Brief psychotic disorder used to be called brief reactive psychosis in DSM-III-R (American Psychiatric Association, 1987). When initially proposed, the new DSM-IV diagnosis of acute stress disorder was called brief reactive dissociative disorder. The relationship between brief psychotic disorder and acute stress disorder needs to be clarified. The stressor criterion was dropped from the main diagnostic criteria set for brief reactive psychosis when it was renamed brief psychotic disorder in DSM-IV. However, a specifier of "with marked stressors" was retained, so the conceptualization did not change.

In contrast, the stressor criterion was retained in the main diagnostic criteria set for brief reactive dissociative disorder when it was renamed acute stress disorder, and placed in the anxiety disorders section of DSM-IV. Brief psychotic disorder can be diagnosed with the single symptom of "grossly disorganized or catatonic behavior." Acute stress disorder includes a criterion of "a reduction in awareness of his or her surroundings."

Most people receiving a diagnosis of brief psychotic disorder with marked stressors should also meet criteria for acute stress disorder, and vice versa. What do such people have, an anxiety disorder or a psychotic disorder? Where is the threshold for transition from adjustment disorder to brief psychotic disorder? DSM-IV-TR has no rules for answering these questions.

As it does for brief psychotic disorder with marked stressors, DSM-IV-TR specifies an environmental cause of schizophrenia in its diagnostic criteria. This is the only specific etiology for schizophrenia in the DSM-IV-TR. The environmental cause of schizophrenia is hidden in the criteria for shared psychotic disorder. The criteria for shared psychotic disorder include:

- A delusion develops in an individual in the context of a close relationship with another person(s), who has an already-established delusion.

- The delusion is similar in content to that of the person who already has the established delusion.

Under the heading, Course, the DSM-IV-TR text for shared psychotic disorder states that, "With separation from the primary case, the individual's delusional beliefs disappear, sometimes quickly and sometimes quite slowly" (page 306). DSM-IV-TR is stating that both the cause and the treatment of brief psychotic disorder are environmental.

What happens if the shared delusion is "bizarre," lasts for more than six months and is accompanied by social and occupational deterioration? By DSM-IV-TR criteria, the person now has schizophrenia, but the schizophrenia by definition had a purely environmental cause, and has a purely psychosocial treatment. If this form of schizophrenia has an environmental cause, then why can't others?

What is the difference between shared psychotic disorder and brief psychotic disorder without marked stressors? Brief psychotic disorder by definition lasts only one day to one month. Why is there no duration criterion for shared psychotic disorder? According to DSM-IV-TR, schizophreniform disorder lasts for one month to six months, after which the diagnosis changes to schizophrenia. One progresses from brief psychotic disorder to schizophreniform disorder to schizophrenia over a period of six months.

The intent of these criteria is to prevent the psychiatrist from making the grave diagnosis of schizophrenia too quickly. Some cases in fact remit and do not go on to chronic illness. Why isn't there a similar progression for shared psychotic disorder? Problems like this are pervasive in the section of DSM-IV-TR called, Schizophrenia and Other Psychotic Disorders.

Throughout DSM-IV-TR, there are problems with the rules for deciding what is the "primary" disorder in a given case. According to DSM-IV-TR criteria for major depressive disorder (page 344), a diagnosis of schizophrenia excludes a primary diagnosis of depression, and the depression is "superimposed" on the schizophrenia. This is an arbitrary assignment based on ideology, not science. The judgment that a clinical depression is secondary to schizophrenia undermines the disease model of depression, even though it is based on a disease model of schizophrenia. Why? If depression can be secondary to schizophrenia then it is not necessarily an independent biomedical disease. If this is true in people with schizophrenia, it can be true in other people. If it can be true in other people, it can be true in many, most, or all cases of depression.

If depression can be secondary to schizophrenia, it can be secondary to other things, such as trauma. But saying that depression is secondary to trauma is absurd. It's like saying that a broken bone is secondary to hitting a tree while skiing. The statement has no medical meaning. What would a primary broken bone be?

The logic of psychiatric vocabulary is medically absurd in many respects. For instance, what does it mean to say that schizophrenia causes auditory hallucinations? Such statements, which are common, require an assumption that schizophrenia and voices are separate things, one a cause, the other an effect. But there is no schizophrenia separate from its symptoms. The voices are the schizophrenia. Schizophrenia cannot cause itself. DSM-IV-TR needs to be revised to ensure that this class of logical error is eliminated.

This is true in all areas of the manual. Psychiatrists frequently explain that depression causes loss of appetite and poor sleep. There is no entity of depression separate from its symptoms. "Depression," in this way of speaking and thinking, has been reified and concretized into an entity capable of causing its own symptoms.

In the trauma field, things are clearer. Contact with the ground after falling out of an airplane without a parachute causes trauma. Confusion may arise from the fact that the word *trauma* is often used to refer both to the event and to the traumatic impact of the event. This is only a semantic problem, however. It is not a logical error to say that trauma causes trauma.

Finally, the word *schizophrenia* is antiquated and misleading. It means *split mind disorder*. Split mind disorder does not describe the DSM-IV-TR entity named schizophrenia and there is nothing about splitting of the mind in the diagnostic criteria, text, current academic literature, or research. No-one submits research grants designed to study how the mind gets split in schizophrenia.

The idea that schizophrenics have split minds and therefore should receive a diagnosis of schizophrenia, originated with Bleuler. His clinical description of schizophrenia matches the DSM-IV-TR diagnostic criteria, text, and supporting literature for dissociative identity disorder, not schizophrenia (Gainer, 1994).

12

ANXIETY DISORDERS

Upon completion of my residency training in 1985, I worked for three years as the Medical Director of the Anxiety Disorders Clinic at a University teaching hospital in Winnipeg, Canada. I am a co-editor of a book on panic disorder (Walker, Norton, and Ross, 1991), and I have completed two drug company contracts on generalized anxiety disorder, one of which I published (Ross and Matas, 1987). In the neighborhood of two thousand individuals with posttraumatic stress disorder (PTSD) have been treated in my Trauma Program in Dallas since 1991. In addition, I was on the DSM-IV-TR Committee which initially reviewed acute stress disorder. These are my qualifications to comment on the anxiety disorders.

From a trauma model perspective, PTSD is not the core diagnosis, around which other comorbidity revolves. PTSD is just one facet of the trauma response. It is arbitrary which of the DSM-IV-TR disorders gets to be PT-D. We have PTSD, but we could just as easily have posttraumatic psychotic disorder (PTPD), posttraumatic mood disorder (PTMD), posttraumatic dissociative disorder (PTDD), or posttraumatic substance abuse disorder (PTSAD). The symptoms listed in the DSM-IV-TR criteria for PTSD are only one slice of the trauma response.

Logically, one could have a DSM diagnosis called stress disorder (SD). It would be identical to PTSD but without Criterion A, the traumatic event. There would then be endogenous biological theories for SD which completely ignored the trauma. It is because PTSD is only one element of the overall trauma response that it does not receive special treatment in this chapter. For logical consistency, PTSD should really be PTAD, posttraumatic anxiety disorder.

Phenomenology

A major problem with the anxiety disorders is their extensive comorbidity with each other and with major depressive disorder. I noticed while doing drug company contracts for generalized anxiety disorder and major depressive disorder that the Hamilton Anxiety Scale includes depression items, while the Hamilton Depression Scale includes anxiety items. Even the psychometric definitions of anxiety and depression overlap.

The divisions between simple phobia, panic disorder, generalized anxiety disorder and social phobia are arbitrary. The anticipatory anxiety and elevated baseline anxiety in panic disorder is indistinguishable from generalized anxiety disorder. Inversely, almost everyone with generalized anxiety disorder has had at least a few panic attacks, even if they don't have enough to support a diagnosis of panic disorder. I learned this when I completed 60 subjects in a study comparing buspirone to diazepam and placebo for treatment of generalized anxiety disorder (Ross and Matas, 1987).

Panic attacks in panic disorder can be triggered by exposure to an environmental phobic stimulus. The panic of panic disorder doesn't look much different from the panic of simple phobia, however. All that differs between panic disorder and simple phobia is the number of phobic stimuli and the occurrence of spontaneous panic. Social phobia could be redefined as a simple phobia in which the single phobic stimulus is social situations. The fact that many different social situations function as phobic stimuli is irrelevant; we do not diagnose one hundred different dog phobias, one for each species of dog.

The similarities between all these disorders are much more striking than the differences. I regard the entire complex of diagnoses as a single panic-phobic anxiety disorder. From a trauma model perspective, the important research question is, what are the phenomenological differences between trauma pathway panic-phobic anxiety disorder and non-trauma pathway cases?

Once the basic logic of the trauma model is grasped, from reading the chapters of this book on mood disorders and psychosis, the predictions for other sections of DSM-IV-TR are apparent. Trauma pathway cases of panic-phobic anxiety disorder will have more comorbidity, including much higher rates of comorbid PTSD.

Non-trauma pathway cases will tend to fit single diagnoses of generalized anxiety, panic, simple or social phobia more easily. Having trauma and one of the panic-phobic anxiety disorders will increase one's chances of having others. Once the trauma dose exceeds threshold, virtually no-one will meet criteria for only one DSM-IV-TR anxiety disorder. In comparison, individuals with a non-trauma pathway to one of these disorders will be at much lower risk for having others. The trauma dose threshold must be determined mathematically, using receiver operating analysis or a similar procedure.

In panic disorder, when the number of panic attacks is held constant or controlled for in analyses, there will be an increasing amount of phobic avoidance per unit of panic as trauma dosage increases. A person with six spontaneous panic attacks per month but no trauma will have less agoraphobia than another person with six panic attacks per month who has a trauma history. Agoraphobia without panic attacks will be rare in people without significant trauma.

Obsessive compulsive disorder (OCD) belongs to a second sub-category within the DSM-IV-TR anxiety disorders section. I assessed cases of clean, non-trauma pathway OCD while working in the Anxiety Disorders Clinic in Canada. However, other cases were much more complex. I learned from these cases that the content of the compulsion, obsession or phobia is important, both for predicting comorbidity and for planning treatment.

A semen phobia is much more likely to be trauma driven than a height phobia. It is much more likely to be accompanied by PTSD, a sexual dysfunction, a personality disorder and other comorbidity. A woman who has panic attacks only she drives by a topless bar is more likely to have been sexually abused than a woman who panics only at supermarkets. Similarly, obsessions and compulsions with a sexual content are more likely to be symptoms of unresolved sexual trauma than simple counting and checking compulsions. None of these relationships are specific and one cannot infer a trauma history from any single symptom. Nevertheless, the relationships are testable scientific predictions.

In OCD there is always magical childlike thinking. In some cases, there are discrete ego states from whom the magical thinking, obsessions and compulsions arise. One will be much more likely to encounter such discrete ego states during hypnosis or sodium amytal interviews in trauma pathway cases. This prediction could be tested by having the clinician attempting to evoke an ego state do so while blind to the trauma history and comorbidity profiles of subjects.

Non-trauma pathway OCD cases are more likely to be endogenous and biological in etiology. Therefore they will have higher rates of comorbid Tourette's Syndrome, other tic disorders, and developmental and learning disabilities than trauma pathway cases. The trauma pathway cases will have higher rates of comorbid disorders in the trauma spectrum, including PTSD, dissociative disorders, borderline personality disorder, psychoses and substance abuse.

By definition, all cases of PTSD are trauma pathway cases. However, a prediction can be made about who will be at higher risk for PTSD in response to a single major traumatic event in adulthood. The person primed by childhood trauma will have had more active psychiatric disorders prior to the adult-onset single event, and will be more likely to develop PTSD. The risk will vary with childhood trauma dose.

The question of whether there are distinct dissociation-predominant and anxiety-predominant subtypes of PTSD may or may not prove to be interesting. If there are distinct subtypes, they probably vary by characteristics of the trauma, rather than endogenous variables. For instance, intrafamilial, deliberate and human-induced trauma may cause more dissociation. There may be a variation by total trauma dosage, with dissociative symptoms emerging at higher dosages. Alternatively, dissociation and anxiety may function as a single trauma-response factor.

These relationships are unclear to me because my clinical experience is with inpatients who exhibit ceiling effects. All of them have high scores on both anxiety and dissociation. All of them have at least one dissociative disorder and one anxiety disorder.

Natural History

Trauma pathway cases to anxiety disorders will have an earlier onset and a more complex and chronic course. They will have fewer periods of spontaneous remission. The picture will be increasingly severe the more ongoing cumulative trauma there is throughout the life cycle, and the fewer the restorative and healing experiences. Social supports, medical status, finances and many other variables will influence both phenomenology and course.

In PTSD, priming by childhood trauma will predict delayed onset. However, primed individuals will exhibit a bimodal response pattern. Because they have more reason to numb out, suppress and forget, they will be more likely to block out the trauma, through formal amnesia or simple denial, and therefore not exhibit symptoms initially. On the other hand, if their defenses are already overwhelmed and they are already decompensated, they will be at higher risk for immediate, florid PTSD.

In comparison, individuals exposed to the same or similar events in adulthood who have not been primed by childhood trauma, will tend to have a less variable, intermediate response. This prediction leads to two trauma response curves illustrated in Figure 12.1.

Figure 12.1 Priming Predicts Delayed Onset in PTSD

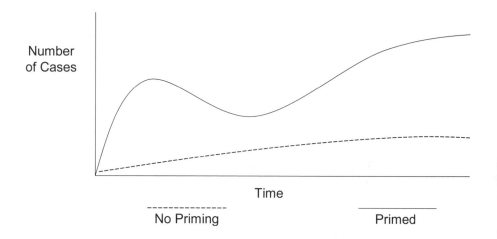

When adult victims of the same major traumatic event are divided into two subgroups (with and without childhood priming), the trauma group will continue to yield newly emerging cases of active PTSD for longer, and will have more total cases over time.

The natural history of PTSD should be studied in the context of a full range of comorbidity. Let's assume that after a major traumatic event in adulthood, such as a bombing, transportation disaster or natural disaster, 25% of exposed individuals develop PTSD within a year. They have never had such symptoms prior to the traumatic event.

What about other conmorbidity? The trauma model predicts that 25% or more of exposed individuals will develop major depressive episode for the first time in their lives within one year of the event. PTDD (posttraumatic depressive disorder) is as intrinsic to the trauma response as PTSD. Similarly, there will be new cases of PTSAD (posttraumatic substance abuse disorder).

The prevalence of new cases of the various Axis I diagnoses within one year of the traumatic event will occur in a hierarchy of frequency. The same logic will apply to the Axis II disorders, if one tabulates the emergence of new symptom and behavior patterns within the first year after the event. These symptoms will not meet DSM-IV-TR criteria for an Axis II diagnosis only because their duration is too short. The hierarchy will be similar to the hierarchy of comorbidity in dissociative identity disorder. The natural history of the PTSD will be worse, the greater the degree of comorbidity.

Epidemiology

The general predictions of the trauma model will hold for the anxiety disorders. Rates of PTSD will rise more quickly with trauma dose than rates of panic disorder or social phobia, but the difference will not be dramatic. The dose-response curve for PTSD will be shifted left compared to the other anxiety disorders, and will plateau at a higher overall rate. These relationships are shown in Figure 12.2.

Figure 12.2. PTSD and the Other Rates of Anxiety Disorder with Increasing Trauma

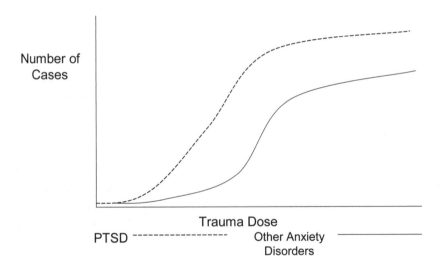

The risk for comorbidity in each anxiety disorder considered separately will rise with trauma dose. This pattern will hold most strongly for comorbid depression; the rate of comorbid depression will rise faster with increasing trauma than the rate of comorbid eating disorders, for instance.

The reciprocal relationship will also hold. When depression is assigned primary status, rates of comorbid anxiety disorders will rise faster with increasing trauma than rates of other disorders. This will be so because anxiety and depression are more intertwined with each other in nature, and as part of the trauma response, than, say, psychosis and eating disorders.

Twin And Adoption Studies

The general logic of the trauma model will also apply to twin and adoption studies for anxiety disorders. In twins, concordance rates for each anxiety disorder will be driven upwards by increasing trauma; the difference in the trauma dose-concordance curves for monozygotic and dizygotic twins will not be striking, demonstrating that the effects of the environment predominate over the effects of the genome. These relationships are illustrated in Figure 12.3.

Figure 12.3 Concordance Rates for Anxiety Disorders in Monozygotic and Dizygotic Twins as a Function of Trauma Dose

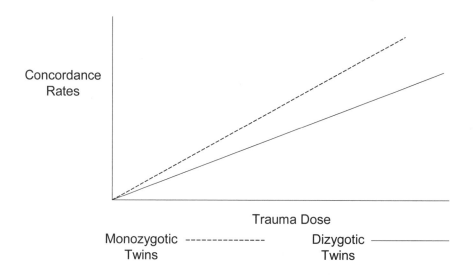

The twin concordance − trauma dosage data could be analyzed by individual anxiety disorder, prevalence of one or more anxiety disorders, total number of anxiety disorders, or scores on continuous measures of anxiety.

Cross-fostering and adoption data would show the standard pattern predicted by the trauma model. It would be interesting to study the prevalence of SD, stress disorder occurring in the absence of a traumatic event. The twin and adoption data would demonstrate the necessity of the traumatic event for development of the symptom profile of PTSD.

Biology

There is no single biology for all the anxiety disorders. They are not a group of unified biomedical diseases. Once the biology of trauma is parceled out, the remaining biology of anxiety disorders, assuming it has any specificity for the anxiety disorders at all, will be absent in PTSD and acute stress disorder, or, at least, it will be present at no more than the baseline rate for the general population. Non-trauma OCD and panic-phobic anxiety disorder will have separate biological abnormalities, again assuming that any biological specificity is ever found for any DSM-IV-TR disorders.

If there is one, the endogenous biological abnormality causing spontaneous panic attacks should be in the midbrain and areas modulating arousal, such as the locus coeruleus. The biological abnormalities causing OCD should be in the cerebral cortex or brain regions involved in integration of identity, perception, and memory, such as the hippocampus.

In PTSD, dysregulation of candidate systems such as the hypothalamic-pituitary-adrenal axis will be due to the normal biology of trauma, rather than genetically abnormal responses. The pathology will arise from genetically normal errors in feedback, double binds created in regulatory systems, system failure caused by excessive input, and similar problems. PTSD arises from the failure of natural selection to solve all problems of adaptation, rather than from defects peculiar to individuals with PTSD. We all have the gene for PTSD; we just have different thresholds for its activation, and different levels of trauma exposure.

Treatment Outcome

Setting aside PTSD and acute stress disorder, treatment failures for the other anxiety disorders will include many trauma cases. In PTSD, immediate-onset florid and delayed onset cases will have more priming by childhood trauma, and therefore will require a more complete version of trauma therapy. In contrast, adult onset single-traumatic event cases will have less comorbidity and require a simpler treatment plan. A more modest level of self-blame will exist in adult-onset cases, therefore cognitive therapy focused on the locus of control shift will be less essential.

Trauma pathway cases of OCD may be differentiated from non-trauma cases by higher responsiveness to selective serotonin reuptake inhibitors (SSRIs) and chlomipramine (Ross, 1997). Non-trauma cases should have lower scores on the Dissociative Experiences Scale and other measures of comorbidity, and lower rates of discrete ego states. Their responsiveness to noraderenergic and serotonergic antidepressants might not differ much, whereas trauma pathway cases might exhibit a wider gap in response rates to the two subtypes of antidepressant. Generally, trauma pathway OCD cases should respond better to psychotherapies derived from the therapy of dissociative identity disorder, because they can more plausibly be defined as cases of dissociative disorder not otherwise specified.

In the phobias, trauma-driven phobias will respond less well to strict behavioral therapy, and will require more attention to the meaning and function of the symptom.

Revisions To DSM-IV-TR

Required revisions of DSM-IV-TR were described in the section on phenomenology. The anxiety disorders should be restricted to the panic-phobic group. OCD should be in a separate category. PTSD and acute stress disorder should be in a third section of DSM-IV-TR for trauma disorders, which should include brief psychotic disorder with marked stressors and the adjustment disorders.

The relationship between PTSD and the dissociative disorders needs to be explicit in future DSMs. In DSM-IV-TR, brief reactive dissociative disorder was redefined as an anxiety disorder, then renamed acute stress disorder. It was then inserted into the anxiety disorders section while the problem of its relationship to the other dissociative disorders was ignored.

I have heard it said that there cannot be a trauma disorders section of DSM-IV-TR because the manual is atheoretical, and classification is not based on theories of etiology. That argument is inconsistent with the name and diagnostic criteria for PTSD. In fact, the etiology of PTSD is already traumatic and the traumatic etiology is incorporated in the diagnostic criteria. DSM-IV-TR is already doing what it is not supposed to do.

A trauma theory of PTSD, acute stress disorder, brief psychotic disorder with marked stressors, conversion disorder, dissociative amnesia, adjustment disorder, and acute stress disorder is already incorporated in DSM-IV-TR. It follows that the theme of trauma should be organized and explicit in future DSMs. As DSM-IV-TR stands, disorders defined as stress, trauma or conflict-driven are scattered across the psychotic, somatoform, anxiety, dissociative and adjustment disorders sections. To stretch a point, the substance-induced mood and psychotic disorders could be redefined as due to neurotransmitter receptor stress.

Overall, the theme of trauma needs integrated attention across the entire DSM system. Up till DSM-IV-TR, trauma has been dealt with in hodge-podge fashion by dissociated committees which do not communicate with other. The dissociated political structure of the DSM process has resulted in inclusion and exclusion criteria for different categories that are often absent, contradictory, or present in only one direction.

13

SUBSTANCE-RELATED DISORDERS

Substance abuse has never been integrated into psychiatry. This is true at many levels including politics, sociology, funding, professional credentialing, and public attitudes. The professional substance abuse world has its own conferences, networks, and treatment centers which overlap only slightly with psychiatry. Yet substance abuse appears on Axis I in DSM-IV-TR.

Treatment for substance abuse in our culture is based on a contradiction. Academic bioreductionist psychiatrists hope to find the gene for alcoholism. At the same time, according to AA, you have to work your steps and make a commitment to sobriety before treatment for alcoholism can be effective. Depending on the school of thought, the alcoholic is either a victim of bad genetics or simply making bad choices.

There are three models for substance abuse in our culture: a biomedical disease model; a moral model, in which substance abuse, violence, divorce and other social problems are due to the moral disintegration of our culture and the family; and a paramilitary model, in which the DEA and other federal agencies wage war on drug suppliers.

None of these models have stemmed the tide of increasing substance abuse in the western world. An alternative approach would be to view cocaine and heroin abuse as a business problem. The suppliers of these drugs are businessmen. If this approach were taken, the supply of heroin and cocaine in North America could be reduced by 95% in a month. The suppliers would be awarded contracts by the federal government in which they were paid more for keeping heroin and cocaine out of North America than they could make by selling it.

The contract fee would be set on a sliding scale such that the suppliers were incentivized to reduce the supply to zero. If the supply were reduced by 50%, profit from sales and the contract fee would be 110% of the amount derived from sales with no reduction in supply. If supply were reduced by 75%, gross revenues would be 120% of baseline. If they were reduced by 100%, gross revenues would be 130%. As gross revenues rose under the contract structure, supplier costs would drop, therefore net revenue would increase more steeply than gross revenue.

The suppliers would be responsible for policing the importation of the drugs into North America, and for distributing the proceeds of their government contracts. The function of the DEA would be to monitor the availability of heroin and cocaine in North America in order to set the contract fee for that month.

In this approach, the supply side of the drug problem would be treated as a business problem. The suppliers would be treated as rational businessmen. Successful implementation of this approach would render the search for a gene for cocaine abuse irrelevant. In the absence of the drug, the gene would never be activated, and the phenotype of cocaine abuse would never occur.

The purpose of my outlining this business approach to the drug problem, is to illustrate several points about the trauma model of substance abuse. The endogenous biology of substance abuse, if it exists, is absolutely dependent on environmental promoters for its activation. Substance abuse cannot be understood or solved independently of politics, sociology, culture, morals, and money.

Finally, the heroin and cocaine problems could be solved easily if the political will existed. The solution would require no input from medicine, psychiatry, or biology. The extremely slim likelihood of this ever actually happening is irrelevant to the point I am making, namely that substance abuse does not come anywhere near fitting the cystic fibrosis model of mental illness. You could not eradicate cystic fibrosis in North America with a business plan.

According to the trauma model, only two things are required for substance abuse: the drug, and human suffering. The demand side of the drug problem is driven by trauma, while the supply side is driven by economics.

DSM-IV-TR includes separate diagnoses for alcohol, amphetamines, caffeine, cannabis, cocaine, hallucinogens, inhalants, nicotine, opioids, phencyclidine, sedatives, hypnotics, or anxiolytics, polysubstance, and other. According to DSM-IV-TR, these are all separate mental illnesses.

There is no diagnosis for watchamickwingit abuse in DSM-IV-TR because watchamickwingit has not yet been synthesized in clandestine laboratories. If watchamickwingit does become a widely used designer drug over the next decade, however, it will have to be included in future editions of DSM. Academic psychiatrists will ask whether the gene for watchamickwingit abuse is on the same chromosone as the gene for alcoholism.

The table in DSM-IV-TR (page 193) which lists these 13 different categories of drug, also lists 13 different "diagnoses associated with class of substance." According to DSM-IV-TR, there are potentially 13 x 13 = 169 different mental disorders related to substance abuse. Heavy substance abusers could easily have forty or fifty different psychiatric disorders.

The table on page 193 of DSM-IV-TR illustrates another problem. According to the American Psychiatric Association, nicotine, caffeine and alcohol are on the same list as heroin and cocaine. They belong to the same medical category of substances of abuse. Why, then, in our culture, are nicotine, caffeine and alcohol sold legally, while heroin and cocaine are supplied only by vile, morally reprehensible criminals? The moral attitudes do not fit with the medical classification.

Which substance is illegal and which is promoted by Hall-of-Fame athletes on prime time television is arbitrary, from the DSM-IV-TR perspective. In day-to-day operational reality, psychiatry adheres to both the moral and biomedical models simultaneously while ignoring the contradiction. Psychiatrists classify alcohol in the same category as heroin but have very different moral attitudes towards the two substances. This is so despite the fact that far more children are killed in alcohol-related traffic accidents per year than ever die from heroin and cocaine.

The medical wards are full of patients in treatment for the damage caused to their bodies by alcohol abuse. Nationally, the medical costs of treating chronic alcoholism far outweigh the costs of treating medical complications of heroin or cocaine abuse. Psychiatric thinking about substance abuse is riddled with inconsistencies and contradictions.

Within the trauma model, substance abuse is not a specific disease. It is simply one of many forms of addiction and acting out. Its purpose is to take the person from here to over there. Here may be intolerable due to loneliness, boredom, physical pain, fear, depression, or conflict. Over there may equal stoned, unconscious, thrilled, hallucinated, transcended, or distracted. The specifics of over here and over there do not matter. Nor does the specific make of vehicle used for transportation from here to over there make a fundamental difference.

This logic is analogous to the behavioral analysis of phobias. The principles of behavioral analysis and treatment of specific phobias do not vary by the content of the phobia. If the phobia section of DSM-IV-TR followed the same logic as the substance abuse section, it would include dozens of different psychiatric disorders with long Latin names, such as arachnophobia. Instead, the specific phobia section of DSM-IV-TR (page 406) lists a number of different subtypes of phobia including "animal type, natural environment type, blood-injection-injury type, situational type and other type."

The principles of the trauma model are those of behavioral analysis.

Phenomenology

The trauma model predicts that substance abuse is an intrinsic component of the trauma response. It is possible that different types of trauma lead to preferential abuse of difference substances. For instance, heroin might soothe the consequences of neglect, while alcohol might dampen the long-term consequences of physical abuse. Any such relationships will be very difficult to prove because of the extensive co-occurrence of different types of trauma and the difficulty of finding individuals who abuse only one substance.

The possible specificity of relationship between type of trauma and type of substance abused could be studied in animal models. Laboratory animals subjected to active physical abuse versus neglect could be offered different drugs in different trays. They might consume one drug preferentially over another in a way that varied with type of trauma.

Among psychiatric inpatients, the concept of the *dual diagnosis* patient has no utility. It is difficult to find a psychiatric inpatient with substance abuse problems who has fewer than four DSM-IV-TR disorders lifetime. Many have five or ten. The number of different substances of abuse should vary with the number of types of trauma and the total trauma dosage, as shown in Figure 13.1.

Other predictions concerning the phenomenology of substance abuse are the same as those for other sections of DSM-IV-TR. Both the amount of comorbidity and the number of substances abused will increase with increasing trauma.

The relationship between substance abuse and other forms of comorbidity is particularly complicated. Hallucinogen intoxication can cause psychotic and dissociative symptoms, but so can withdrawal from alcohol. Depression can be a symptom of drug intoxication or

Figure 13.1. The Relationship Between Trauma Dose and Number of Substances Abused

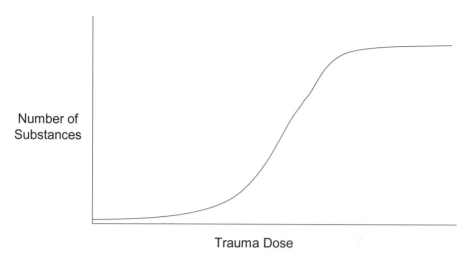

Number of Substances

Trauma Dose

drug withdrawal. Alternatively, drugs and alcohol can be taken to self-medicate depression.

Symptoms can be misattributed in many different ways.   Incorrect diagnoses of alcohol blackouts can be made by professionals who do not consider dissociative identity disorder. A careful history reveals that the blackouts preceded substance use by a decade, and the blackouts can be provoked by a request for an alter personality to take executive control. Such attributional errors can be made in all possible combinations and directions.

Natural History

In any given substance abuse case, a key consideration is whether trauma preceded the substance abuse. If not, the substance abuse cannot be an element of the trauma response. The trauma model predicts that the worse the natural history, the more severe the trauma history, and the greater the degree of comorbidity.

One could estimate the total amount of alcohol consumed, say, between ages fifteen and twenty-five. When alcohol consumption is held constant or included as a covariate in analyses, the trauma dosage will predict bad outcomes at age fifty independently of alcohol consumption between ages fifteen and twenty-five.

Epidemiology

Substance abuse illustrates the fundamental role of culture, religion, politics, and economics in the epidemiology of mental illness. The lifetime prevalence of alcoholism varies dramatically by culture in a way that cannot be explained plausibly by genetics. Substance abuse is the only DSM-IV-TR mental disorder whose prevalence is affected by advertising and legislation.

I was taught in my psychiatry residency that depressed women have more male relatives with alcoholism and antisocial personality disorder in their families than comparison, non-depressed women. I was taught that a common gene for depression expresses itself differently in men and women in these families; as depression in the women, and alcoholism and antisocial personality in the men.

If we accept the mood disorder spectrum model of depression, alcoholism and sociopathy, we must abandon the single disease – single gene model of these three DSM-IV-TR disorders. The mood, substance abuse and personality disorder sections of DSM-IV-TR become arbitrary distinctions between variants of a common biogenetic disease. This contradiction was never pointed out to me by my teachers, who endorsed both the mood disorder spectrum theory, the validity of the DSM system, and the single disease – single gene model.

From a trauma model perspective, it is depressing to be a woman in an extended family full of alcoholic antisocial men. The men molest their children and beat up their wives.

Twin And Adoption Studies

The concordance rates for alcoholism in monozygotic and dyzygotic twins should vary by culture, as shown in Table 13.1. In cultures with very high rates of alcoholism, concordance will be higher in DZ twins than among MZ twins in low-consumption cultures. That this pattern is due to cross-cultural variations, not genetics, could be demonstrated by cross-cultural adoption studies or studies of immigrant twins who had moved in and out of high and low-consumption cultures at birth or in early childhood.

According to the trauma model, the availability of alcohol in a culture outweighs the contribution of a gene for alcoholism, assuming such a gene exists at all. The definitive data would be provided by studies of identical twins separated at birth and reared apart. In general, any reduction in the concordance for a mental disorder in twins reared apart, compared to twins reared together, is conclusive proof of the contribution of the environment. Since there are so few MZ and DZ twins separated at birth and reared separately available for study, especially given the base rates of the different DSM-IV-TR disorders, we must rely on adoption data.

Table 13.1. Concordance Rates for Alcoholism in Different Cultures

Low Alcohol Culture		High Alcohol Culture	
MZ	DZ	MZ	DZ
++	+	++++	+++

A woman adopted at birth into a multigenerational incest family will have a higher risk for depression, while a male adopted into the same pedigree will have an increased risk for alcoholism and antisocial personality. Risks will drop to the base rate for the population in individuals adopted out of the pedigree at birth. Such data would prove the over-riding influence of differential socialization in the pedigree, and the negligible effect of genetics.

The prediction can be taken one step further. The risk for depression will increase for any girl adopted into the pedigree, but will rise even higher if the girl is a victim of incest. There is a two-strike effect. The first strike is simply growing up in the family, with its disturbed dynamics, modeling, socialization, and other pathology. The second strike is intrafamilial incest. The woman with two strikes will have much more extensive comorbidity in general, including both depression and substance abuse.

A question then arises. Are women genetically programmed to respond to trauma with depression, while men are programmed to respond with alcoholism and antisocial personality? If one assumes the answer to this question is, 'Yes,' one has ruled out a gene for an endogenous disorder as such. One must speak of gender differences in the trauma response.

But men with anorexia nervosa do not develop amenorrhea. This is not because they lack a gene for "amenhorrhea disorder." That would be an absurd way to talk about the data. The difference in anorexia symptoms between men and women is due to the normal genetics of normal gender differences. Following this logic, if women are more prone to depression in response to trauma, this is due to the normal biology of being female, not to a gene for depression as such.

The gene for depression should express itself at the same rate irrespective of adoption pattern, if depression is primarily an endogenous biomedical disease. If girls adopted into multigenerational incest families experience a greater increase in risk for depression than boys adopted into the same families, we cannot conclude that the female response to trauma is more inherently depressive until we control for quantity and quality of trauma dosage. There could be some intrinsic gender differences, but they are probably of the same significance as the fact that males with anorexia nervosa do not develop amenorrhea. The gender difference has no impact on treatment planning, and is biologically accidental with respect to the etiology of the disorder.

Biology

The premorbid biology of substance abuse is impossible to study in end-stage alcoholics, or IV drug users with AIDS and hepatitis. There is no way to tell whether a given biological abnormality is cause or effect of the drinking. The only exception to this rule would be specific genetic differences, which could not be caused by the substance abuse.

Setting aside molecular biology, study of the biology of substance abuse must begin with high-risk children of addicts, prior to the children starting to use themselves. Even here, however, the mother cannot have abused substances while pregnant. This requirement rules out the children of the most severe cases of addiction in women, which complicates the research. But the search for a biological cause of substance abuse is misconceived for two reasons; 1) the biological abnormality is meaningless in the absence of the substance of abuse, and 2) even if you have the abnormality, you can just say no to drugs. If this were not true, AA would be a waste of time.

It is also true that culture is intertwined with biology. Without the genes for tongue, palate and vocal cords, there would be no English language. Nor would there be toothbrushes if there were no genes for teeth. But there is no gene for tooth brushing, and there is no gene for speaking English. The gene for alcoholism is like the gene for tooth brushing. Tooth brushing is a complex, human, cultural, and sociological behavior. It is driven, among other things, by technology and TV ads. The same is true for alcoholism.

People with obsessive compulsive disorder (OCD) who brush their teeth for sixty minutes a day do not have an abnormal tooth brushing gene. They may or may not have an abnormal gene for OCD. But to say that there a distinct genetic abnormality for each different specific obsession and compulsion would be absurd. Should we postulate the existence of one gene for compulsive checking, one for counting, one for hand washing, and a fourth for ironing your trousers for two hours per day? Specific genes or other biological causes for different types of substance abuse are no less absurd than the same logic applied to OCD.

Research into biological treatments for alcoholism should focus on blocking the normal biology of intoxication and avoidance. I'll drink to that.

Treatment Outcome

The trauma model predicts that for all DSM-IV-TR categories and treatment modalities, treatment failures will tend to be trauma cases. Treatment failures can be randomized to further conventional treatment versus conventional treatment plus trauma therapy. Assuming honest and accurate patient report, substance abuse and eating disorders are handy for such treatment outcome studies because they provide concrete, objective outcome criteria. For eating disorders these are weight and binge-purge episodes, while for substance abuse they are grams or milliliters of substance ingested over time.

Revisions To DSM-IV-TR

Future DSMs should drop the fiction that each different substance of abuse represents a different mental disorder. There should be one disorder only, substance abuse, with modifiers for substance(s) abused. The different modifiers on page 177 of DSM-IV-TR, such as dependence, intoxication, and withdrawal should not be different "diagnoses associated with class of substance," but should themselves be modifiers of the single diagnosis, substance abuse.

DSM-IV-TR is three steps short of the ultimate proliferation of substance abuse disorders. There could be separate diagnoses for whiskey, vodka and gin abuse. Each could be caused by a different gene, and have a distinct biology and treatment plan. Why should we stop the program of micro-subdivision into different mental disorders at the point arrived at in DSM-IV-TR? Why not extend the process to its logical conclusion? Why not different diagnoses for rye whiskey and scotch whiskey abuse? Why not different diagnoses for different brands of rye whiskey?

The program of micro-subdivision has been stopped at its current point because the absurdity of pressing it further would become apparent even to psychiatrists. A future edition of DSM should be less than one hundred pages in length. The micro-subdivision process should be reversed throughout the manual. Unfortunately, there is a sociological micro-subdivision parallel to that in DSM-IV-TR within the professionals treating substance abuse, and among the consumers of their services. We have not just AA, but Narcotics Anonymous, Sex and Love Addiction Anonymous, Gamblers Anonymous and Overeaters Anonymous.

These organizations should give rise to many more organizations within substance abuse alone, if they follow the logic of DSM-IV-TR. Any behavioral health care system offering "a full continuum of services" should provide evening groups for Rye Whiskeyaholics Anonymous, because the counselors at Scotch Whiskeyaholics Anonymous haven't walked a mile in the right shoes, and really don't understand the problem of Rye Whiskey abuse. This would be only a further micro-subdivision of services that are already absurdly subdivided.

The concept of special treatment services for "dual diagnosis patients" is a permutation of the DSM-IV-TR logic. The dual diagnosis concept is mistaken for two reasons. First, virtually everyone with serious substance abuse problems has other psychiatric comorbidity – there are no "single diagnosis" patients. Secondly, even dual diagnosis patients are rare, given the hundreds of separate mental disorders in the DSM-IV-TR system.

My suggested revisions to DSM-IV-TR flow directly from the trauma model. The problem is not the substance. The substance is merely the vehicle. The purpose of substance abuse is to get away from here, to over there. The year, make and model of car, or whether it is a car, boat, plane, or train is not of fundamental interest. Neither the biology nor the treatment plan vary by class of substance abused, except in minor details.

14

SOMATOFORM DISORDERS

As noted in DSM-IV-TR (page 445), somatization disorder was originally named hysteria, and then Briquet's Syndrome. Many of the women with somatization disorder studied by Briquet in the nineteenth century had histories of childhood sexual abuse, an observation replicated by Morrison (1989), who found, one hundred years later, that 60% of women with somatization disorder report childhood sexual abuse. The traumatic origins of somatization disappeared from mainstream psychiatry over one hundred years ago.

Phenomenology

The DSM-IV-TR section on Somatoform Disorders is one of the most poorly thought out sections of the manual. The distinctions between the different types of somatoform disorder are arbitrary, and rules for diagnosing one of them rather than another are unclear. I will analyze these problems later in the chapter, and until then will discuss somatic symptoms in general, independently from DSM-IV-TR rules for classifying them.

Childhood sexual abuse is a major cause of psychosomatic symptoms. Sexual abuse is more predominant in causing somatization than it is in causing depression or borderline personality disorder. For other sections of DSM-IV-TR, sexual abuse is important, but other forms of trauma such as physical and verbal abuse, neglect and loss play a bigger role than they do in somatization, with a caveat.

DSM-IV-TR lists 10 pain symptoms, 5 gastrointestinal symptoms, 5 sexual symptoms, and 13 pseudoneurological symptoms in its criteria for somatization disorder. Sexual abuse is not linked to all of these symptoms to the same degree. The relationship between sexual abuse and individual somatic symptoms predicted by the trauma model is shown in Table 14.1. The symptoms driven by sexual abuse arise logically from the body systems that bear the brunt of the trauma, including oral, anal, and vaginal penetration.

The somatic symptoms most related to childhood sexual abuse are those which should occur in a previously well-adjusted woman who is raped by a stranger. Persistent psychosomatic symptoms following a mugging or car accident should be more likely to include muscle pain, stiffness, weakness, paralysis and double vision.

Table 14.1. Relationship Between Sexual Abuse and Different Somatic Symptoms

Symptom	Sexual Abuse
Rectal pain; pain during menstruation, intercourse or urination; sexual indifference; erectile or ejaculatory dysfunction; irregular menses; difficulty swallowing or lump in throat; aphonia; urinary retention; hallucinations; loss of touch or pain sensation; blindness; deafness; seizures; amnesia; loss of consciousness other than fainting.	++++
Pain in abdomen; nausea; bloating; vomiting other than during pregnancy; diarrhea; intolerance of several different foods.	++
Pain in head, back, joints, extremities, chest; excessive menstrual bleeding; vomiting throughout pregnancy; impaired coordination or balance; paralysis or localized weakness; double vision.	+

Excessive menstrual bleeding is excluded from the symptoms highly related to sexual abuse on the assumption that it usually has an endogenous biological cause. Vomiting throughout pregnancy is included in the DSM-IV-TR symptom list for somatization disorder only because of psychoanalytical theories about conflict over pregnancy and vomiting up the fetus. It is clear to me that the vomiting of hyperemesis gravidarum is an epiphenomenon of heightened sensory arousal occurring during the first trimester of pregnancy.

The sequence of events in hyperemesis is: 1) heightened sensory sensitivity to sound, vibration, light, smell, taste, and touch; 2) smells trigger nausea, and 3) vomiting if the cycle escalates or the source of the odor is not removed. As in migraine, vomiting is the end-point in the cycle, not the core symptom. The sexual abuse victim develops aphonia, blindness or deafness in order not to see, hear, or speak of the abuse.

Natural History

The natural history of somatic symptoms can be profoundly affected by therapy. Untreated, somatic symptoms can lead to unnecessary medical and surgical interventions, dependency on doctors, substance abuse and a chronic patient-victim role. Since the somatic symptoms do not respond to conventional treatment, and engender hostile countertransference, the individual may escalate his or her complaints in order to get taken seriously. This strategy backfires and earns the patient an additional diagnosis of factitious or borderline personality disorder.

Epidemiology

The general predictions of the trauma model hold for somatic symptoms. The greater the degree of trauma, the more somatic symptoms and the more comorbidity. Somatic symptoms occur most frequently in cultures with the highest rates of childhood trauma. Similarly, within a given culture, the highest density of somatic symptoms is seen in multi-generational incest families.

Twin And Adoption Studies

The logic of trauma model predictions concerning somatic symptoms is the same as that for other diagnostic categories. The concordance for somatic symptoms will be higher in traumatized dizygotic twins than in monozygotic twins who have not been abused or neglected. The traumatic origin of somatic symptoms will also be demonstrated by adoption studies. As in other diagnostic categories, a subgroup of somatizing people will not have a traumatic etiology, and will exhibit different patterns of twin concordance, and risk with adoption.

Mothers will pass somatization onto their daughters in the pattern shown in Table 14.2, which parallels the logic for transmission of psychotic symptoms in families with psychotic pedophile fathers.

Biology

The focus in study of the biology of somatization should be on the biology of the genetically normal response to incest. There is unlikely to be a specific biology of somatization independently from trauma.

Treatment Outcome

The general predictions of the trauma model hold for somatization. Treatment failures will do better with trauma therapy. Somatoform symptoms carry a high risk of pathological entanglement in the medical-surgical system. Reduction in baseline medical costs, and a reduction compared to untreated controls are predicted by the model. The potential savings in unnecessary medical and surgical interventions due to trauma therapy could be very large. One reason such studies are not funded at present is the fact that behavioral health care coverage is often carved out from general medical insurance coverage. The managed care company that spends more on behavioral treatment will experience only increased costs from trauma therapy, even with a major reduction in medical costs. Therefore the behavioral health managed care company experiences no incentive to provide that treatment.

Table 14.2. Risk for Somatization in Daughters of Different Women

Mother		Daughter	
Married to Pedophile	Somatic Symptoms	Incest	Somatic Symptoms
+	++++	++++	++++
+	+	++++	+++
-	++++	-	++
-	+	-	+

Revisions To DSM-IV-TR

There are several problems with somatization disorder, the main diagnosis in this section of DSM-IV-TR. The first is a practical one. I doubt that even 5% of psychiatrists in North America can state the diagnostic criteria from memory. I don't mean list all 33 items, I mean state from memory that the diagnosis requires four pain symptoms, two gastrointestinal (GI) symptoms, one sexual symptom, and one neurological symptom. This is one reason why the diagnosis is almost never made in psychiatric hospitals.

Why are two GI symptoms required but only one neurological one? Why not the other way around? In DSM-III-R, it was necessary to have 13 symptoms from the entire list of 33 items. Now only eight are required, and they can't be just any eight. Why? What is the biomedical foundation of the different number of symptoms required in each sub-category? Clearly, there isn't one.

Setting aside the arbitrary rules about number of symptoms, the general idea of somatization disorder is quite reasonable. But when the rules for the other somatoform disorders are analyzed, the entire section collapses under its own arbitrary rules and uncertainties, as follows.

Undifferentiated somatoform disorder is defined in DSM-IV-TR (page 445) as "unexplained physical complaints, lasting at least 6 months, that are below the threshold for somatization disorder." However, in the diagnostic criteria themselves, only one symptom is required to make the diagnosis.

If the one symptom is a conversion symptom, however, the diagnosis is conversion disorder. If the one symptom is pain, the diagnosis is pain disorder. Why are only pain and conversion separate disorders? Why is there no diarrhea disorder, nausea disorder, or lump in the throat disorder? Why have a few of the 33 symptoms listed under somatization disorder been given separate diagnostic status when they occur alone, and not others? The foundations for these decisions by the Somatoform Disorders Committee of DSM-IV-TR are not scientific.

Why is undifferentiated somatoform disorder called "undifferentiated?" In the schizophrenia section of DSM-IV-TR, undifferentiated identifies a subtype of schizophrenia with undifferentiated symptoms. The symptoms of undifferentiated somatoform disorder, in contrast, are perfectly well differentiated, but fewer in number than required for somatization disorder.

The somatoform section also includes a diagnosis of somatoform disorder not otherwise specified (SDNOS). One of the subtypes of SDNOS is "unexplained physical complaints (e.g., fatigue or body weakness) of less than 6 months duration that are not due to another complaint" (DSM-IV-TR, page 469).

It appears that SDNOS becomes undifferentiated somatoform disorder (USD) after 6 months, but the actual names of the disorders do not indicate a logical progression. The clinician has to guess that SDNOS changes to USD because the rules are not stated.

Pseudocyesis, or false pregnancy, is included under SDNOS, but it is much more clearly defined and has more symptoms than UDS. Also, it can last longer than 6 months. There are no duration criteria for conversion disorder or pain disorder.

A number of sexual symptoms are listed under somatization disorder. However if there are only sexual symptoms, according to DSM-IV-TR rules, one can diagnose a Sexual Disorder. There are no rules in DSM-IV-TR that tell the clinician when to diagnose a Somatoform Disorder and when a Sexual Disorder.

Similarly, amnesia is a symptom of somatization disorder, but amnesia occurring by itself is a dissociative disorder. Why is dissociative amnesia not a somatoform disorder like pain disorder or conversion disorder?

The same problem occurs in the diagnostic criteria for body dysmorphic disorder, which seems much more logically grouped with the delusional disorders than the somatoform disorders. Indeed, DSM-IV-TR (page 468) states that, "Individuals with Body Dysmorphic Disorder can receive an additional diagnosis of Delusional Disorder, Somatic Type if their preoccupation with an imagined defect in appearance is held with a delusional intensity."

DSM-IV-TR is saying that the same single symptom can result in two different concurrent diagnoses. That makes no sense. Additionally, DSM-IV-TR states (page 466) that in individuals with body dysmorphic disorder, "Frequent mirror checking and checking of the "defect" in other available reflecting surfaces (e.g., store windows, car bumpers, watch faces) can consume many hours a day. Some individuals use special lighting or magnifying glasses to scrutinize their defect."

What is this but "delusional intensity?" According to the DSM-IV-TR text for the disorder, most or even all cases of body dysmorphic disorder are of delusional intensity, and therefore should receive the additional diagnosis of delusional disorder, somatic type. Why, then, even have the somatoform diagnosis?

The rules for when an imagined defect like obesity should be attributed to an eating disorder, namely anorexia nervosa, rather than to a somatoform disorder are vague. Also, there are no rules for when chest pain, nausea, and a lump in the throat should be diagnosed as a limited symptom panic attack, and when they are better classified as USD. If the logic and vocabulary of the anxiety disorders section were followed, conversion disorder and pain disorder would be subtypes of specific somatoform disorder.

On the other hand, if the logic of the Somatoform Disorders section of DSM-IV-TR followed that of the psychosis section, we would have brief somatoform disorder lasting up to one month, then somatophreniform disorder lasting up to six months, then somatization disorder. If there were insufficient symptoms after six months for somatization disorder, we would go so SDNOS. There is no integration of rules and principles across the manual. This fact highlights the scientifically arbitrary nature of the rules in any one section.

I favor the adoption of a simple somatoform disorder and somatization disorder as the two major diagnoses. Pseudocyesis, pain and conversion disorders should be incorporated under simple somatoform disorder. Body dysmorphic disorder should be eliminated, and patients diagnosed with a delusional disorder. Undifferentiated somatoform disorder should be eliminated. Hypochondriasis should be moved somewhere else, perhaps the personality disorders section.

The duration criterion for somatization disorder should be retained, and shorter-duration cases should be simple somatoform disorder. The algorithm for different numbers of symptoms from different symptom sublists should be eliminated, and we should go back to the DSM-III-R rule that a threshold number of symptoms from the entire list is required. The threshold number should be set by receiver operating curve studies.

These revisions to DSM-IV-TR would make scientific testing of the trauma model of somatization possible. As presently organized, the Somatoform Disorders section of DSM-IV-TR cannot be studied scientifically because its rules are arbitrary and vague. They cannot generate adequate inter-rater reliability.

15

DISSOCIATIVE DISORDERS

Multiple personality disorder has been my area of identified subspecialty for twelve years, ever since I became Medical Director of the Dissociative Disorders Clinic at St. Boniface Hospital in Winnipeg, Canada in 1988. It has been a major interest of mine within psychiatry for twenty-one years, ever since I diagnosed my first case as a third-year medical student in Edmonton in 1979 (Ross, 1984).

I have published more original research data on multiple personality and dissociation than anyone in the world. The only other person in the world who has written more than one single-author book on multiple personality and dissociation is Frank Putnam (1989; 1997), who has written two. *The C.I.A. Doctors: Human Rights Violations By American Psychiatrists*, is my fifth book on the subject, one of which has gone into a second edition (Ross, 1989; 1994; 1995; 1997; 2004; 2006).

Despite this work and expertise, my interest throughout my career has been on general psychopathology. I fell into the world of multiple personality much like the White Rabbit fell into Wonderland, by accident and with alarm. In that world, however, I devised the trauma model, which is a unified field theory of general psychopathology. My patients with multiple personality disorder have been my teachers, from whom I have learned the logic of the human trauma response.

I believe absolutely that individuals suffer from psychiatric disorders. These disorders can be classified in a rational system, and can be diagnosed with excellent reliability and validity, in principle. The DSM-IV-TR cannot do that very well, but I believe absolutely in the need for a DSM system. The present edition, DSM-IV-TR, needs a lot of work, but we have to have a DSM, otherwise psychiatry will never be a real branch of medicine. The dissociative disorders belong in the DSM system, because they are both reliable and valid.

Because there are so many misconceptions and errors of logic and scholarship about dissociation, I have included one of my papers as an Appendix to this book. The paper, entitled "Errors of Scholarship Concerning Dissociation," addresses and corrects many of these errors.

Phenomenology

Multiple personality disorder was renamed dissociative identity disorder (DID) in DSM-IV, which was published in 1994. The dividing line between DID and most cases of dissociative disorder not otherwise specified (DDNOS) is arbitrary. Most cases of DDNOS are partial forms of DID which lack either clear switching of executive control, full amnesia barriers between identity states, or clear differentiation and structure of identity states. They are partial forms of DID with the same patterns of childhood trauma and comorbidity.

Phenomenologically, the dissociative disorders fall into three separate subcategories. The first is chronic, complex dissociative disorders including DID and most cases of DDNOS. The second is chronic cases of depersonalization disorder without a significant number of other dissociative features. The third is relatively simple, brief dissociative disorders such as dissociative amnesia for single events and dissociative fugue.

There is good agreement between four different methods of diagnosing chronic, complex dissociative disorders, as shown in Table 15.1. In this study, 210 general adult psychiatric inpatients were interviewed with the Dissociative Disorders Interview Schedule (DDIS) (Ross, 1997). A second interviewer blind to the results of the DDIS interviews then administered the Structured Clinical Interview for DSM-IV-TR Dissociative Disorders (SCID-D) (Steinberg, 1995) to 110 of these subjects. I then interviewed 50 of the patients clinically, blind to results of the DDIS and SCID-D interviews. All patients interviewed with the DDIS also completed the Dissociative Experiences Scale (DES) (Bernstein and Putnam, 1986). An eight-item subscale of the DES called the DES-T, with a cutoff score of twenty, was used to define whether an individual did or did not have DID/DDNOS in the study.

Chronic, complex dissociative disorders never occur without extensive comorbidity. The trauma model predicts that trauma dose, DES score and severity of comorbidity will correlate with each other at $r = 0.40$ or greater in large samples of dissociative disorder cases.

The phenomenology of the chronic, complex dissociative disorders is described in my other books (Ross 1994; 1995; 1997; 2000), which include extensive references. One of the most interesting problems in the phenomenology of dissociation is the relationship between dissociation and psychosis. In a study of 103 inpatients with DID, I found that 74.1% met criteria for a psychotic disorder on the Structured Clinical Interview for DSM-III-R, a commonly used structured interview (Ross, 1997). This included 49.5% of subjects with schizoaffective disorder and 18.7% with schizophrenia.

TABLE 15.1. Rates of Agreement Between Four Different Methods of Diagnosing Chronic, Complex Dissociative Disorders (Cohen's Kappa)

DDIS-SCID-D	DDIS-Clinician	SCID-D-Clinician
0.74	0.71	0.56
DDIS-DES-T	SCID-D-DES-T	Clinician-DES-T
0.81	0.76	0.74

There are four main differences between the truly psychotic person and an individual with complex, chronic dissociation. The dissociative person has fewer negative symptoms of schizophrenia, much less thought disorder, more trauma, and more comorbidity. This is true for groups of patients, but not necessarily for every individual. One person with schizophrenia may have more severe trauma than another person with DID.

Psychiatry needs to take the problem of how to differentiate dissociation and psychosis seriously. The conceptual system of twentieth century psychiatry, the DSM-IV-TR, and most psychological tests and measures of psychosis cannot differentiate dissociation and psychosis. This is a problem for phenomenology, diagnostics, research and therapeutics.

A second area of conceptual and empirical confusion is the relationship and overlap between dissociation and attention deficit disorder. My experience tells me that many traumatized, dissociative children are receiving false positive diagnoses of attention deficit disorder. The problem is, we have no reliable and valid measures for making the differentiation.

Natural History

The chronic, complex dissociative disorders are highly trauma-related, therefore their onset is after the onset of the trauma. The trauma itself is usually chronic and complex. The relationship between pure depersonalization disorder and trauma is unclear to me and the trauma model makes no specific prediction in this regard. However, as for all DSM-IV-TR disorders, the more severe the symptoms and the more malignant the natural history of the depersonalization disorder, the higher the trauma dose.

Dissociative fugue appears to be linked to what we would usually call *stress* rather than to the extreme traumatic events required for PTSD. The cases I have seen are an escape from general life stresses including finances, relationships and loneliness. The natural history of fugue is often full remission. Recurrent fugues are usually features of DID or DDNOS. Chronic, recurrent fugue is either very rare or non-existent in the absence of DID or complex DDNOS.

Pure dissociative amnesia is usually not recurrent, is usually linked to a specific severe traumatic event, and usually has a benign natural history. It is very similar to simple conversion disorders in its onset and natural history.

Epidemiology

The lifetime prevalence of dissociative disorders in the general population has been studied in Turkey (Akyuz, Dogan, Sar, Yargic, and Tutkun, 1999) and Canada (Ross, 1997) using the DDIS.

Table 15.2. Lifetime Prevalence of Dissociative Disorders in the General Population

	Canada (N=454) %	Turkey (N=994) %
Dissociative Amnesia	7.0	0.9
Dissociative Fugue	0.2	-
Depersonalization Disorder	2.4	0.2
Dissociative Identity Disorder	3.1	0.4
Dissociative Disorder NOS	0.2	0.6
Dissociative Disorder of Some Type	11.2	1.7

The results of these two surveys of random samples of the general population are shown in Table 15.2.

Like all psychiatric research, these two studies have methodological limitations, however they provide the only available data. The dissociative disorders should be more common in highly traumatized populations, which would include children living in Vietnam in the 1960's, and in Bosnia in the 1990's. Other populations predicted to have high rates of dissociative disorders include starving children in Africa, child prostitutes in Thailand, child victims of monsoons in Bangladesh, south-east Asian boat children, and street children in Rio de Janeiro.

Twin And Adoption Studies

The general predictions of the trauma model apply to DID and DDNOS. The risk for a chronic, complex dissociative disorder drops to zero in children adopted at birth out of multigenerational incest families into healthy, stable families. In the opposite direction, risk rises from zero to over 80% if the trauma dose delivered by the adoptive family is set high enough. The above-threshold trauma dosage is delivered by many families in the western world.

Concordance for complex DID in twins is driven entirely by trauma. Identical twins discordant for DID are discordant for trauma, with few if any exceptions. Concordance rates for DID do not differ in dyzygotic and monozygotic twins, once trauma dose is controlled for, or at most differ only a little. These predictions hold for cases of DID with severe trauma histories and extensive comorbidity.

There may be a non-pathological form of DID without trauma or comorbidity which shows higher concordance among identical than among fraternal twins. Dissociative fugue is so rare that twin studies cannot be done. The trauma model makes no specific prediction about twin concordance patterns in pure depersonalization disorder.

Biology

The biology of the chronic, complex dissociative disorders is the biology of trauma. Pathological dissociation should be correlated with hippocampal damage caused by high levels of cortisol. The hippocampal damage should be measurable with both anatomical and functional brain scans. Increased risk for memory error is a predicted consequence of hippocampal damage.

Treatment Outcome

The general treatment outcome predictions of the trauma model hold for DID and DDNOS. There are only minor differences in the treatment plans for DID and DDNOS. The trauma model predicts that DID patients will demonstrate the highest level of response to trauma therapy in well-designed studies. The outcomes in more rigorous studies will closely resemble those in the one prospective, systematic treatment outcome study for DID published to date (Ellason and Ross, 1997).

The successfully treated childhood-onset DID case will exhibit a dramatic reduction in symptoms and health care utilization, accompanied by a major improvement in occupational and social function and subjective well being. These changes will be accompanied by normalization of hippocampal function on PET scan.

If these predictions are correct, the psychotherapy of DID by Master's level clinicians will be proven to result in repair of damage to central nervous system tissue, a revolutionary finding in western medicine that could not have been predicted ten years ago. The prediction could not have been made ten years ago because we lacked the brain scan data, a trauma model, and a sufficiently developed field of trauma studies.

Revisions To DSM-IV-TR

The main problem in the DSM-IV-TR dissociative disorders section is the categorization of partial forms of DID as DDNOS. This problem existed in DSM-III (Ross, 1985). Partial forms of DID are not "atypical," as they were in DSM-III vocabulary, and they are not "unspecified," as they are in DSM-IV-TR vocabulary. They are like moderate pneumonia compared to severe pneumonia. DID, partial form should be separated out from DDNOS and be placed under DID as a modifier.

A second problem arises from cases which meet criteria for both dissociative amnesia and depersonalization disorder. These are usually partial forms of DID, and therefore should be diagnosed as DDNOS by DSM-IV-TR rules. However, DDNOS cannot be diagnosed because the individuals meet criteria for two of the other dissociative disorders. They clearly have only one dissociative disorder falling within the chronic, complex sub-category. These cases should also be classified under DID with a partial form modifier.

It makes no sense to have PTSD, acute stress disorder and the dissociative disorders in separate sections of DSM-IV-TR. This has occurred for historical and political reasons, not because of a rational classification system. Likewise, the conversion disorders are clearly dissociative disorders in the spheres of sensation and motor function. This is how they are classified in ICD-10 (Ross, 1997). If the conversion disorders are simple dissociative disorders, then somatization is a chronic, complex dissociative disorder. The somatoform disorders need to have a rational relationship to PTSD, acute stress disorder and the dissociative disorders.

16

FACTITIOUS DISORDERS

In my Trauma Programs, I see a great deal of factitious behavior and some patients warrant a formal DSM-IV-TR diagnosis of factitious disorder. I have done a lot of thinking about factitious disorders in order to arrive at their place within the trauma model. They are trauma disorders. I never see patients with factitious disorders who did not suffer serious neglect and emotional trauma in childhood.

Faking illness in order to get into the patient role is symptomatic of profoundly impaired attachment systems. The only way such individuals can form attachments is to be in the patient role. The factitious dissociative identity disorder patient, for instance, is much more severely traumatized and damaged than the high-functioning childhood-onset case treated to stable integration with outpatient therapy alone.

There are two main problems concerning factitious disorders: the DSM-IV-TR rules for the diagnosis, which I will analyze at the end of this chapter; and hostile professional attitudes towards patients with factitious disorders.

For all other disorders in medicine, one "makes" a diagnosis. Doctors don't "make" a diagnosis of factitious disorder – they *catch* the patient. People with factitious disorders are regarded as fakers and con artists. They do not belong to the category of legitimate patient. When caught by the doctor, they are exposed rather than treated. The exposure is hostile in tone, manner and vocabulary. The patient is rejected from the health care system, while the doctor congratulates himself on not getting tricked.

Catching a factitious disorder is gratifying for the ego of the doctor making the catch. Previous doctors who were fooled by the patient are regarded as competent, ethical colleagues, not marginal physicians. The factitious patient is viewed as well studied, clever and manipulative. Therefore the doctor making the catch is particularly clever himself, since his competent colleagues were fooled.

Unfortunately, however, the factitious disorder does not spontaneously remit when caught. The patient goes to another hospital and carries on with the factitious behavior. One result of the hostile countertransference towards this group of patients is the fact that we have no prospective follow-up data on factitious disorders in the world medical literature. No-one has published a defined treatment protocol for factitious disorders, and there is no detailed teaching in medical schools about how to detect or treat them.

Factitious patients in my Trauma Programs are actually more severely disturbed than the rest of the population. They require more care, not less. Patients have retracted their factitious dissociative identity disorder and done productive work while in my Trauma Programs. They have been accepted and supported by the other patients and staff during the process. This has been achieved through extensive team meetings and staff discussions, and by understanding that the trauma model applies to this subgroup within our population.

Why do I see cases of factitious dissociative identity disorder in my Trauma Programs, but no cases of factitious borderline personality disorder? Why does no-one fake borderline personality? The choice of disorder is driven by professional countertransference. Factitious patients fake disorders which generate a positive countertransference. Borderline personality disorder does not do the job. Patients in general are well aware of the hostile countertransference towards borderlines in conventional psychiatry.

Phenomenology

Factitious disorders do not exist in a vacuum. The trauma model predicts that they are accompanied by extensive psychiatric comorbidity on both Axis I and Axis II. This often includes mood disorders, substance abuse, personality disorders, and dissociative disorders. The most extreme cases, called Munchausen's Syndrome in the medical literature, probably have a 100% prevalence of chronic, complex dissociative disorders.

The greater the number of medical and psychiatric disorders faked, the higher the trauma dose, and the higher the scores on measures of general psychopathology. For instance, I reviewed the medical records as an expert witness for the defense in a case of Munchausen's Syndrome. The Munchausen's patient had filed a lawsuit against her therapists for iatrogenic multiple personality disorder. Prior to moving to the state in which the therapists practiced, she had committed a number of documented antisocial acts.

Prior to meeting the therapists she was suing, the woman had almost died from cardiac arrest caused by low potassium levels, which were secondary to her eating disorder. Her medical records filled six large three-ringed binders. They included numerous claims of numerous different surgeries, cancers and other disorders which were refuted by prior and subsequent records. For instance, she claimed to have had a kidney removed for cancer, but subsequently had two normal kidneys on an IVP X-ray.

The claim of iatrogenic dissociative identity disorder was itself an element of her factitious disorder. She was consciously faking iatrogenic dissociative identity disorder in order to extract money from her therapists' insurance companies. When she arrived in the state where her therapists worked, she changed her name prior to meeting them in order to evade legal authorities in her home state. She used this new name as the name of her host personality throughout therapy. Despite her claim that she had provided her therapists with a complete list of all her alter personalities, none of them had her real, legal name. This could only occur in one of two circumstances: a factitious disorder; or real pre-existing dissociative identity disorder with complete suppression of the alters carrying the real name and personal history. In either scenario, the dissociative identity disorder could not be iatrogenic.

The medical record included a hand written letter by the patient's mother, dated prior to first contact with the therapists being sued, in which the mother stated that she thought her daughter had Munchausen's Syndrome. The patient appeared on national television as a case of iatrogenic multiple personality disorder, and she was championed publicly by psychiatrists who claim that all cases of multiple personality are iatrogenic.

During the lawsuit, hostile professional countertransference was aimed at the therapists being sued by the plaintiff's experts. The patient was a victim in the eyes of her experts. She was able to extract from her expert witnesses the positive countertransference she had previously gotten from her therapists. Instead of being viewed as competent victims of a clever con artist, the therapists being sued were blamed for the patient's behavior by the plaintiff's experts.

The case illustrates the point that the choice of factitious disorder is driven by professional countertransference, plus secondary gain. The secondary gain of alleging iatrogenic multiple personality in a lawsuit outweighed the secondary gain obtained during therapy for factitious multiple personality, therefore the patient flipped from childhood-onset to iatrogenic multiple personality during the period of the lawsuit. The positive professional countertransference was held constant – only the personnel providing the countertransference changed. First it was the therapists, then it was the plaintiff's experts. Another constant in the equation was the fact that the woman maintained the victim role throughout.

The case settled out of court for an undisclosed amount. Because of the structure of the legal system, and the willingness of plaintiff's experts to act out their hostile countertransference in the courts, cases of what I call *factitious iatrogenic multiple personality* are heavily reinforced during lawsuits. The cost of dealing with the errors of logic and scholarship committed by the plaintiff's experts, and the difficulty of overcoming their dogmatic testimony, given their moral self-righteousness and appeal to their own authority, means that cost-of-defense settlements can run into hundreds of thousands of dollars. It becomes a rational business decision on the part of the insurance company to settle for large amounts of money rather than taking the case to trial, even if the insurance company predicts that it will win a zero verdict.

Even if frivolous, such lawsuits are rational business ventures for plaintiffs' lawyers. The cost of losing the occasional case is outweighed by the revenues obtained from others, especially if several truly iatrogenic cases are also brought to trial.

I describe the dynamics of such cases in detail because they illustrate the complexity of factitious disorders. The cases of factitious iatrogenic multiple personality illustrate how convoluted the dynamics can become. The cure lies in correcting the countertransference errors of the professionals.

My main point about the phenomenology of factitious disorders is their reinforcement by professional countertransference. This occurs even when a patient is "caught" and ejected from the health care system. The rejection reinforces the tenacity and increases the guile of the patient, who has just received unwitting instruction on how not to get caught at the next hospital.

The person with factitious iatrogenic multiple personality who obtains a favorable settlement or who wins at trial, is told by her experts that she has achieved a great victory. This is true financially. However, the emotional cost to the victorious litigant is increased self-disgust, cynicism, and scorn for human beings, including her own experts.

Natural History

The natural history of a factitious disorder depends primarily on the countertransference of the professionals and the degree of reinforcement by secondary gain. If the factitious disorder is "caught," the countertransference is hostile, and the natural history becomes more malignant. If the factitious disorder is mistaken for a "real" disorder, it is reinforced by positive countertransference, as in cases of factitious iatrogenic multiple personality, and again the natural history becomes more malignant. In those cases, the plaintiff's experts assess the person as having *real iatrogenic multiple personality*, to coin another term. In most factitious disorders, the "real" disorder being faked is more straight forward, but the same logic is in effect as in factitious iatrogenic multiple personality.

In my Trauma Programs, we maintain a positive countertransference when we "catch" a factitious disorder because we understand the factitious behavior as a symptom of a severe and genuine psychiatric disorder. Within the trauma model, factitious disorders are as "real" as depression or substance abuse.

The trauma model predicts that positive countertransference maintained subsequent to the diagnosis of factitious disorder will be a powerful predictor of positive treatment outcome. The inverse will be true for negative countetransference. The fact that we lack a valid measure of countertransference is a measurement problem. It is a technical problem, not a conceptual limitation of the trauma model.

Epidemiology

The epidemiology of factitious disorders is entirely socially determined. For instance, if a diagnosis of dissociative identity disorder automatically resulted in a guilty verdict and a doubling of sentence in criminal cases, the prevalence of malingered dissociation would drop to zero in that social system. People who actually had the disorder would fake not having it. The utility of factitious dissociative identity disorder in the legal setting depends entirely on two things: its ability to extract positive countertransference from the jury; and the rules of the system. From a biomedical perspective, the rules are arbitrary.

Similarly, if low back pain resulted in a drop in salary and disqualification from disability programs, workers would fake good backs rather than bad ones.

There can be no epidemiology of factitious disorders independent from the rules of the social system and the countertransference errors of the members of the system. Generally, then, the prevalence of factitious disorder varies with its reinforcers.

At the same time, trauma contributes to the prevalence, given that factitious behavior is an attempt to correct for the attachment deficits induced by neglect and emotional abuse. The trauma model predicts that sexual abuse will have negligible affect on the prevalence of factious disorders, while neglect is a major predictor. This is the inverse of the predictors for somatoform disorders, as illustrated in Table 16.1

Table 16.1. Effects of Sexual Abuse and Neglect on the Prevalence of Factitious and Somatoform Disorders

	Prevalence of Disorder	
	Factitious	Somatoform
Sexual Abuse	+	++++
Neglect	++++	+

Twin And Adoption Studies

The general predictions of the trauma model hold for twin and adoption studies of factitious disorders. Identical twins discordant for severe neglect will be discordant for factitious disorder. Fraternal twins concordant for severe neglect will have higher concordance for factitious disorder than identical twins discordant for neglect. Adoption in and out of neglectful families will have profound effects on the prevalence of factitious behavior.

It follows from this logic that children who live in orphanages for prolonged periods should have higher rates of factitious disorder than children separated from their parents at the same age but adopted shortly thereafter. Studies of this prediction would have to control for the effects of sexual abuse and other trauma occurring both before and after separation from parents.

Biology

There is no specific biology of factious disorder independent of the biology of trauma. Even if there was a biology of factitious behavior, it could not be activated or maintained in the absence of social reinforcement. The trauma model assumes that other disorders such as bipolar mood disorder may have a substantial endogenous biological component to their etiology. The DSM-IV-TR definition of factitious disorder makes a predominantly endogenous biological etiology impossible.

Treatment Outcome

Predictions about treatment outcome were made above in the section on natural history. The nature of the countertransference is the most important predictor of outcome. When there is a positive countertransference and trauma therapy is delivered, the outcome for the factitious disorder improves. Since it then becomes possible to address the underlying trauma to attachment systems, the prognosis also improves for other forms of comorbidity.

Revisions To DSM-IV-TR

The DSM-IV-TR definitions of factitious disorder and malingering are unscientific for several reasons. Factitious disorder is defined as conscious faking of symptoms in order to get into the patient role. Faking of symptoms for secondary gain is called malingering. Factitious disorder is an Axis I diagnosis, while malingering is not regarded as a psychiatric disorder, and is classified in a section of DSM-IV-TR called V Codes.

This is an arbitrary distinction because getting into the patient role is itself a form of secondary gain. Why should a person should have a psychiatric disorder when he fakes symptoms in his relationship with a psychiatrist, but no psychiatric disorder if he fakes symptoms in his relationship with a jury? The distinction is based on turf considerations, not true distinctions occurring in nature. In any case, many if not most factitious patients fake symptoms in many social contexts; should they receive two diagnoses for the same behavior, factitious disorder and malingering, depending on the social context?

A further problem with the DSM-IV-TR definitions of factitious disorder and malingering is the requirement that the symptoms be consciously faked. This requirement assumes that the same symptom can occur unconsciously, and in fact this assumption is stated explicitly in the Somatoform Disorders section of DSM-IV-TR (page 486). There it is stated that the same patient may have both consciously produced and unconsciously produced somatic symptoms, in which case both a somatoform disorder and a factitious disorder should be diagnosed. Again, we have two diagnoses for the same symptom, this time depending on a conscious-unconscious distinction.

The conscious-unconscious distinction is unscientific. There are no valid and reliable measures for making the distinction, and there are no data showing that psychiatrists can make it in a reliable fashion. Also, conscious and unconscious are not in reality dichotomous categories. They are more like a continuum. A given symptom can be more or less conscious on different days.

In criminal cases, a great deal hinges on psychiatric judgments about whether a person has consciously or unconsciously produced symptoms. The judgments are unscientific, despite the pretensions of the testifying experts. DSM-IV-TR needs to be revised to eliminate the conscious-unconscious distinction and the arbitrary distinction between secondary gain in the form of the patient role and all other forms of secondary gain.

The crucial fact in factitious disorders is that they do not pre-exist the social context in which they first arise and have the purpose of accruing secondary gain. They are not iatrogenic. It is the iatrogenic-factitious distinction which is fundamental. Unfortunately, we lack valid measures for making this distinction as well. I operationalized the factitious-iatrogenic distinction for dissociative identity disorder in a way which makes it scientifically testable (Ross, 1997). This can be done for other disorders. The conscious-unconscious distinction is either much more difficult or impossible to operationalize.

17

EATING DISORDERS

Eating disorders provide hard, objective measures of treatment outcome. These are weight, electrolyte levels, and being alive. The number of binge and purge episodes per week is an objective criterion, but it can be faked or inaccurately reported. Anorexia nervosa carries as high a mortality rate as any psychiatric disorder – in severe cases, simply being alive can be a positive outcome. The eating disorders are highly influenced by culture.

In my Trauma Programs, the prevalence of DSM-IV-TR eating disorders on structured interview is about 40%, but this is only part of the story. I would say that over 75% of patients have highly pathological eating patterns. The problems include overeating, massive over-reliance on junk food, traumatic triggering by food, food phobias, projection of false memories onto food, mood regulation with food, and obsessive rituals concerning food. All of these are trauma-related.

I have had a specific interest in the eating disorders since I did a six-month rotation in the Eating Disorders Clinic as a resident in 1985, at which time I ran an outpatient cognitive therapy group for women with bulimia. It was evident to me in 1985 that most people with eating disorders have not been sexually abused. However, trauma in the broad sense is a major factor in most eating disorders. It is debatable whether "trauma" should include general life stress and conflict. The risk of broadening the term is dilution of its meaning to the point that it becomes trivial. This is called a Type I error in science. One could include too many things in the category of trauma.

The risk of narrowing the meaning of trauma is missing real trauma effects in nature. This is called a Type II error. Analysis of data always involves striking a balance between Type I and Type II errors. It is rarely possible to eliminate either. I will adopt a broad definition of trauma for this chapter. Psychological trauma includes extreme degrees of parental perfectionism, parental double binds, high performance standards, inconsistent withdrawal of love for failure to follow changing rules, and a range of parental behaviors occurring in apparently "normal" or "pillar of the community" families.

Such transactional patterns can lead to obsessive compulsive, depression, phobic, and eating disorder symptoms. For instance, mother sets performance demands for her daughter so high that they are unattainable. Extraordinary effort by the daughter results in failure. This by itself would cause serious problems with mood and self-esteem. The family system is more complex and traumatic than that, however, because the rules and performance expectations are constantly changing. Failure to predict correctly which rule or performance demand is active is itself a cause for a performance rating of failure.

Failure is an occasion for negative character evaluation by the mother. Failure is always due to the daughter's not caring enough and not trying hard enough. Failure disappoints and wounds the mother who has tried so hard to teach her daughter the right way to do things. The daughter learns that obsessive fearfulness on her part is an indicator of caring enough to worry. She stays up at night ruminating. She believes that worrying may earn her a partial success rating.

The family environment causes low self esteem and depression, and compulsive attempts to do everything correctly and with the ultimate degree of thoroughness. Perfect performance, which would finally earn the mother's conditional love, is strived for but never attained. The fear of negative performance evaluation and negative character evaluation traps the daughter between phobic avoidance as a strategy for failure risk-reduction, and compulsive performance at tasks which can potentially be mastered. In order to have a manageable world, the world has to be contained within a small perimeter. As a result, the daughter develops agoraphobia. The cost of this strategy is to be inadequate in the wider world.

The punitive mother is identified with and introjected, in psychoanalytical terms, resulting in highly self-punitive cognition. The daughter can make everything OK if she can reduce her world to a manageable number of variables and control enough of them to earn a positive performance evaluation from her introjected mother. The targets of control could include percent body fat, dust in the house, the number of germs on the kitchen counter, the academic and extracurricular performances of her children, or anything else in the restricted universe.

This type of family system can cause an eating disorder with extensive comorbidity in the absence of physical abuse, sexual abuse and neglect. The mother is regarded as devoted to her family, an evaluation made by neighbors and acquaintances of the daughter a generation later, and the father is a hard working, good provider. These facts make it the daughter's fault if she has any criticisms of her parents, and makes her conclude that her own anger, resentment, loss and loneliness are not legitimate. She cannot trust or tolerate her feelings because these are evidence of her bad character, which is in turn the cause of her inadequate performance.

Phenomenology

The majority of people with eating disorders do not report childhood sexual abuse. However, in the subgroup of eating disorders with sexual abuse, there is a set of specific dynamics and cognitive errors. These are shown in Tables 17.1, 17.2 and 17.3.

Table 17.1. Motives For Bingeing And Purging In Sexual Abuse Victims

- Weight and Body-Image Management
- Purging the Body of Bad Feelings
- Mood State Management
- Filling Up Inner Emptiness
- Maintaining an Illusion of Control
- Undoing Fellatio and Intercourse

The motives for bingeing and purging in people with histories of childhood sexual abuse include weight and body-image management. This motive is universal in eating disorders. The structure and logic of the eating disorder do not vary depending on whether there has been sexual abuse – what varies is the content. The bulimic person with a sexual abuse history will be particularly preoccupied with secondary sexual characteristics, and disgust for the body will be focused on the sexual organs.

Similarly, purging is almost always designed to get rid of bad feelings. In the sexually abused person, the bad feelings will be sexual or linked to the sexual abuse. Purging to rid the body of semen from long ago is one of the less common motives, but is not rare. I am not referring to a postulated unconscious motive here, rather I am thinking of patients who have stated this as their conscious motive.

The motives for anorexia in sexual abuse victims are shown in Table 17.2.

Table 17.2. Motives For Anorexia In Sexual Abuse Victims

- Phobias Related to Fellatio
- Starving Off Secondary Sex Characteristics
- Suicide by Starvation
- Punishment of Other Ego States
- Suppression of Menstruation
- Internal Negotiation With Other Ego States
- Re-enactment of Childhood Trauma
- Cleansing the Body
- Maintaining an Illusion of Control

Other ego states may be punished for a variety of reasons including: sexual arousal; causing rejection; being blamed for the abuse; eating too much; saying the wrong things; or being too fat. The starvation is inflicted on one ego state by another. Suppression of menstruation may be motivated by a general fear and disgust of secondary sexual characteristics, or by the fact that menstruation is a specific traumatic trigger.

Cleansing the body is a major motive for anorexia in many cases. In the sexual abuse survivor, some of the feelings may be derived directly from the sexual abuse. One woman with dissociative identity disorder and anorexia nervosa had a child alter personality who would not eat. The child alter personality believed that any fat in her body was stored semen from long ago. The content of the feelings, and their specific origin, does not determine the treatment plan, however, just as the content of a phobia does not affect the need for a desensitization hierarchy.

Maintaining an illusion of control is the primary motive in most eating disorders. In the sexual abuse survivor, the bad body has bad sexual feelings, but there are other intolerable emotions as well, including anger and sadness.

Table 17.3. Motives For Obesity In Sexual Abuse Victims

- Make the Body Unattractive to Perpetrators
- Insulation Between the Self and Outside World
- To Suppress Promiscuous Ego States
- To Fill Up Inner Emptiness
- To Punish the Self

The motives for obesity in sexual abuse victims are listed in Table 17.3.

They are self-evident, except for the suppression of promiscuous ego states. This motive can occur in obese people with full dissociative identity disorder (DID), dissociative disorder not otherwise specified, or no dissociative disorder, and does not depend on the degree of differentiation of the ego state. I learned it from a DID patient whose prostitute alter personalities would not take executive control if the body was overweight.

There may be a specific cutoff weight, such as eighty pounds overweight. The person may lose weight easily until she approaches the cutoff point. Then anxiety will increase dramatically and weight loss will slow down and stop.

The general relationship between the severity of sexual abuse and the severity of the eating disorder is shown in Figure 17.1. The figure is illustrative – the exact relationship is not necessarily as depicted. The sexual trauma dose could be measured by the Dissociative Disorders Interview Schedule and the severity of eating disorder by one of the standard eating disorder scales.

Figure 17.1. The Relationship Between Trauma Dose and the Severity of the Eating Disorder

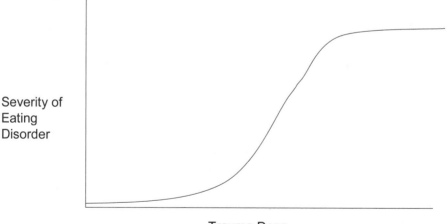

Severity of
Eating
Disorder

Trauma Dose

The general predictions of the trauma model will hold for the eating disorders. The degree of comorbidity will increase with the severity of both the trauma and the eating disorder.

Natural History

The general predictions of the trauma model hold for the natural history of the eating disorders. The more severe the trauma, the more malignant the course of the eating disorder. Eating disorders appear to remit gradually with advancing years in many but not all cases. This may be because of declining concern with body image, or because accumulated life experience provides other preoccupations.

A measure of spiritual malaise and emptiness should predict the natural history of an eating disorder. The more empty the person, the greater the drive to fill the void with food, or avoidance of food.

Epidemiology

The higher the trauma dose in a population, the higher the prevalence of eating disorders. However, a large subgroup of eating disorder patients has not experienced overt abuse or neglect, therefore other factors must have a significant affect on the epidemiology. The gender ratio in eating disorders in North America is about 10:1 female to male. The childhood abuse ratio is probably about 1.5:1. I derive this number from an assumption that physical abuse and neglect have a 1:1 ratio in boys and girls, while sexual abuse has a 2:1 ratio girls to boys. Whatever the exact numbers, it is evident that the gender ratio of eating disorders is skewed far out of proportion to the abuse ratio.

Several measures of parental behavior might predict eating disorders independently of abuse. In a given family or population, the higher the scores on measures of parental perfectionism, the lower the scores on measures of parental unconditional love, or the higher the scores on measures of negative characterological attributions by parents, the higher the prevalence of eating disorders. The more pathological the parental scores on these measures, the lower the scores of their children on measures of self-esteem.

Bulimia should be less common in cultures which value chubbiness in women. This prediction could be tested by presenting pictures of a series of women with varying per cent body fat to men in various cultures, which would yield an ideal number for each culture. This number should predict average binge/vomit episodes per month in girls and women across cultures. The average per cent body fat of women in magazines in a culture should show a significant negative correlation with number of binge/vomit episodes per female per month. The number of women on diets in a culture should correlate with the prevalence of bulimia. One could develop a measure of male preferences in female body type that would have the same predictive power.

It would be interesting to know if the ready availability of excess fat grams predicts the prevalence of anorexia nervosa in a culture. If the possibility of being obese is not readily available, pathological thinness may have no meaning or function. One cannot create an illusion of self-control by controlling fat intake if there are no excess fat grams available in the diet, or if everyone is malnourished. The prevalence of anorexia nervosa among starving refugee populations should be zero.

Measures of parental control, perfectionism and absence of unconditional love should predict restrictive eating patterns in daughters. Boys in anorexia families should prefer excessively thin girls to a greater degree than their friends - they should adopt the male perceptions that reinforce their sisters' distorted body images. There should be a significant correlation between the number of breast implants and liposuction procedures in a culture, and scores on measures of eating disorders.

Twin And Adoption Studies

The general predictions of the trauma model hold for twin and adoption studies of eating disorders. However, there is a gender effect. Controlling for the effect of trauma, concordance for eating disorders should be as high among dizygotic female twins as it is among monozygotic male twins. This will occur because the etiology is environmental, and fraternal twin girls share the environmental pressures to the same extent as identical twin boys. This finding would refute the equal environments assumption for eating disorders.

Parents treat identical twins the same to a much greater degree than they do fraternal twins. Therefore when one monozygotic male twin experiences the pressures to have an eating disorder, so will the other. The similarity in degree of environmental pressure holds for all sisters, whether they are twins or not. Concordance in non-twin sisters should approach that in monozygotic twin sisters. These relationships are illustrated in Table 17.4

The risk for eating disorders will rise much further for girls adopted into a family or culture that promotes eating disorders than it does for boys. This finding will prove that the difference in gender rates for eating disorders is not endogenous-genetic.

Table 17.4. Concordance Rates for Eating Disorders in Different Siblings

	Male	Female
MZ Twins	+++	++++
DZ Twins	++	+++
Non-Twin Siblings	+	++

Biology

There is no specific biology of eating disorders independent of the biology of trauma. There are, however, specific biological complications, including weight, electrolyte, immune system and hormonal imbalances. Everyone recognizes that end-stage anorexia nervosa involves profound biological changes which reinforce and perpetuate the disorder.

Treatment Outcome

Trauma therapy will improve the outcome for eating disorders because they fall within the addictions model component of trauma therapy.

Revisions To DSM-IV-TR

The DSM-IV-TR section on eating disorders does not have any major problems. Future editions need to guard against a proliferation of subtypes of eating disorder.

18

SEXUAL AND GENDER IDENTITY DISORDERS

Surgical and chemical gender reassignment is a very radical thing to do to another human being. The procedure should not be undertaken without a careful assessment for a chronic, complex dissociative disorder. It is not surprising that many transsexuals report a positive outcome from gender reassignment – the positive outcome is experienced by a female identity who has achieved a complete chemical and surgical victory over the male identity of the body.

Gender identity disorder (GID) is defined in DSM-IV-TR as having a female identity housed in a biologically male body (or vice versa), but the diagnosis has nothing at all to do with dissociative identity disorder (DID) according to DSM-IV-TR. The two are regarded as completely separate disorders and the text and diagnostic criteria for gender identity disorder do not even mention dissociative identity disorder.

What more graphic demonstration of a dissociation between biological and psychological identity could there be than that provided by gender identity disorder? I have spoken with many opposite-sex alter personalities in DID cases, and have seen many of them integrated successfully into the host personality. The outcome of these integrations has been a psychological identity congruent with the biological identity in 100% of cases.

I have evaluated only a handful of DID patients with gender identity disorder diagnoses (Ross, 1994), so cannot speak from a large experience base as I can for other comorbidity. But I understand the consequences of failing to assess for pathological dissociation prior to surgical reassignment. Why? Because I have spoken with male alter personalities trapped in chemically reassigned bodies.

In a subgroup of cases, gender identity disorder is a partial form of dissociative identity disorder. The question is whether the host psychological identity has achieved a complete suppression of the biological identity, and therefore experiences no intrusions from it. If

165

the suppression is incomplete there will be intrusions that resemble the Schneiderian symptoms of DID. The intrusions will be from a dissociated component of the psyche whose psychological gender identity is congruent with the biological identity of the body.

If suppression fails, and intrusions occur, they will be denied or disavowed by the host personality seeking victory in the internal war. Chemical reassignment should reinforce the dissociation and reduce the internal conflict. The male transsexual will feel more secure in his female identity for both hormonal and psychological reasons – the inner enemy has been vanquished. These dynamics will occur only in the subtype of gender identity disorder with a false negative diagnosis of DID or DDNOS. The most extreme skepticism about DID should occur in academic Departments of Psychiatry whose Professors are involved in chemical and surgical gender reassignment.

The DSM-IV-TR definition of gender identity disorder and chemical/ surgical reassignment contradict each other. If gender identity disorder is a psychiatric disorder, then it cannot be treated by surgery on the body. The disorder must be in the mind for it to appear in DSM-IV-TR as a mental disorder. Castration is a rational procedure only if the body is wrong. The mind must be right about its gender identity for castration to make sense. But if the mind is right, there is no mental disorder. There is a body disorder.

Scientifically, however, there is nothing biologically wrong with the body of a male transsexual. It is a normal 46XY male body. This being so, the transsexual gender identity is a delusion. Chemical/surgical gender reassignment for gender identity disorder is really plastic surgery for delusional disorder, somatic subtype. It is like doing liposuction for someone with anorexia nervosa. This is an inescapable conclusion of classifying transsexualism as a mental disorder in DSM-IV-TR. Chemical/surgical reassignment makes sense only if transsexualism is not a mental disorder.

Gender identity disorder should be in a separate section from the disorders of sexual arousal, desire and orgasm. These in turn should be in a separate section from the paraphilias, the DSM-IV-TR term for sexual perversions.

The reason that the lobby to get homosexuality excluded from DSM was successful was two-fold: the lobby was strong enough politically; and there was no scientific argument in favor of retaining homosexuality in the DSM system. The other paraphilias are retained in DSM-IV-TR only because the lobby in favor of excluding them has no strength.

If paraphilic behavior is truly compulsive and ego-dystonic, and is properly classified as a mental disorder, it should be a form of obsessive-compulsive disorder (OCD). The content of obsessions and compulsions is not relevant to their classification as OCD according to DSM-IV-TR rules, just as the content of specific phobias is not relevant. The sexual obsessions and compulsions have been placed in a separate section of DSM-IV-TR for historical and ideological reasons, in a manner which violates the rules for OCD and specific phobias.

Bringing the argument full circle, why do we not prescribe amputation of the hands for hand-washing compulsions? What is the difference between that procedure and surgical reassignment for male transsexuals? The consent of the obsessive-compulsive patient to hand amputation would result in his being defined as delusional and legally incompetent. The consent would be the reason not to operate. Why do psychiatrists not follow the same rules and reach the same conclusions concerning gender identity disorder?

Phenomenology

Disorders of sexual desire, arousal and orgasm can be consequences of childhood sexual abuse. Rates of sexual dysfunction are very high in survivors of serious childhood sexual abuse, however the majority of people with sexual dysfunctions have not been sexually abused. The trauma model predicts that a history of severe, chronic childhood sexual abuse increases the risk for sexual dysfunction dramatically, although it is not the most common cause of such problems.

The general predictions of the trauma model hold for sexual dysfunction. Severe cases of sexual dysfunction are accompanied by extensive comorbidity and trauma. Sexual dysfunctions caused by sexual abuse should be accompanied by other somatic symptoms from the genito-urinary, reproductive and gastrointestinal systems.

Natural History

The sexual dysfunctions should start earlier, be more severe, and persist longer, the more severe the trauma. Factors predicting a more favorable outcome for a given trauma dose, in the absence of therapy, should include: an otherwise healthy relationship with a sexual partner;

other positive life experiences; absence of secondary gain for the sexual dysfunction; understanding the psychological nature of the problem; motivation for change; clear cognitive errors concerning sexuality; self-study and reading about the problem; and absence of other obsessions, compulsions and addictions.

There seems to be a very low rate of spontaneous remission in gender identity disorder. Its natural history should be affected by the same factors modifying the course of sexual dysfunctions.

Epidemiology

The sexual and gender identity disorders will be more common in cultures, families and populations with more childhood sexual trauma. There may be a universal base rate of gender identity disorder that is not caused by trauma.

Twin And Adoption Studies

Twin studies of gender identity disorder might yield interesting results. When trauma cases are excluded from the analysis, there might be a higher concordance in identical than non-identical twins. When only twins concordant for trauma are considered, the difference in concordance rates between MZ and DZ twins should disappear.

If some cases of gender identity disorder are caused by biological factors, twin and adoption studies could establish whether the caused is inherited. Any cause which is not genetic, is environmental. Intrauterine infections, radiation exposure, abnormalities of maternal hormone levels, poor maternal nutrition, birth complications, and effects of maternal drug abuse during pregnancy are all environmental causes of mental illness. Most biological causes of mental illness should be environmental, according to the trauma model.

Among genetic mental disorders, if any exist, there are two subgroups: inherited diseases; and diseases due to mutations. The mutations may have an environmental cause. Ultimately, one might say, even inherited genes for mental illness have an environmental cause, since they have been selected by the environment over millennia.

Setting these considerations aside, twin and adoption studies can show whether gender identity disorder is inherited. I predict that it is not. The risk for sexual dysfunctions should rise and fall dramatically depending on the type of family one is adopted into or out of, as is true for most other DSM-IV-TR disorders. Concordance for sexual dysfunctions in twins should be driven primarily by the environment, not the genome.

Biology

There may be a subtle causative biological abnormality in some cases of gender identity disorder. There is a set point theory of sexual desire, analogous to the set point theory for obesity. The idea is that some people just have more sexual drive than others. Actuarial data on rapidly increasing rates of obesity in North America over the last fifty years provide conclusive proof of the role of the environment in the majority of cases of obesity. I assume that the sexual dysfunctions are driven primarily by the environment as well, and that they have no specific biology except perhaps in a small subset of cases.

Treatment Outcome

Treatment of simple cases of sexual dysfunction involves simple cognitive-behavioral protocols. More complex cases will require trauma therapy, which will result in improved outcome for prior treatment failures. In the DID and DDNOS subtypes of gender identity disorder, treatment will be trauma therapy. There will be three outcomes: 1) realignment of psychological gender identity with biological identity; 2) resolution of internal conflict and desire for chemical/surgical reassignment, with no change in psychological gender identity; and, 3) treatment failure.

The second outcome will result from the dominant host personality accepting a compromise. The dominant female host in a male body (or vice versa) will agree not to pursue chemical/surgical reassignment in trade for an agreement by the other identity states that they will not seek executive control.

Revisions To DSM-IV-TR

The necessary revisions to DSM-IV-TR were described in the opening section of this chapter. Gender identity disorder should stand by itself or be moved to the dissociative disorders. The sexual dysfunctions should be moved to the somatoform disorders.

19

SLEEP DISORDERS

Disordered sleep is commonly a component of a DSM-IV-TR disorder other than the sleep disorders. Disordered sleep is a diagnostic criterion for mood disorders and posttraumatic stress disorder, for instance, and is extremely common in the other anxiety disorders and substance abuse. Many sleep disorders such as narcolepsy and sleep apnea are clearly medical disorders of the brain. Others, such as sleep terrors, remit spontaneously without treatment. This leaves the primary sleep disorders for consideration.

Simple insomnia without other comorbidity is rarely or ever due to trauma. Trauma-driven serious insomnia is always accompanied by extensive comorbidity. The only sleep disorder of any interest from a trauma model perspective is sleep walking. I will discuss only sleep walking in the rest of this chapter.

Phenomenology

Sleep walking usually remits spontaneously in childhood or early adolescence, especially when it is unrelated to trauma. In trauma cases, it is accompanied by a wide range of other trance and dissociative symptoms. The prevalence of sleep walking and selected other symptoms in dissociative identity disorder is shown in Table 19.1.

Table 19.1. Prevalence of Sleep Walking and Other Symptoms in Dissociative Identity Disorder

Symptom	%
Going into Trances	92.0
Sleepwalking	55.9
Imaginary Companions	48.0

The behavior that occurs during sleep walking can have clear meaning and purpose, ranging from murder to re-enactment of childhood trauma to symbolic expression of conflicts and impulses. Behaviors occurring during the day in people with chronic, complex dissociative disorders can be indistinguishable from sleep walking. Sleep walking is a classical

171

example of dissociated executive control – the normal, alert waking self is deactivated and a rudimentary, sleep-like self is in control.

Trauma-driven sleep walking occurs on a spectrum as show in Figure 19.1.

Figure 19.1. The Spectrum of Trauma-Driven Sleep Walking

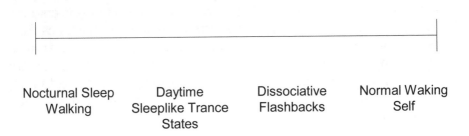

| Nocturnal Sleep Walking | Daytime Sleeplike Trance States | Dissociative Flashbacks | Normal Waking Self |

As one moves right on the spectrum of trauma-driven sleep walking, the self in executive control becomes less sleeplike and more oriented to the present. The executive self fully absorbed in a flashback is not "sleepy" but has the quality of a REM dream self. It is "lucid" but not oriented to the present. At no point on the spectrum is the person actually asleep by EEG criteria.

Sleep walking could be considered a form of dissociative possession disorder, a diagnosis included in DSM-IV-TR in the section for proposed diagnoses requiring further study. The possessing self in sleep walking has an identity. It is just more rudimentary and sleeplike than the usual spirit, demon or alter personality. What is the difference between sleep walking and possession by a sleeplike spirit?

Natural History

The natural history of trauma-driven sleep walking differs from that of simple sleep walking. It lasts longer, occurs more frequently, involves more complex behaviors, and has more negative consequences, the more severe the trauma.

Epidemiology

The risk for trauma-driven sleep walking increases with increasing trauma dosage and increasing comorbidity.

Twin And Adoption Studies

Twin and adoption studies will demonstrate both the traumatic nature of sleep walking in the trauma subgroup, and the endogenous, developmental nature of the disorder in non-trauma cases. In the absence of trauma, concordance for sleep walking will be greater in monozygotic than dizygotic twins. However, dizygotic twins concordant for severe trauma will have higher concordance rates for sleep walking than monozygotic twins discordant for trauma. Discordance for trauma will reduce the concordance rate for sleep walking in both types of twin because one twin will have the traumatic risk and the other will not. These relationships are shown in Table 19.2.

Table 19.2. Concordance Rates for Trauma and Sleep Walking in Monozygotic and Dizygotic Twins

| | Concordance for Sleep Walking | |
	MZ	DZ
Trauma in Both Twins	++++	+++
No Trauma	++	+
Trauma in One Twin	+	-

Adoption studies will show the general pattern predicted by the trauma model.

Biology

There should be two biological subgroups in sleep walking. One should have the biology of trauma, and the other should not. There could be a two-hit effect. It is possible that the endogenous abnormality in sleep walking gives rise to a benign, spontaneously remitting form of the disorder. It could be that this abnormality interacts with trauma to produce the more malignant form of sleep walking which lasts beyond adolescence. This possibility cannot be tested until a specific abnormality in simple sleep walking has been identified. If such an abnormality exists it may be hard to detect as a signal because of the background noise caused by the biology of trauma.

Treatment Outcome

Simple sleep walking does not require treatment. Complex sleep walking should respond to trauma therapy. The symptom decay curve of the sleep walking should parallel the decline in scores on the Dissociative Experiences Scale.

Revisions To DSM-IV-TR

As mentioned above, trauma-driven sleep walking should be moved to the dissociative disorders section. Other disorders of sleep are accounted for by the trauma model in terms of other comorbidity, such as depression and anxiety, of which they are a component. Some sleep disorders such as narcolepsy and sleep apnea are clearly endogenous biomedical disorders and do not belong in DSM-IV-TR. Beyond that, I have no specific comments on the sleep disorders section of DSM-IV-TR.

20

IMPULSE-CONTROL DISORDERS

The amnesia occurring in intermittent explosive disorder was acknowledged in DSM-III, published in 1980, but deleted from DSM-III-R, published in 1987. It was not re-introduced in DSM-IV, published in 1994, or in DSM-IV-TR, published in 2000. From my perspective, the impulse control disorders are always dissociative in nature. Impulses from outside the sphere of the executive self over-ride the control of the executive self in a manner experienced as ego-alien and ego-dystonic by the executive self. The impulse control disorders are classical examples of dissociated executive control.

This is true at a phenomenological level no matter what etiology is proposed or proven. Dissociated executive control is occurring in the impulse-control disorders whether the cause is biological, psychological, or a combination of the two. Intermittent explosive disorder rarely occurs without comorbidity and a history of trauma.

Phenomenology

Serious impulse dyscontrol is probably always accompanied by other dissociative symptoms. In the trauma subgroup of the disorder, the impulse dyscontrol episodes are a form of dissociative flashback in which past traumatic emotion and behavioral reactions are activated and intrude into the executive self. The verbal, visual and cognitive elements of the past trauma are dissociated from the feelings and behavior, with intrusion of the feelings and behavior, but ongoing suppression of the visual, verbal and cognitive elements. The intermittent explosions are triggered by environmental or internal cues, just like the episodes more commonly thought of as trauma flashbacks. Intermittent explosive disorder episodes, spontaneous age regressions, and dissociative flashbacks are all closely related to each other.

Natural History

The natural history of the impulse–control disorders is the natural history of trauma disorders in general.

Epidemiology

The prevalence of impulse-control disorders will vary with the prevalence of chronic childhood trauma

Twin And Adoption Studies

Twin and adoption studies will demonstrate that impulse-control disorders are environmentally induced. Concordance rates should be the same in MZ and DZ twins when the cause of the disorder is intrauterine infection, maternal starvation, or maternal substance abuse during pregnancy. Exceptions to this rule will occur only when there are two amniotic sacks and the biological insult is contained within one of them. When the cause is childhood psychological trauma, concordance rates will be driven by the trauma rather than the genome.

As for other disorders, the risk for impulse-control disorders will depend on the rates of trauma in adoptive families.

Biology

The biology of impulse-control disorders is the biology of trauma. If abnormal temporal lobe spikes or other EEG abnormalities occur during the explosive episodes, they are aspects of the biology of trauma, rather than genetically caused. The etiological question is whether the environmental trauma was biomedical or psychological. The two subtypes of environmental trauma, biomedical and psychological, may be pathways to the same or similar biology and behavior.

Treatment Outcome

In trauma cases with extensive comorbidity, the impulse-control disorder will respond to trauma therapy, assuming there is a real commitment to the work of therapy.

Revisions To DSM-IV-TR

The text and diagnostic criteria for impulse-control disorders need to take a broad range of dissociative symptoms into account. It is not clear why this section of DSM-IV-TR even exists. Following the logic of the anxiety and somatoform disorders section, impulse-control disorders could be classified as simple forms of borderline personality disorder. Or, alternatively, borderline personality disorder could be reclassified as a chronic, complex impulse-control disorder. Serious impulse dyscontrol rarely occurs without other dysregulations, including ones of mood, identity, and perception of self and others.

Trichotillomania should be classified as a form of obsessive-compulsive disorder. There is no difference between OCD and trichotillomania even though DSM-IV-TR (page 620) states that, "The repetitive hair pulling in Trichotillomania must be distinguished from a compulsion, as in Obsessive-Compulsive Disorder. In Obsessive-Compulsive Disorder, the repetitive behaviors are performed in response to an obsession..."

I have never seen a non-compulsive case of trichotillomania. Why, out of all the behaviors carried out by human beings, are fire setting (pyromania), hair pulling (trichotillomania), shoplifting (kleptomania) and gambling given status as separate Impulse Control Disorders in DSM-IV-TR? Why doesn't DSM-IV-TR have categories for Self Mutilation Disorder, Vehicular Speeding Disorder, Fast Food Over-Consumption Disorder, Credit Card Over-Utilization Disorder, Tattoo Over-Utilization Disorder or Migratory Game Bird Excessive Killing Disorder? Why is substance abuse not an Impulse Control Disorder?

The inclusion, exclusion, and classification rules for DSM-IV-TR impulse control disorders are not based on science.

21

BORDERLINE PERSONALITY DISORDER

The word "borderline" has three distinct meanings in psychiatry. The first is the operationalized DSM-IV-TR definition of the disorder: in order to be borderline by DSM-IV-TR rules, you must meet five out of nine criteria for the disorder. The DSM-IV-TR criteria are a behavioral checklist and can be studied empirically like any other symptom or behavioral measure in psychiatry.

The second meaning of "borderline" is a metapsychological one. Borderline is a postulated intrapsychic structure, the core elements of which are splitting, denial and projective identification. One can be structurally borderline in this sense but meet criteria for virtually any combination of Axis I and II DSM-IV-TR disorders. This meaning of borderline is not scientifically testable as formulated. There is no evidence that this meaning of borderline has any inter-rater reliability or validity.

The third meaning of borderline is less pleasant. The word borderline is a rationalization for hostile countertransference. As soon as a patient is identified as "borderline," it becomes professionally acceptable to talk about her in a manner that would be forbidden if the diagnosis was depression. In my residency, I was taught to have a belittling, demeaning attitude towards borderlines. I was taught that borderlines are bad, manipulative, dangerous, highly prone to regression and untreatable. They are not legitimate patients, do not have a right to be in the hospital, and are incapable of acting in their own best interests.

I was taught to counter-manipulate and out-maneuver borderlines. The goal was to block their admission to the hospital, or, if that was impossible, to discharge them as quickly as possible. At the same time, borderlines were provocative, fascinating, and the subject of much interest and discussion. We gave each other knowing looks and pronounced the word "borderline" in a special way that provided tacit approval for our collective hostile countertransference, which was simultaneously an erotic fear and fascination.

There was zero discussion of sexual misconduct by psychiatrists during my four years of residency training. I learned later that the most common dyad for sexual misconduct by a psychiatrist is a young, attractive female borderline patient and a middle-aged male psychiatrist. The sexual misconduct is the extreme acting out of the collectively sanctioned hostile countertransference.

I view borderline personality disorder as a trauma disorder. It could be called reactive attachment disorder of adulthood. The trauma which gives rise to borderline personality is a complex and variable mix of "parental rejection and neglect, difficult infant temperament, inconsistent child-rearing practices with harsh discipline, physical or sexual abuse, lack of supervision, early institutional living, frequent changes of caregivers, large family size, association with a delinquent group, and certain kinds of familial psychopathology" (DSM-IV-TR, page 88).

This description of a typical borderline childhood on page 88 of DSM-IV-TR is in fact part of the text for conduct disorder. On page 116, the same childhood is described again in the text for reactive attachment disorder of infancy or early childhood: "By definition, the condition is associated with grossly pathological care that may take the form of persistent disregard of the child's basic emotional needs for comfort, stimulation, and affection; persistent disregard of the child's basic physical needs; or repeated changes of primary caretaker that prevent formation of stable attachments (e.g., frequent changes in foster care). The pathological care is presumed to be responsible for the disturbed social relatedness."

On page 652 of DSM-IV-TR the typical borderline childhood is described: "Physical and sexual abuse, neglect, hostile conflict and early parental loss and separation are more common in the childhood histories of those with Borderline Personality Disorder."

I view borderline personality disorder as a normal human response to chronic childhood trauma. The trauma giving rise to borderline personality is multidimensional, and causes profound harm to the individual's attachment systems.

Phenomenology

Borderline personality disorder never occurs without comorbidity. In inpatient settings, the comorbidity is always extensive. Occasionally, a person will look borderline or narcissistic only while hypomanic or manic, and will have no personality disorder when his bipolar mood disorder is in remission. Most of the time, however, the numerous chronic Axis I and II symptoms are so intermingled that they are impossible to disentangle.

I have never met a borderline who had a childhood that was anywhere near normal or happy. I have given dozens of workshops in which I have asked whether anyone has ever seen a borderline with a normal childhood, and not one out of thousands of professionals have ever raised a hand. The "tough" childhood is part of the phenomenology of the disorder.

Self-destructive, addictive, inconsistent and self-defeating behaviors are the hallmark of borderline personality disorder.

Natural History

According to DSM-IV-TR, borderline personality disorder may burn out with increasing age. It is hard to be borderline at 55 years of age because it takes a lot of energy. Also, the older one gets, the more distant the traumatic childhood. This natural history could be an artifact, however. The most severe borderlines may all be dead, homeless or brain damaged by age 55, due to drugs, alcohol, suicide, murder, smoking, bad diet, inadequate exercise, obesity, and other long-term consequences of unhealthy lifestyles.

Epidemiology

Borderline personality disorder affects 2% of the general population according to DSM-IV-TR (page 652). It is a marker of the degree of chronic childhood trauma in a population. Borderline personality is at the core of the trauma model, and all the general predictions of the trauma model apply to it.

Twin And Adoption Studies

Borderline personality should confirm the predictions of the trauma model concerning twin and adoption studies. The prevalence of borderline personality disorder will fall from 10% or higher in severe trauma pedigrees to zero when a child is adopted into a healthy family at birth. The reverse effect will occur when the adoption goes in the opposite direction.

Concordance for borderline personality in twins will be driven by trauma. Although temperament may provide a risk factor for the disorder, the prevalence will be over 80% once the trauma dose is set high enough. Empirical studies of temperament as a risk factor for borderline personality are almost impossible to conduct because the trauma is so pervasive and starts so early, and because a child followed closely from birth in a prospective study would have to be apprehended by Child Protective Services. Nevertheless, the idea of a temperament carrying greater vulnerability or risk makes intuitive sense.

Biology

The biology of borderline personality disorder is the biology of trauma.

Treatment Outcome

Trauma therapy will have a profound positive impact on the natural history of borderline personality disorder. However, a subgroup will be unmotivated and untreatable. These trauma therapy treatment failures await the development of an alternative model and treatment method.

Revisions To DSM-IV-TR

Borderline personality disorder should be grouped with the other Axis I trauma disorders. Just as conduct disorder evolves into antisocial personality by DSM-IV-TR rules, so should reactive attachment disorder evolve into borderline personality disorder. Conduct disorder and oppositional defiant disorder are childhood variants of borderline personality, and vice versa. In the adult sections of DSM-IV-TR, the impulse control disorders should be grouped with borderline personality disorder as well, since they too are variants of conduct disorder, oppositional defiant disorder and reactive attachment disorder. All these disorders are variants of each other – if I had to assign primary status to one, I would choose reactive attachment disorder.

Borderline personality disorder is not a discrete entity which one either has or does not have. It is a trauma behavioral checklist. One can be either more or less borderline, compared to other people, and compared to oneself at different points in time. Since there are nine criteria for borderline personality in DSM-IV-TR, and since only five are required for the diagnosis, two people can both be borderline but share only one symptom in common. This makes no sense, and proves that DSM-IV-TR borderline personality is not a discrete entity. Two people are unlikely to have the same "disease" if they each have five symptoms but share only one.

The term "borderline personality disorder" is historically derived and has no scientific meaning at a phenomenological level.   The name should be dropped.   This is especially true because of the hostile countertransference evoked by the term borderline.   I favor reactive attachment disorder of adulthood.

22

OTHER AXIS II DISORDERS

Like borderline personality, the other DSM-IV-TR personality disorders can all be understood as elements of the trauma response. If you read the DSM-IV-TR diagnostic criteria for the different Axis II disorders from the perspective of the trauma model, they are a description of the trauma response. For instance, you would expect someone treated in a harsh, mean, inconsistent manner by his parents to be paranoid and suspicious of others and their motives as an adult. DSM-IV-TR (page 629) describes paranoid personality disorder as "a pattern of distrust and suspiciousness such that others' motives are interpreted as malevolent." From a trauma-cognitive perspective, paranoid personality is caused by overgeneralization from childhood experience.

Similarly, DSM-IV-TR (page 629) describes schizotypal personality disorder as "a pattern of acute discomfort in close relationships, cognitive or perceptual distortions, and eccentricities of behavior." The magical thinking of the wounded child, combined with the many, many times over-learned lesson that other people, especially adults, cause extreme discomfort, should lead directly to symptoms of schizotypal personality.

DSM-IV-TR (page 629) describes schizoid personality disorder as "a pattern of detachment from social relationships and a restricted range of emotional expression." This picture is a predictable outcome of neglect and failure of parents to offer and foster secure attachments.

The dominant model in academic psychiatry today states that the Cluster A personality disorders (paranoid, schizoid, and schizotypal) are variants of the genetic disease of schizophrenia. They represent either partial penetration of the gene for schizophrenia, or expression of a fewer number of loci than are required for the full disease of schizophrenia. The details of the postulated genetic machinery do not matter. The basic idea is that the Cluster A personality disorders are schizophrenia spectrum variants of the full disease.

The trauma model offers alternative testable research hypotheses for Cluster A personality disorders, as it does for those in Cluster B (antisocial, borderline, histrionic, and narcissistic) and Cluster C (avoidant, dependent, obsessive-compulsive, and not otherwise specified).

DSM-IV-TR recognizes the relationship between trauma and personality disorders in a limited way. It states (page 632) that, "When personality changes emerge and persist after an individual has been exposed to extreme stress, a diagnosis of Posttraumatic Stress Disorder should be considered."

The phenotype of a personality disorder can emerge and persist as a component of PTSD, according to DSM-IV-TR. The trauma model predicts that careful inspection of childhood histories will yield a traumatic origin for the personality disorder in the majority of cases. In most cases, there is no independent "personality disorder" separate from the trauma response.

The traumatic nature of the personality disorders has been difficult to appreciate for a number of reasons. The first is lack of a testable model which predicts the traumatic origins of Axis II symptoms. The second is the difficulty of determining a "pre-morbid" personality structure in children. There are two sub-reasons that account for this difficulty: 1) there may have been no premorbid period without trauma, and 2) the personality is so plastic and unformed in young children that it does not exist as a developed structure prior to the trauma. Third, the Axis I disorders of which the Axis II disorders are supposed to be spectrum variants, may themselves be trauma-driven. There must be a testable model which predicts the traumatic origins of the Axis I disorders.

Finally, the trauma can be subtle, or it can stretch the boundaries of the term. Harsh criticism, emotional absence, punitive perfectionism, borderline double binds, and other parental pressures are not usually thought of as "trauma," but they can certainly have a traumatic impact on development.

The predictions of the trauma model concerning the Axis II disorders follow the general logic of the model. I separated out borderline personality because it is probably the most highly trauma-related of all the Axis II disorders.

23

CHILDHOOD DISORDERS

I am not a child psychiatrist, however I do have comments on the section of DSM-IV-TR entitled, "Disorders Usually First Diagnosed in Infancy, Childhood, or Adolescence."

From my perspective, the childhood disorders can be grouped into three categories: neurological disorders, mixed neurological-trauma disorders, and trauma disorders. It is clear that many childhood DSM-IV-TR disorders are biomedical brain diseases. They are not psychiatric disorders. According to my definition, biomedical brain diseases have physical causes and minimal or no psychological etiology. Any biomedical disorder can be worsened or improved by countless psychological and sociological factors including insurance coverage, non-compliance, competing priorities, addictions, and health care policy. But the fundamental etiology is biomedical.

Psychiatric disorders may have significant endogenous biological components to their etiology, but their biology is profoundly interactive with the environment at genetic and biochemical levels. Psychiatric "disease" arises from a complex interactive dance between the genome and the environment. The causality is bi-directional: genome out, and environment in. There are myriad feedback loops in both directions. However, few if any psychiatric disorders require any specific endogenous biological abnormality for their full expression. The biological abnormalities that do contribute are diagnostically non-specific from a DSM-IV-TR perspective, and they do not breed true according to DSM-IV-TR categories.

In truly genetic biomedical disorders like cystic fibrosis, the fundamental etiology is relentlessly unidirectional: genome out. In non-genetic biomedical diseases, there may be an environmental promoter like a carcinogen, or an environmental cause like a virus or bacterium. In non-genetic biomedical diseases, there is always a component of host susceptibility, and a range of resistance across individuals, but by and large the environmental agent acts on biology that is within the normal range, and psychology does not come into play.

It is the interactive dance between genome and environment which makes psychiatry a distinct specialty from neurology. The interaction with the environment is much more fundamental and essential to the basic disease process in psychiatry than it is in neurology. The genome, somatic tissue, sociology and psychology all participate in the dance, and none can be reduced to the other. The dance makes psychiatry complicated but not "soft." Trauma model psychiatry is a clinical science and a legitimate branch of medicine. Its disorders work by higher order, more complex biological rules than those in neurology.

The DSM-IV-TR childhood disorders I would assign to the neurological group, the trauma group and mixed neurological-trauma or intermediate group are listed in Figure 23.1.

Table 23.2. Mixed Neurological-Trauma Disorders in DSM-IV

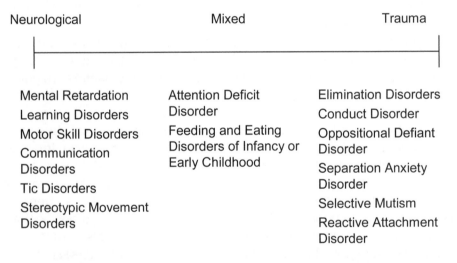

Neurological	Mixed	Trauma
Mental Retardation	Attention Deficit Disorder	Elimination Disorders
Learning Disorders	Feeding and Eating Disorders of Infancy or Early Childhood	Conduct Disorder
Motor Skill Disorders		Oppositional Defiant Disorder
Communication Disorders		Separation Anxiety Disorder
Tic Disorders		Selective Mutism
Stereotypic Movement Disorders		Reactive Attachment Disorder

The trauma model does not apply to the neurological disorders because their etiology is physical not psychological. The cerebral cortex and limbic system do not participate in the fundamental disease process in neurological disorders, not in the way they do in psychiatric disorders. In pure neurological disorders, the cortex and limbic system are passive. They may be damaged by the direct physical impact of the etiological agents, and this may give rise to cortical or limbic symptoms, but the cortex and limbic system are not active participants in creation of the disease. This distinction may become meaningless in gray-zone cases, but it is clear if we compare a height phobia to a brain tumor.

In psychiatric disorders, the etiology involves dysregulation of the basic functions of the cortex and limbic systems. The dysregulation is driven by the environment but can become autonomous. A good example is the damage to hippocampal neurons caused by high levels of cortisol, which in turn are caused by trauma. There is initially nothing abnormal about the hypothalamic-pituitary-adrenal axis or the hippocampus. The damage is caused by system overload.

In an analogy drawn from physics, one might say that trauma activates the system to a higher energy level. At the higher level, phenomena emerge which do not take place and cannot be observed at lower energy levels. Trauma puts the mind and brain in a linear accelerator. The atoms in the accelerator were physically normal prior to being accelerated.

The only trauma disorder I might reassign to the mixed group of childhood disorders is separation anxiety disorder. Some cases may have an endogenous dysregulation which promotes the separation anxiety.

Conceptually, one of the most interesting disorders in the childhood section of DSM-IV-TR is attention deficit disorder (ADD). This is because it presents a scientific puzzle. The differentiation of dissociation, attention deficit, depression, and specific learning disabilities, is sometimes easy but often impossible. We have no measures for making these differentiations in a reliable fashion. There are probably numerous pathways to the phenotype of ADD, including birth injury, intrauterine infection, maternal drug use during pregnancy, psychological trauma, and complications of vaccinations.

Disentangling the role of psychological trauma in ADD is a complex but important task. ADD medication failures may include an over-representation of trauma pathway cases.

As mentioned in the chapter on borderline personality disorder, conduct disorder, reactive attachment disorder and oppositional defiant disorder are variants of each other. They should be condensed into a single diagnosis with subtype specifiers. They evolve into Cluster B personality disorders.

Tourette's Syndrome is one of the childhood neurological disorders. However, it gives rise to a specific trauma prediction. From my perspective, the obsessive-compulsive symptoms common in Tourette's Syndrome are tics occurring in the cognitive areas of the brain. There is no reason that the pathophysiology of tics should be limited to the motor cortex.

Looking from the vantage point of obsessive compulsive disorder (OCD), some cases of OCD have concurrent Tourette's or tic disorder. These should tend to be the non-trauma cases. They should have low dissociation scores. Trauma pathway cases of OCD, in contrast, should have more extensive psychiatric comorbidity and fewer tics. Tourette's Syndrome should co-occur with trauma pathway OCD at the base rate for Tourette's in the general population.

All the general predictions of the trauma model apply to the trauma disorders in the childhood section of DSM-IV-TR.

24

AXIS III DISORDERS

Medical disorders are listed on Axis III in DSM-IV-TR. The endogenous biomedical disorders, such as cystic fibrosis, are not directly affected by trauma in their basic disease process. However, the outcome of cystic fibrosis will be worse in third world countries for financial reasons. It will be worse in trauma families with physical abuse, neglect and parental inconsistency. Chest physiotherapy, antibiotics and enzyme replacement will be haphazard in trauma families.

Other biomedical disorders could be classified as mixed endogenous-environmental. A good example is coronary artery disease. The risk factors for heart attack are: family history, high blood pressure, high cholesterol, smoking, obesity, and lack of exercise. Victims of chronic childhood trauma will have higher rates of all of these risk factors due to self-neglect and unhealthy lifestyles. Elimination of childhood trauma would have a dramatic impact on the prevalence of coronary artery disease.

Obesity is of particular interest because it is so common in North America and has so many negative health consequences. In my Trauma Programs, I see many women who are one hundred pounds overweight. At any given time, there is often more than one person who is over two hundred pounds overweight. I have worked personally with several women who have lost eighty pounds during trauma therapy.

In trauma disorders, obesity has several different functions. These were described in the chapter on eating disorders. Obesity illustrates one of the pathways by which psychological trauma can interact with the biology of the body. The different pathways are listed in Table 24.1.

Psychological trauma is an endemic public health problem throughout the world. In some areas, it is epidemic, as it has been in Bosnia in the 1990's. Psychological trauma probably takes as big a toll on the health of the human race worldwide as do the infectious diseases. It is possible that psychological trauma is the number one public health problem on the planet. This is so in part because endemic infectious diseases cause psychological trauma.

Table 24.1. Pathways to Interaction Between Psychological Trauma and
Biomedical Illness

Pathway	Examples
Psychological Defense	Obesity
High Risk Behavior	Stress Fracture From Exercise
	AIDS
	Sexually Transmitted Disease
	Hepatitis from Dirty Needles
Unhealthy Lifestyle	Coronary Artery Disease
Behavior Directly Affecting the Body	Electrolyte Imbalance in Eating Disorders
Biology of Trauma	Hippocampal Damage
Somatic Symptoms/ Factitious Disorder	Iatrogenic Complications of Unnecessary Procedures and Treatment
Substance Abuse	Cirrhosis, Pancreatitis

Public health measures are often more important in the war against
endemic disease than interventions at the level of the individual patient.
Examples of this principle include clean water supplies, adequate
sewage disposal, and air pollution controls. Other interventions at the
population level are mediated through the individual person, but are
mass programs. Examples include vaccinations, silver nitrate eye drops
for newborns, and Pap smears.

For PTSD and the other trauma disorders, prevention can result from the
activities of intelligence agencies, anti-terrorist groups and diplomats. If
the CIA, the FBI and the State Department prevent a major terrorist
bombing, or a war, they prevent many trauma disorders. Mass programs
mediated through the individual person include rape crisis centers and
battered spouse shelters. The effects of psychological trauma are a
major component of family practice, internal medicine and pediatrics,
though they receive insufficient attention.

IV. TRAUMA THERAPY

25

GENERAL PRINCIPLES OF THERAPY

The two core elements of trauma therapy are the problem of attachment to the perpetrator and the locus of control shift. Each of these has its own chapter. There are also general principles which govern the treatment – the general principles may be stated explicitly at some point in therapy, but much of the time they are implicit in the work. Many are not intrinsic to trauma therapy and are components of generic psychotherapy.

Trauma therapy is cognitive-behavioral in most of its techniques and strategies, but it is psychodynamically informed and uses many systems principles. Expressive techniques are used, but they result in changes in cognition, and could therefore be thought of as a subset of cognitive-behavioral therapy. Throughout the chapters on therapy I will assume a general familiarity with the principles and techniques of cognitive therapy (Beck and Emery, 1985; Beck, Rush, Shaw and Emery, 1979; Linehan, 1993; Follette, Ruzek, and Abueg, 1998). Sometimes I will not describe the cognitive strategies for different dynamics, conflicts and errors in thinking in detail because they should be self-evident to anyone familiar with cognitive therapy.

As in the rest of the book, in the treatment section of *The Trauma Model*, my references will be illustrative only. I make no effort to provide complete references. Entry into the relevant literature can be made through the web sites of the International Society for the Study of Dissociation (www.issd.org) and the International Society for Traumatic Stress Studies (www.istss.org) and my own web site (www.rossinst.com). Surveys of the relevant literature have been completed by Courtois (1999), Brown, Scheflin and Hammond (1998), Follete, Ruzek, and Abueg (1998), Michelson and Ray (1996), and van der Kolk, McFarlane, and Weisaeth (1996).

The Intrinsic Worth Of Human Beings

Several basic assumptions of trauma therapy are *ascientific*. They cannot be tested scientifically and cannot be proven or disproven. They are absolute.

These assumptions are, first, that human beings have value, simply because they are human beings. Second, people are intrinsically worthy of respect and deserve to be treated decently. Third, human life has meaning.

In therapy, these assumptions are stated explicitly when there is a reason to do so. Otherwise, they are the implicit foundation of the work throughout. I might tell someone that there is a reason I am investing so much time and energy in her treatment, which can amount to hundreds of hours if I am the primary therapist. She is worth it. She may disagree with me on this point intellectually, and in her feelings and self-esteem, but on the other hand, she agrees with me enough to come for appointments.

The power of trauma therapy is derived from the techniques, strategies and principles described in *The Trauma Model*, but that is not the whole story. Much of the power of the therapy comes from the implicit affirmation of value and worth delivered by the therapist through body language, tone of voice and facial expression. Trauma therapy for complex comorbid cases requires hundreds of hours of professional time.

The therapist is a busy, skilled professional who could be seeing other clients or doing other things. But no, he or she is spending hundreds of hours with the client over a period of years. Why? Because the client is interesting, worthy, valuable and capable of healing and growth. The message delivered implicitly by the therapist's focus on the client corrects a lifetime's worth of negative cognitions about the self, the world and the future. This is why technically marginal therapists can have good outcomes.

Clients with dissociative identity disorder (DID) often make two cognitive errors about their intrinsic worth. The first is that they have no worth. As a reaction formation defense against this primary cognitive error they then make a secondary grandiose cognitive error. They believe that they are special and interesting because they have DID. The secondary cognitive error breeds entitlement. It can be corrected by simple education. Alternatively, it can be reinforced by the therapist who is more interested in the DID than the person.

People in renal dialysis are not special because their kidneys are failing. They require special technical care, but they are special simply because they are human beings. The same is true of DID. The grandiose cognitive error can cause a psychiatric disorder not included in DSM-IV-TR: dissociative identity disorder identity disorder (DIDID). The person with DIDID is similar to someone with a factitious disorder – without her diagnosis she is nothing. (The treatment involves correcting the misperception that a diagnosis makes you special. In fact, it simply makes you ill.) One must also correct the underlying cognitive error of worthlessness, which is the locus of control shift.

A permutation of the cognitive error about DIDID is the belief that the abuse caused the person's creativity, and that without the abuse the person would have been boring and ordinary. First of all, ordinary does not equal boring. (A more accurate way to look at the situation, I believe, is to conclude that the creativity was intrinsic to the person, and would have been there even if the person had been adopted at birth into a healthy family. The intrinsic creativity of the person was harnessed to create defenses against the trauma, but was not caused by the trauma.)

GWEN

The belief that one's creativity was caused by childhood abuse creates a double bind. The creativity becomes disgusting because it was created by the parents' perversity, but at the same time it is the survivor's best attribute. Letting go of the symptoms and the patient role would mean losing one's best attribute. The survivor therefore holds onto her pathology in order to be special and creative. Doing so, however, keeps her trapped in the role of disgusting product of abuse. The solution to the double bind is to endlessly create and then trash one's creations, whether they be poems, paintings, children or relationships.

The trauma model assumes that self-worth, safety and meaning are basic human needs. Trauma survivors may kill themselves in the midst of material plenty in order to find safety in death. One problem with that strategy, from a Christian perspective, is the risk that death will not be a safe or pleasant state. If the client has traditional Christian beliefs about the afterlife, they can provide therapeutic leverage against suicide. Although suicide is a comprehensible plan of action, it is never acceptable within the trauma model. I am absolutely opposed to euthanasia for survivors of psychological trauma.

Adult Responsibility

People with arthritis of the hip are not given a license to kill. They are held to the same moral and legal standards as everyone else. The same should be true for trauma disorders, including DID. Trauma patients usually experience their symptoms as involuntary, and often plead for special status because of their symptoms. This is particularly true for episodes of age regression, flashbacks, triggering and trauma re-enactments.

There are several proofs that the symptoms are in fact voluntary. The first is that people can recover – from alcoholism, bulimia, posttraumatic stress disorder, panic disorder and many other Axis I and II disorders. If the symptoms were truly involuntary, all forms of psychotherapy would be useless. If all forms of therapy are useless, therapy should stop immediately. This logical consequence is unacceptable to the client, so its opening premise must be abandoned.

Second, the symptoms are not randomly distributed in time and space. Vietnam veterans are more likely to have combat flashbacks when a civilian helicopter flies overhead than when they are brushing their teeth. A woman abused as a child in a green bedroom will be triggered by the color green more than by blue. The symptoms have a social context, and usually communicate meaning or have specific functions.

Third, behavioral interventions have a profound impact on the frequency of symptoms, in both directions. This is particularly evident in an inpatient setting. Unit rules which are permissive or which reinforce and reward acting out rapidly increase the amount of acting out. For instance, extravagant displays of care and concern by nurses in response to superficial self-mutilation, accompanied by application of copious amounts of gauze dressing in public, quickly result in two thirds of the patients having gauze dressings.

In the opposite direction, a policy of transfer off the Unit for acting out dramatically reduces the amount of behavioral disturbance. This would not occur if the symptoms were involuntary. It is more accurate to say that there is a defensive illusion of involuntariness. Reinforcing the illusion reinforces the patient role.

A therapist can take the principle of adult responsibility to an absurd extreme. Just because patients are responsible adults does not mean they can instantly become symptom free by willpower alone. Failure to become completely symptom-free on demand is not evidence of lack of motivation or perversity. It is part of the natural history of trauma disorders. Some people are too damaged to make a full recovery.

I often compare psychological trauma to falling out of an airplane without a parachute. Hitting the ground causes serious problems. You don't just get up and walk away. Similarly, when you arrive at the Emergency Department from a major car wreck, you don't just hop up and leave after five minutes of treatment. Sometimes you die. Sometimes you are paralyzed for life. Sometimes you make a full recovery. Full recovery requires a lot of work, a lot of expert help, and a lot of time. Trauma therapy is physiotherapy for the psyche. There may be some passive range-of-motion exercises conducted by the physiotherapist, but mostly it takes a lot of hard work by the patient.

In my Trauma Programs, I hold patients to the same behavioral standards as any other inpatients. In fact, the behavioral standards are tougher in the Trauma Program than on the general adult unit. The expectations for hard work are much, much higher in the Trauma Program. In the current managed care climate, little if any real treatment is delivered in general adult psychiatry. There is no individual therapy, and only a small amount of simplistic group therapy. Length of stay is too short for any therapeutic effect from changes of medications. Most of the staff's energy is devoted to paperwork, the mechanical aspects of discharge planning, and insurance verification and certification.

Symptoms are not involuntary for a fourth reason. Inpatients rise to staff expectations. This is true independently of any specific Trauma Program rules or behavioral interventions. When expectations for focused, hard work are set high, there is more work and less acting out.

When someone insists on the involuntary nature of his or her symptoms, I use a version of *reductio ad absurdum*. I ask whether the person suffers from a seizure disorder. Does a seizure occur in which the person involuntarily walks to the fridge, opens the door, gets out a beer, opens it, and then with absolutely no control, takes a sip? Is it really true that the drinking is caused by brain seizure activity? In cognitive therapy group, everyone is amused by the question, and the individual person denies having a seizure disorder which causes his or her acting out.

If it is not a seizure disorder, then it is a choice. The trauma survivor is responsible for his or her choices, just like everyone else. The counter-argument may be that the person did not choose to be abused as a child, and therefore did not choose to have the symptoms. The counter-counter-argument by the therapist is, "You are not responsible for becoming a victim. But you are responsible for remaining one."

Adult responsibility is a non-negotiable principle of trauma therapy.

Informed Consent

Informed consent is essential in all psychiatric treatments. There is no requirement that written informed consent be obtained in private practice, but it is required for hospital treatment. I always obtain written informed consent for participation in research projects, and always have the consent form reviewed by a committee prior to starting the project. I would also obtain written informed consent for any specific procedure such as formal induction of hypnosis or a sodium amytal interview, neither of which I have done in the last eight years.

The professional atmosphere is very adversarial and litigious in the United States. Although it is not necessary, it is always best to err on the side of caution in obtaining consent. Real consent is an ongoing process. With or without an initial written consent form, clinical records should reflect an ongoing discussion of the goals of therapy and progress to date. This does not need to be legalistic.

In an inpatient medical record, a brief daily note might read, "Patient has reached initial treatment goal of remission of active suicidal ideation. Is now working on consolidating reversal of the self-blame (the locus of control shift) which drives the suicidal ideation through continued cognitive and expressive group therapy. Should be ready for transition to the partial hospitalization program in three days. Patient in agreement with this discharge date."

This note does not read like an informed consent document but it contains the clinical reality of the situation. The patient is participating actively in the core work of the Trauma Program, has met her primary inpatient treatment goal, and is in agreement with the discharge date. Informed consent is implicit in these facts.

An element of informed consent is ongoing cost-benefit analysis. The analysis is applied to the defenses, the treatment, and the current life situation. For instance, a selective serotonin reuptake inhibitor (SSRI) antidepressant may be part of the treatment. In one case, the antidepressant was working effectively to reduce depression, panic, and obsessive-compulsive symptoms. However, it had also suppressed the woman's libido.

At this stage of therapy, the anti-panic effect was probably coming from the suppression of the libido. There was still a lot of unresolved conflict about sexuality. Suppressing the sex drive relieved the anxiety and conflict, which was a benefit. The cost was that the parts of herself responsible for sexual arousal and function were suppressed and not available for therapy, or for sexual relations in the present. The parts had acted out destructively twenty years earlier but had been suppressed since then.

This cost of the antidepressant was balanced by the benefit of reduced symptoms. Also, the woman was better able to do other therapeutic work which needed to be completed before the arena of sex was worked on directly. The work was staged or sequenced. Throughout this period there was an ongoing discussion of the cost-benefit of the antidepressant, and ongoing confirmation that she would continue to take it. Written informed consent was not required because it was outpatient therapy, and because a single document would not have dealt adequately with the ongoing, process nature of the consent.

The Patient Not The Diagnosis

This simple rule is too often forgotten in treatment. Everyone pays lip service to it, but not everyone follows it. The treatment is always for the person as a whole, no matter how dissociated he or she might be, and is not for the diagnosis. Within the trauma model, the diagnosis is usually a coping strategy, and is not the problem in and of itself. The goal of treatment is to build healthier, more flexible and more adaptive coping strategies, not simply to erase diagnoses. When diagnoses go into remission that is a good thing because it is a marker of positive growth, but it is not the basic goal of therapy.

The symptoms and diagnoses are important because they provide measurable indicators of treatment outcome, and because they cause suffering. But treatment is about building the positive, not simply removing the negative. *Strengthening the heart*

Trauma diagnoses are not like warts. When someone goes to the doctor to have a wart removed, he or she sits passively while the doctor, or physician's assistant, performs the procedure. The patient is the patient and the wart is removed. Trauma therapy doesn't work like that. The defenses are part of the person. The therapist works *with* the defenses. They are part of the person just like the hopes, dreams, sense of humor and personal history.

This principle is best illustrated by auditory hallucinations. In conventional psychiatry, the voices are mental warts. The antipsychotic medication removes them, or at least is supposed to do so. In trauma therapy, the voices are as much the patient as the patient. The therapist talks to the voices, forms a treatment alliance with them, negotiates with them, and may joke around with them about the foibles and cognitive errors of the executive self, while the executive self is listening.

The desire of the executive self to get rid of the voices is a form of resistance. The voices hold thoughts, feelings, conflicts and elements of the personal narrative which the executive self has denied or disavowed. The problem is not the voices, it is the executive self's resistance. Treating the person as a whole is important not for ideological reasons, or because it is "holistic." *Treat the patient not the diagnosis*, is a tactical principle. I advocate it for empirical reasons more than theoretical ones. It is an element of the treatment package designed to foster arrival at the treatment goals.

If treating the diagnosis not the person worked better, I would reverse my stance, because that strategy would be better for the person as a whole. An example of this approach is the treatment of diabetic coma in an Emergency Department; treating the "whole person" in order to reverse the coma would be absurd, and against the person's best interests.

The Diagnosis Does Not Determine The Treatment Plan

In medical school I was taught to do diagnosis and differential diagnosis. The differential diagnosis was the list of possible diagnoses, which I had to narrow it down to the single correct diagnosis. If a person had more than one diagnosis, usually one was primary. For instance, there could be a pneumonia secondary to chronic obstructive lung disease.

When I went into my psychiatry residency, I was told that I was still a doctor. My job was still diagnosis and differential diagnosis. The diagnosis determined the treatment plan. Not so within trauma psychiatry.

In non-trauma cases, it is obvious that diagnosis plays a role. The person with non-trauma schizophrenia requires different treatment from the person with non-trauma generalized anxiety disorder, who in turn would not benefit from the treatment plan for bulimia. In clean, single-diagnosis, non-trauma cases, the single disease model works fairly well. There are far too many sub-diagnoses in DSM-IV-TR to have truly differentiated treatment plans for all of them, which is one reason why most of the DSM-IV-TR diagnoses are rarely used by general psychiatrists. But, roughly speaking, in single disease cases, the DSM-IV-TR diagnosis can determine the treatment plan.

The problem is that most severely disturbed people do not fit the single disease model. They do not have psychiatric warts. They have extensive comorbidity and require a combination of medication and trauma therapy. Most often, the medication is an SSRI antidepressant, which is effective for the eating disorder, depression, PTSD, obsessive-compulsive disorder, panic disorder, elements of the personality disorder, impulse control, and myriad other symptoms.

Within the trauma model, the treatment plan is determined by the conflicts, which are disavowed, acted out or otherwise avoided by the defenses and diagnoses. The idea is to go around the defenses to the real work of therapy, not to spend inordinate amounts of time and effort on the defenses themselves. The defenses tend to melt away when they are no longer needed.

Stages of Therapy

Like life in general, all therapies can be divided into stages. For instance, there are the stages of death and dying: denial, anger, bargaining, acceptance, and hope. In the real work of dying, one goes back and forth from stage to stage, does more than one at a time, avoids one stage by hiding in another, and hopefully in the end comes to some resolution. The stages of death and dying are never neatly checked off in a tidy sequence. But the list of stages provides a helpful guide, a map of the territory.

The same is true for the stages of trauma therapy. There are many permutations and combinations of stages on the long path to recovery. In one scheme, with which I agree, trauma therapy is divided into three stages: stabilization, safety and education; the active work phase; and resolution or completion. The names of the stages may vary by author, but there is overall consensus among trauma therapists (Courtois, 1999).

There is no use trying to do trauma therapy if the client is broke, depressed, homeless and being stalked by her ex-boyfriend. Basic safety has to be established and there has to be initial stabilization. Millions of impoverished and starving people in Asia and Africa have experienced massive psychological trauma, but their basic needs for food, shelter, health, education and safety must be met before aid in the form of psychotherapy is even considered.

One of the classical cognitive errors is dichotomization, also called all-or-nothing thinking or black-and-white thinking. Using my best powers of dichotomization, I divide trauma therapy into two stages: the PTSD stage and the grief stage. These could be regarded as two sub-stages within the working phase of therapy.

In the PTSD stage of therapy, there are many active symptoms and the feeling tone tends to be one of fear, horror, anxiety, and panic. There is a lot of acting out and addictive behavior, and there can be a lot of anger. There is a lot of instability and turmoil. The second stage of therapy is very different. Everything is quieter. There is less agitation, switching of states, acting out and entrenchment in the victim role. The tone is one of sadness and grief.

Memory content in the PTSD stage is focused on the traumatic events. These are the bad things that happened that should not have happened. Everything fits with the conceptual system of DSM-IV-TR PTSD, which is focused on the traumatic event and its consequences.

In the second, grief stage of therapy, memory content is focused on the good things that should have happened, but didn't. The task is to mourn the loss of the parents one never had. The parents one never had were consistent, loving, affectionate parents who were reasonably healthy, who provided basic security and stability, and who set limits and kicked your butt when you needed it.

False memories may occur in the PTSD stage, but rarely in the grief stage. During the grief work, the language is simpler, the extravagant defenses and behavior melt away, the bad deeds of the perpetrator, real or imagined, are not the focus, and it is the whole gestalt of childhood which must be mourned, not some particular bad hours, days, or weeks.

"Mom and dad just weren't there for me," is a summary of the grief stage.

The grief stage is left till later because it is deeper, more painful, and more defended against. Not uncommonly, a client will hide in the PTSD stage of therapy to avoid the more difficult grief work. It is easy not to be sad when you are acting out, terrorized by flashbacks, stoned, or a wretched victim of other people's malevolence. All of these are avoidance strategies.

There is a later, less pressured stage of recovery in which the work is consolidation, integration and resolution. Integration is the fundamental process throughout therapy, but it comes to fruition in this final stage. There are now very few psychiatric symptoms, and it is highly unlikely the person will need inpatient treatment. The person is functioning reasonably well in personal relationships and is beginning to realize his or her potential in the workplace or career. The benefits of the therapy are obvious to loved ones and family members, unlike in the earlier stages, where there may have been internal progress, but the payoff was not yet visible externally.

Educating spouse, loved ones and family members about the stages of therapy can be helpful to them. In the first third of therapy, they may hear from the therapist and client about all the hard work being done and all the progress being made, but they may not see much change outside therapy. This is par for the course in the first third of therapy. The trick is not to let the first third drag on for too long.

Addiction Is The Opposite Of Desensitization

I realized early in the year 2000 that addiction is the opposite of desensitization. What is addiction? The problem in addictions is the place you are at, which I call *here*. Here is intolerable due to feelings and conflicts. The intolerable feeling could be fear, anger, anxiety, emptiness, boredom, or sadness. The purpose of the addiction is to take you from *here* to *over there*. Over there is stoned, passed out, thrilled, or otherwise distracted.

The particular addiction is simply the vehicle for getting from here to over there. It doesn't matter fundamentally whether you drive in a European, American or Japanese car. It's all about getting away from here. The particular mode of transportation could be chosen for any one of countless reasons including price, availability and personal preference.

There are countless drugs of addiction. These include heroin, alcohol, cocaine, anger, self-mutilation, binge eating, shoplifting, the victim role, the PTSD phase of therapy, sadomasochistic sex, internet sex, and depression.

Desensitization is the opposite of addiction. The two have a reciprocal relationship with each other: the more you do of one, the less you do of the other. Desensitization involves turning around to face the thing you are avoiding, which always boils down to grief. Trauma therapy is always desensitization of a grief phobia. The unresolved grief is the phobic stimulus which is being avoided.

Desensitization involves setting up a hierarchy and learning to tolerate the phobic stimulus one step at a time. While working through the desensitization hierarchy, one builds healthier, more adaptive coping skills, since life is sure to offer more pain and conflict in the future. When the person has been desensitized, there is no need for the avoidance strategies. Trauma therapy is analogous to desensitization for a simple phobia in that you don't really remove the avoidance tactics as such, rather you remove the need for them, and they resolve spontaneously as a result of this work.

It's All Avoidance

The maxim, *desensitization is the opposite of addiction*, leads directly to a second principle of trauma therapy: *it's all avoidance*. It doesn't matter what the addiction, defense, or acting out strategy is, it always serves the purpose of avoidance, either of feelings or conflict. This is handy because it keeps things simple.

The locus of control shift is a universal strategy of avoidance among trauma survivors, and attention to it is a core component of trauma therapy. The trauma model is easy to remember because, in the end, the same thing is always being avoided. The fundamental work of therapy is mourning the loss of the parents you never actually had. The auditory hallucinations, negative self-talk, drug addictions, borderline behavior, panic attacks, and compulsive rituals all serve the same purpose. Therefore a different plan of treatment is not required for each one, and the diagnosis does not determine the treatment plan.

Just Do It

I include this section in the hope that Nike will eventually make me a corporate sponsor. Therapy always boils down to a Nike commercial. You have to say 'No' to drugs. This is true whether your drug is a drug, a behavior, a symptom, a social role, as it is in factitious disorders, or an otherwise normal activity. One can be addicted to food, sleep, exercise, sex, or entertainment, all of which are good and normal in and of themselves.

This is the basic twelve step principle of trauma therapy. You have to be serious about recovery. Sobriety is a choice and a decision. The commitment to sobriety cannot be made by the therapist, warden, governor, parent, spouse or child of the survivor. You have to do it yourself. Until the fundamental commitment has been made, no real work will be done. You have to walk the walk, not just talk the talk.

Just do it is a good principle for several reasons. First, it takes all the heat off the therapist. Within a rigid, hard core twelve step approach, all treatment failures can be accounted for: the addict has not worked his steps. Treatment failures are never the fault of the twelve step model or the counselor. The counselor never stops to consider that there might need to be fourteen steps. The twelve step approach is a great stress reducer for the counselor.

At the same time, it is absolutely true that only the addict can make the fundamental choice for recovery. Just do it is not a cop out for the therapist. Defining the addiction as a choice bumps the client out of the helpless victim/patient role into the role of adult problem-solver who is using effective strategies to regulate mood and soothe the self. The only problem, from the therapist's perspective, is the overall negative cost-benefit of the particular strategies being used. There is short-term gain but long-term pain.

The road from helpless victim who needs 24-hour protection from herself to recovery is a long one. It is a lot easier to get there from the starting point of smart, dedicated, hard-working, adult problem-solver who is using sub-optimal strategies. Since the second road is so much shorter, its causes much less despair and hopelessness. The trip on the second road is do-able. The trip on the first road is infinite. This is one of the tactics that contributes to the amazing reductions in scores on the Beck Depression, Hopelessness and Suicide Scales we see over an average inpatient length of stay of twelve days.

I always compare the person's addiction of choice to alcohol because alcohol is very concrete, and our culture is saturated with the assumptions of the twelve step approach to alcoholism (Everyone agrees that treatment will not work if the addict is not committed to sobriety. Also, alcohol is absolute and black and white. You either drink or you don't. You are clean or still using. For the serious alcoholic, there is no recreational gray zone in the middle)

We know it is a fact that many alcoholics have drunk heavily for years, then gotten sober and stayed sober for decades. This can in fact be done. How does the alcoholic reach sobriety?

When I explain the Nike approach to therapy, patients usually protest that it isn't so easy. They can't just decide to get better. I agree with them. I compare their situations to the alcoholic's. The alcoholic drank for years. He didn't just wake up one morning and decide to get sober. There is a long, difficult journey from heavy addiction to the commitment to sobriety. But one day the alcoholic got there. This was a major landmark in his recovery process.

What happened after the alcoholic made a serious commitment to sobriety? Then the hard work started. There were relapses for a while. The alcoholic got on and off the wagon a few times. But eventually that day, that minute, that second arrived when the alcoholic drank his last drink. From that moment on, the bottle has not touched his lips for twenty years. We know for a fact that this can be done.

That was the second when the commitment became complete, real and final. It was a choice and a decision. No-one could make it but the alcoholic. Once the decision was made, what happened? Many AA meetings, a lot of help and support, a lot of structure, and a lot of hard work. The same principles and steps are required no matter what the addiction.

In the desensitization of simple phobias, the treatment principles, structure, plan and steps do not vary according to the content of the phobia. The content of the phobia is the content of the therapy, certainly, but healing takes place at the level of process and structure, not content. The same is true for the trauma therapy of addictions.

Since the commitment to sobriety is a choice, I ask the patient when she is planning to make the choice.

The answer is usually something like, "I'm hoping I'll be strong enough to stop cutting soon."

My reply is, "Oh, you're hoping you will be strong enough to be able to choose to stop cutting soon. But you're already making all kinds of choice all the time. You're already strong enough to make choices. So what are you waiting for?"

"I have to do more work on my memories first."

"No you don't. That's an avoidance strategy. Since this is a decision, and you have made lots of difficult decisions in the last few weeks, you could make this decision now."

"But I'm not ready yet," the patient will reply.

"That's because you're choosing not to be ready. Tell me, which decade are you thinking you might decide to choose to stop cutting?"

"This decade."

"What year?"

"This year. In a few months."

"Oh, in a few months. If you could decide in a few months, then you could decide to stop cutting now. What's stopping you?"

"I'm not ready."

"But that's a choice."

"You mean I could just decide to stop cutting now, and that would be it? It's that easy?"

To which the ever-paradoxical Dr. Ross might reply, "No, it's that hard. It's easy to make the decision. The hard part is staying sober and facing what you've been avoiding. But you could decide now if you wanted to."

This is a good tactic because it maximizes the peer pressure in group therapy, and exerts maximum leverage on the survivor's identity as committed-to-recovery. Few patients want to admit in public that they are not serious about recovery and are deliberately choosing to maintain their addictions. It is quite common for patients to make a serious commitment to sobriety during a 45-60 minute piece of work in my cognitive therapy group.

The most serious and frequent addictions among inpatients are self-mutilation and suicidal ideation. Rumination about suicide provides control, a safe place (death), a distraction, reinforcement of the locus of control shift, and a soothing heroin high all rolled into one. You have no time to be sad, lonely or scared if you're busy stock piling pills, rehearsing your funeral, and writing suicide notes. Suicide is the ultimate avoidance strategy. You have to say 'No' to drugs.

The Problem Is Not The Problem

This principle is derived from family therapy. In my textbook example, young Johnny is brought in by his parents because he is stealing CDs from a local store. A biological psychiatrist might order an EEG, might teach the parents about electrical discharges in the temporal lobe, and might consider a trial of carbamazepine. The parents will be relieved to hear it is a brain problem, not a reflection on their parenting.

A psychoanalyst might conclude that long-term individual psychotherapy is required. The psychoanalyst and the biological psychiatrist share a common assumption: the problem is inside Johnny.

Systems theory provides another approach. Here, the assumption is that Johnny is the identified patient. The problem, in this case stealing CDs, is not the problem. The problem is the solution to some other problem. In the simple world of textbook examples, the real problem in the family is that the parents are drifting closer and closer to divorce. The only remaining topic of mutual interest, and the only one on which they share any joint passion, is Johnny's bad behavior.

The function of the symptom is to prevent divorce. Having read all the textbooks, the family therapist might then make a paradoxical intervention. He might define Johnny as a hero who is taking on symptoms and the patient role in order to prevent divorce. The therapist will then prescribe the symptom. Johnny will then rebel against the therapist's prescription, because he doesn't want to be a suck-hole, and the presenting problem is resolved. The stealing stops. The work of therapy then becomes marital therapy. You could never get to a treatment plan of marital therapy from an opening assumption that the problem is inside Johnny.

The same logic applies in trauma therapy no matter what the problem. It could be suicidal ideation, treatment non-compliance, auditory hallucinations, explosive anger, spousal battery, flashbacks, or amphetamine abuse. The problem is not the problem. It is the solution to some other problem. The therapist's job is to figure out what problem is being solved by the symptom, behavior or addiction, then to help the client find a healthier, more adaptive solution to the problem.

The symptom always has a social context and a function. In the language of Nicholas Spanos (1996), with which I agree, symptoms and behaviors are "rule-governed and goal-directed." The principles of social psychology are extremely useful in trauma therapy.

The Principle of Therapeutic Neutrality

I always maintain therapeutic neutrality, even when I am not being neutral. Therapeutic neutrality is more like a Zen discipline than a rigid rule for how to behave. There are moral absolutes in therapy. I am never neutral about whether child abuse is OK, for instance. Child abuse is always wrong, always the responsibility of the adult, and never justified. If the patient is currently abusing a child, mandatory reporting will occur the same day I find out about it.

I am never neutral bout whether rape, suicide, IV heroin use, self-mutilation, attacking hospital staff, deliberately hurting co-patients' feelings, or hoarding razor blades under your mattress are OK. Neutrality has nothing to do with not caring or not taking a position. Neutrality is a very distinct position, and it requires a great deal of self-discipline to maintain it. I am never neutral about the destructive impact of false accusations of incest.

Therapeutic neutrality has several levels to it. One level is neutrality with respect to the historical reality of trauma memories. If there is objective evidence that a given event did or did not take place, I do not remain neutral about it. I am not neutral about whether the Oklahoma City bombing took place. But most of the time, there is no conclusive evidence one way or the other.

Most often, the trauma is child abuse and neglect which happened twenty or thirty years ago. The accused parents may be estranged or dead. Since over half the Trauma Program patients are from outside the immediate geographical area of my three hospitals, family meetings are difficult to set up logistically at the best of times, given an average inpatient length of stay of twelve days.

Even when there are family meetings, the clinician cannot use "clinical judgment" to tell whether an incest accusation is accurate or inaccurate. There is no way to tell the difference between perpetrator denial and true innocence. Nor is there a way to differentiate a confabulated from an accurate accusation. Both parties can be very reasonable and compelling.

The same principle that applies to phobias and addictions applies to trauma memories: the content of the memories does not determine the plan of therapy. I do not need to make a decision about the accuracy of the memories, which may range from zero to nearly 100% accuracy for major details of a given memory, in order to decide what to do in therapy. This is true for a number of reasons.

First, there is no scientific way to determine the accuracy of a memory without outside evidence. This is equally true in both directions: you cannot tell for sure a memory is accurate, and equally you cannot tell it is inaccurate, without outside evidence. There is no time, and there are no resources to investigate events of thirty years ago in any case, beyond the level of ordinary history taking and gathering of collateral information and prior records. Records from previous hospitalizations will not arrive until long after discharge, even if ordered on the first day of admission. In practical reality, the evidence just isn't available the majority of the time.

There is absolutely no way to tell from clinical observation whether a memory is accurate or inaccurate, especially since accuracy within a given set of memories can range continuously from zero to 90% for different details, or range from zero to over 90% from one memory set to another. No memories of any kind are 100% accurate. You can never remember every square inch of the scene being recalled with complete accuracy.

Memories accurate in their major details can be vague, fragmented, without affect and denied by the client. Confabulated memories can be detailed, charged with affect, plausible, compelling and believed absolutely. Subjective confidence in the accuracy of a memory is a very unreliable measure of the objective accuracy of that memory.

One reason to maintain therapeutic neutrality about memories is that there is no scientific way to justify any other position. If a therapist decides to use "clinical judgment" to decide which memories are accurate, errors in both directions are guaranteed. These will reinforce either denial or confabulation. Both confabulation and denial can foster bad decision making outside therapy.

A more important reason to maintain neutrality is the major negative consequence of either "validating" or disconfirming a client's memories. Validation is by far the more common therapeutic error.

As soon as the therapist takes the position that he or she can validate the client's memories, a power imbalance has been created. The therapist is the adult, and the client is the dependent child. The goal of therapy is independence, autonomy and self-validation. This cannot be created from a basis of infantalization and dependency. It may "feel good" to be validated, but it also feels good when the doctor writes the heroin addict a prescription for morphine.

Trauma therapy is not focused on memory content. The bad events are talked about, just like the behaviorist talks about snakes in treating a snake phobia, or talks about blood when desensitizing a blood and needle phobia. If someone has a phobia of spiders, you don't talk to them about heights. But the content of the phobia doesn't determine the treatment plan or the timing, logic or nature of the interventions. In fact, in trauma therapy patients commonly hide in the content of trauma memories in order to avoid their grief.

Let's say a woman in her thirties accuses her father of training her to be a high priestess in a Satanic human sacrifice cult. What is the problem? The problem is in the present, the only place where therapy can have any effect. The problem today is the woman's unresolved ambivalent attachment to her father, which is avoided and acted out in countless destructive ways in the present.

Let's assume the memories are accurate – it is not hard to understand why the woman has ambivalent feelings about her father. She loves him because he is her father, but hates him because of the horrific abuse.

On the other hand, let's assume the memories are entirely confabulated. They surely express profoundly ambivalent feelings about the father in the present. Whether the inaccurate memories were caused by therapy, her own imagination, a fundamentalist religious group, the media or an unknown source does not matter. The target of therapy is the unresolved ambivalence that is dominating the present.

Therapeutic neutrality has another meaning. The neutral therapist has not adopted a position on the victim-rescuer-perpetrator triangle, which is the subject of a separate chapter. Neutrality, from a systems perspective, means maintaining a position as an independent consultant, the only position with any therapeutic leverage. Neutrality in this sense requires good boundaries.

I participated in a session with a young woman who had accused her father of ongoing incest prior to arriving at our Trauma Program. The father attended the session. I began the session by explaining the principle of therapeutic neutrality. I said that the treatment team truly did not know what was going on, and neither believed nor disbelieved either party. I defined the problem as a problem between the two of them. It was clear that this was a major problem, I said, and we were willing to work with them to try to find a resolution of it.

The father stated that his daughter was possessed by a demon and tried to exorcise the accusatory demon in front of me, which I had to stop. What the father identified as a demon, the woman identified as a child alter personality. The child personality took executive control during the session to repeat her accusation.

The father said he had been instructed directly by God that his daughter was possessed and that her possession was a test of his faith. He was therefore not angry at his daughter. Other evidence that she was being controlled by a demon, he said, included her choice of friends, jewelry and clothes, her career plans, and her choice of a future college, which was not a church-run college. None of these choices, in my opinion, were outside the normal range for a conservative suburban late adolescent.

A year later, the young woman was enrolled in a compromise college away from her home which was neither her first choice, nor her father's first choice. She was wearing the same style of clothing and jewelry as a year previously, to which her father still objected. The goal of treatment was not a decision as to whether there was in fact ongoing paternal incest, but normal separation and individuation. The young woman was having a great deal of difficulty achieving this normal developmental goal, but had made a lot of progress in the previous year.

I sometimes say to patients, "Just because I don't believe you doesn't mean I don't believe you."

This statement always causes puzzled looks. So I explain it. The patient assumes that there are only two options: I believe her, or I don't believe her. Since I am not believing her, I must be actively not believing her. This is a cognitive error. I fact I am neither believing nor not believing. I have adopted a third position, therapeutic neutrality.

If the patient persists in a catastrophic reaction to my not "validating" her memory, I remind myself that the problem is not the problem. I tell the patient that she is holding onto the catastrophe in order to avoid her own conflict and feelings. Also, she is trying to engage me in a re-enactment of her relationship with her father, with an undoing dynamic added on top. She feels that her reality was never validated by her father, and she is trying to undo this reality by getting Dr. Ross to validate her.

If I did "validate" her memory I would be colluding with her undoing. I would therefore be reinforcing her defenses and making her road to recovery longer and more difficult. After I explain all of this, patients don't like therapeutic neutrality, but they put up with it. They are healthy enough to choose a doctor who doesn't give them a sedative prescription every time they ask for one. They are working hard on saying 'No' to drugs.

In the memory war that filled much of the 1990's, extremists on both sides of the combat shared a common assumption. Both sides were focused on memory content. There are two kinds of picket signs, Believe the Children, and Voodoo False Memory Therapist. I have been vilified by extremists on both sides. On the one hand, I am a major cause of false memories, harm to families, and therapist malpractice. On the other, I have sold out to the False Memory Syndrome Foundation. On June 1, 2000, these two viewpoints were represented in reviews of my book, *Satanic Ritual Abuse*, on www.amazon.com.

Some reviewers scolded me for believing in Satanic cults, others scolded me for invalidating survivors. Neither side has listened carefully. Let me repeat myself.

Just because I don't believe you, doesn't mean I don't believe you.

Integration Of Opposites

The work of therapy is the integration of opposites. In the history of Western thought, the first thinker about the integration of opposites, was the Pre-Socratic Greek philosopher, Heraclitus, with whom I have a close spiritual affinity. The other major influences on my thought about the problem of opposites are the English poet, William Blake, (*The Marriage of Heaven and Hell*); the German philosopher, Neitzsche, (*The Birth of Tragedy*); and the English novelist, D.H. Lawrence, (*Fantasia of the Unconscious, and Psychoanalysis and the Unconscious*).

My book *Satanic Ritual Abuse* is about the dissociation of opposites in Western civilization, as manifested in the history of Satan, the Catholic Inquisition, and people in the late twentieth century with multiple personality disorder and memories of participation in Satanic cults. The book is not about the content of patients' memories.

One person will come into my Trauma Program an angry, entitled borderline rage-aholic. This person is out of balance. She needs to get in touch with her grief and is avoiding it by hiding in her anger.

The next person comes into the Trauma Program depressed, passive and a walking victim. She too is out of balance. She needs to get in touch with her anger, and has an anger phobia.

Both these patients can benefit from anger management group. Neither know how to feel or manage anger in a healthy fashion. A preliminary phase of the work involves correcting cognitive errors about anger. Anger is a healthy, normal emotion. It is biologically normal to be very angry when you have been treated in an inconsistent, abusive fashion as a child. That is why God made the amygdala, so you can be angry. God looked out over Creation, and saw that it was good, including the amygdala.

Anger is rocket fuel for assertiveness, straightening up your backbone, and meeting your goals in life. It is also the most effective antidepressant on the market. Anger and depression are incompatible states. You cannot be rip-roaring angry, with your adrenalin up and running, and be clinically depressed at the same time.

The victim patient has an anger phobia. She needs desensitization. She needs the structure and containment of anger management group. Step by step, with structure, support and validation (of her anger, not her memory content), she practices actually being angry, and practices de-escalating from the anger. The experience corrects her cognitive error that she will die, explode, go insane, be hated, get stuck in the anger forever, have to kill herself, or go on a murder rampage if she allows herself to feel her anger. As a pure emotion, her anger is valid. What counts is not where it came from, but how she handles it.

The physical set-up of the anger group is not essential. In our inpatient setting, we have a sheet of plywood painted with an oil-based paint. The patients take turns throwing balls of clay at the board, which do not stick, and can be peeled off, reformed and used again. The balls making a very hyper-alerting sound like a gunshot when they hit the board, and the physical energy of the throwing helps to mobilize the adrenalin and anger.

To the passive victim patient, the therapist says, "I want you to let your body throw from the anger that is stored in your body."

The patient straightens up, throws with moderate vigor, and makes some angry statements.

The therapist asks, "See how the depression goes away when you allow yourself to feel your anger?"

The entitled, angry borderline is eager to volunteer to work in anger management group. She gets up and hurls 95 mph pitches while hurling f-words at her parent-perpetrators, and does so with glee. This is a repetition of the angry, acting out behavior she does all day every day, with staff, peers, lovers, therapists and any other bystander who gets in her way.
The therapist says to this woman, "Now I want you to say, 'I couldn't make you love me'."

Before the next pitch leaves her hand, the floodgates open and the tears come pouring out.

The therapist says, "See how you hide in your anger to avoid your grief."

Both these women use dissociation as a defense. They have dissociated their anger from their grief, cannot tolerate ambivalence, and cannot feel both feelings at once. Both can escalate into trance states. When the angry borderline escalates into a trance state, she experiences blind rage. Her eyes become glassy, she is back in the past, and the risk of dangerous behavior is going up every second. She needs to be grounded in the present

When the victim patient goes into a trance state, she becomes little, defenseless, curled up and the risk of a flashback goes up with every second. She too needs to be grounded in the present.

Following the teaching of Heraclitus, the universe is sustained by a tension between opposites. Whether this is true in quantum mechanics, or not, I don't know. It is true in my Trauma Programs. The opposites have been dissociated. The patient switches state back and forth from one to the other in a chaotic fashion, hides in one to avoid the other, and uses addictions, acting out and cognitive errors to avoid the attunement of opposites.

The goal is not the elimination of opposites, it is their attunement. There cannot be a healthy life without anger or sadness. The goal is to feel both, be stuck in neither, and be desperate to escape neither. Much of the work of therapy is simply practicing sitting with the feelings, instead of stuffing, avoiding or acting them out. The conflict of opposites arises from the problem of attachment to the perpetrator, which is the subject of the next chapter.

Integration Of Schools Of Thought

The patients in my Trauma Program are not integrated human beings, no matter what their diagnoses. They are dissociated. Other systems based on pathological dissociation include the federal government, DSM-IV-TR, and the field of psychiatry. Psychiatry is a Tower of Babel. There are countless schools of thought, all engaged in ideological wars with their opponents.

Trauma therapy is based on an integration of schools of thought. I have received negative feedback from professionals at workshops because I am not really doing cognitive therapy, and because I am discounting the existence of the unconscious. I have been accused of superficial band-aid work by psychoanalytically oriented therapists, on the grounds that I do cognitive therapy. I have been trashed by false memory syndrome advocates on the grounds that I do unscientific Freudian therapy.

All these critics are mistaken.

Trauma therapy is not "eclectic." It is based on a coherent model, has a restricted range of applications, is operationalized in this book, is transmissible, and can be subjected to scientific treatment outcome studies. A manual for trauma therapy is in development, as is a measure for determining whether, on review of session tapes, a given therapist is delivering trauma therapy.

Trauma therapy is distinct from narrowly defined, classical Beckian cognitive therapy for depression. It is not family therapy and it is not psychoanalysis. Trauma therapy does incorporate many principles and tactics from all three schools of thought, and from social psychology. It draws on developmental psychology and the biology of mammalian attachment. But it cannot be reduced to any one narrowly defined school of thought. Each of these schools has some of the truth but not all of it.

The same is true for trauma therapy. Trauma therapy is useless for a lithium-responsive clear-cut bipolar patient with no comorbidity, or for a deteriorated schizophrenic with fixed auditory hallucinations.

There is too much investment in semantics and jargon in psychiatry. Often, the different schools of thought are saying much the same thing in different vocabulary. It isn't the vocabulary that matters. It is the overall stance of the school.

In my book, cognitive-behavioral therapy wins by a mile. Why, when much of it can be translated into psychoanalytical vocabulary? Cognitive therapy is superior because, as a field, it has an empirical mindset. The vocabulary is part of the mindset. The terms, concepts and procedures have been operationalized, manualized and subjected to scientific outcome studies across a range of applications. Psychoanalysis, as a school of thought, just isn't trying to get there. Cognitive therapy generates more evidence of its efficacy in a year than psychoanalysis has in a century.

From my perspective, the vocabulary and concepts of psychoanalysis are obscurantist by intent. The goal is not to be testable and never to be tested. The useful concepts and principles of psychoanalytical thinking are threatened most not by hostility from without, but by lack of serious commitment to scientific verification from within. The same problem exists in sectors of family therapy, which are over-invested in untestable, obscurantist vocabulary and concepts.

The trauma model, including its therapeutic component, is formulated so as to be scientifically testable. The requirements of a scientific psychotherapy outcome study are that the therapy have a defined target with sensitive and reliable outcome measures; that it be operationalized and transmissible; and that there be a measure to verify it is being delivered. All these elements are part of the current project, of which this book is a component.

Psychotherapists in general, and psychiatrists in particular, I believe, have a moral, ethical and scientific obligation to try to devise scientifically testable models and treatments. The more the different schools of thought in psychiatry subject themselves to scientific study, the more common ground they will find. Internal medicine doesn't have warring schools of thought the way psychiatry does, because it has more science.

Defenses Evolve Over Time

A common error made by therapists working with trauma, is the belief that defenses are fixed. This idea is derived from the psychoanalytical concept of developmental arrest and fixation. Too many therapists operate as if the past has been frozen in time, preserved without change for decades. This misconception gets applied to the content of memories and to the function of defenses.

Defenses evolve over time. The function, structure and content of a defense may change dramatically over decades. Sometimes, of course, defenses are relatively rigid and unchanging, but certainly in the dissociative disorders field, many therapists have over-estimated the degree of fixity.

It is *as if* the child alter personality has been stored unchanged in a time storage capsule for thirty years, and emerges fresh and unchanged in the therapist's office. It isn't true that a child is present at all, for one thing. Even if a relative discovered a long-lost family movie which showed a switch to the same child alter thirty years ago, and the alter behaved in much the same way it does in the year 2000, my point would be the same. The function of the defense has evolved.

Now, in the present, the alter personality has taken executive control as a defense against feelings and conflicts experienced in the session. The host personality was sad, scared, or anxious, so a child came out to rescue the host. The defense is working in an adult body in the year 2000. The situation, needs, threats and resources have all changed dramatically.

In Vietnam, decades ago, the flashbacks that occurred at night back at base camp were simply flashbacks. Now decades later, they are used as a justification for getting drunk. It is easy to understand why someone with combat-related PTSD would want to drink, but not everyone with PTSD is an alcoholic. Look at the situation from the perspective of alcoholism, and you see someone who is trying to con his AA sponsor into agreeing that it is absolutely necessary to have a drink. The person had PTSD while on tour in Vietnam, but did not meet criteria for alcoholism till several years later.

The focus of trauma therapy is the function of the symptoms and defenses in the present, which is the only place where healing can take place.

Collaborative Empiricism

Collaborative empiricism is a term from cognitive therapy. It means that therapist and client work together in a particular way. The therapist does not impart wisdom from on high. Instead, the two parties work together to test the accuracy of the client's cognitive errors. The errors are tested against empirical evidence, logic, and other contradictory beliefs held by the client.

The therapist might ask, "How can it be true that you are a total failure at everything, and at the same time you have an M.A., and two healthy children?"

The client will respond, "Well, maybe I'm not a total failure, but I'm a failure in everything that's important."

"So sending two healthy children off to college is a trivial achievement? There are more important things in life?"

"My marriage is a mess."

"That's true, but that's not what we're talking about at the moment. You changed topics because your belief that you're a failure was being threatened."

"See, I can't even do therapy right."

"And what do you think is a fitting punishment for that crime?"

"I should be dead."

"Right. I figured you'd say that. Do you deserve to die because you're a total failure at life?"

"Yes."

"Do people who are only partial or moderate failures deserve to die?"

"No."

"So if it was true that you are only a partial failure, you would have to commute your death sentence, wouldn't you?"

"I hate it when you're logical like that."

"I know, that's why I do it. Remember, this is a torture dungeon disguised as a therapy office. Right?"

"Right. We proved that last session."

"So you have a good memory, then. I think you're holding onto the false belief that you are a failure in order to justify keeping the option of suicide open. You are keeping the option of suicide open for a reason. What do you think that is?"

The therapist contributes hypotheses and devises tests for them. The client collaborates in the process. It isn't that one person does therapy to the other. Trauma therapy is a joint project, like building a model airplane together.

I compare therapy to a consultation with an architect. The client brings in hopes, dreams, a life and a vision, and money to pay the professional fee, but cannot design and build a house by herself. The architect contributes technical skill and creativity so that the house can actually be built, not just dreamed of and hoped for. But it is the client's house. Only the client can turn it into a home. The tone of trauma therapy is more like the tone of visits to an architect than the stereotyped, over-cooked, over-private, over-sexualized psychoanalytical session seen so often in Hollywood movies.

In trauma therapy, the joint project is building a self. Not everyone who comes to my Trauma Programs really wants to have a healthy identity. A healthy self takes a lot of work.

Intense Recollection, Not Abreaction

In the 1980's, I was taught at professional meetings that abreaction is a core component of healing. This doctrine was derived from Janet (1965; 1977) and the early Freud (Breuer and Freud, 1986). The idea was analogous to surgical treatment of an abscess. An abscess cannot be cured with antibiotics because there is no blood circulation into the core of the abscess. Therefore, the abscess must be opened surgically and drained. Then antibiotics and natural healing can complete the process of recovery.

In the abreactive model of trauma therapy, the dissociated memory, for which there may be partial or complete amnesia, is a mental abscess. It causes symptoms through leakages of imagery and emotion, by driving pathological defenses, and by robbing the self of its unity and full energy supply. The contents of the abscess are the contents of the memory of the traumatic event, including the visual and cognitive information, the emotions, the physiological arousal and sensations, and any attendant conflicts. All of these must be drained, according to the abreactive model.

The process of drainage requires minute attention to the details of the traumatic events, and reliving them through abreaction. Too often, in the 1980's and early 1990's, there were way too many abreactions, they were way too intense, and the outcomes were bad. Instead of getting better, patients went down the tubes. They regressed, had more symptoms and crises, required more phone calls, extra sessions and hospitalizations, and escalated further and further out of control.

In the extreme cases there were numerous serious boundary violations as the therapist moved deeper and deeper into the rescuer role. The rescuer-victim dyad became more and more enmeshed, and along with it, the third corner of the triangle became malignantly inflated. The crimes of the perpetrator became more and more numerous and bizarre to balance and justify the escalation at the other two corners of the triangle. The therapy became an engine for false memories. There were seminar trainings in hyper-elaborate methods to prepare for and conduct planned abreactions.

During this period, I realized that abreaction is by definition always acting out. Acting out is when you turn your feelings and conflicts into behavior, rather than processing them at a verbal level in therapy. This is particularly true of extreme abreactions in which the person loses all grounding in the present, and is back in the past reliving the trauma with full intensity, clutching her genital area while curled up in the fetal position. I defined such events as *malignant abreaction* in my 1989 text, *Multiple Personality Disorder*, and said that such abreactions need to be stopped as quickly as possible.

I realized in the early 1990's that even mild abreactions are actually mild malignant abreactions. They are symptoms, not therapeutic work. I explicitly define abreaction as acting out in my Trauma Programs. Abreaction is like running down the hallway to get away from your feelings, which patients do not infrequently. You can't get better by running around inside a mental hospital.

Abreactions are contagious and never spontaneous. They have a social context and strategic function. This is very clear in an inpatient setting. Defining abreactions as acting out results in their being treated with the same principles of behavioral management applied to any other form of acting out. Abreactions have no curative effect for the individual, and they destabilize the milieu and make it for more difficult for other patients to do any productive work.

It does not follow that I prohibit the telling of the trauma narrative. Quite the opposite: telling the story to another human being is an essential component of recovery. In trauma therapy, the telling takes the form of intense recollection, not abreaction. It is essential that the client or patient stay grounded in the present, with adult reasoning and cognitive skills hard at work. The opposite error to planned abreaction is intellectualization. The trauma narrative is told with intense feeling, in the present.

Ethics and Boundaries

From 1985 to 2000, more damage was done to clients in therapy for childhood trauma by bad boundaries and basic ethical violations than by false memories, by far, in my opinion. As an expert witness in about fifty malpractice cases, very few of which ever went to trial, I have worked for both the plaintiff and the defense. I have never seen a case of serious malpractice without numerous severe boundary violations.

These include the list of violations shown in Table 25.1

In the most extreme case I have seen, the therapist described ritualized sexual practices with the client designed to convert her Satanic cult alter personality over to the therapy. The dissociative identity disorder and ritual abuse memories were entirely iatrogenic, in my judgment. In writing, the therapist admitted to living with the client as her sexual partner for five years while therapy was ongoing, but blamed her boundary violations on the borderline dynamics of the client.

The false memories in the case certainly caused specific damages, but they were not the most serious or harmful problem. In my view, this is generally true. The extravagant content of the false memories is heavily emphasized by the plaintiff's lawyer and expert witnesses in these cases, while the boundary violations receive comparatively little emphasis. This is a good business strategy in terms of inflaming the jury and increasing the award, but it is not helpful in efforts to police the profession. The defendant therapists conclude that they have been victimized by the perpetrator-run side of the false memory war, and never get it that boundaries are the main problem.

Table 25.1. Boundary Violations in Malpractice Cases

Sexual Involvement

Living Together with the Client

Client Involved in Therapist's Personal Life

Client Acting as Co-Therapist for other Clients

Confidentiality Violations

Bartering Personal Services for Therapy

Employing Client

Using Client as a Consultant on Other Cases

Involving Client in Personal Lives of Other Clients

Providing Supervision to Client when Client is a Therapist

Being a Co-Client in Therapy Provided to Client and Therapist by the Therapist's Colleague

---

It is imperative to maintain good boundaries in trauma cases. Good boundaries are not rigid. They are like the cell wall of an amoeba: fluid, flexible, and permeable, but able to maintain the integrity of the organism. Concerning the more minor boundaries, rules need not be carved in stone. Some therapists can apparently maintain good boundaries while giving selected clients their home phone numbers.

The idea is not to set up totalitarian boundary police. Deviations from the usual boundaries can be negotiated. If necessary, outside parties including lawyers and spouses can be consulted in advance to review and approve or disapprove of proposed dual relationships or other deviations from standard practice.

At the same time, there are no exceptions to some boundaries. It is never acceptable to bill a client's insurance company and have sex with her at the same time, for instance. This behavior gets zero tolerance. Living with a client while therapy is ongoing is never acceptable. It could be perfectly fine to have a therapy session at a mall for desensitization of agoraphobia, but a candlelit dinner in a romantic restaurant late on a Saturday night is always unethical.

The ethical rules and boundaries for trauma therapy are those of standard general therapeutic practice. There are no special exceptions for trauma survivors. They are more likely to be harmed by special exceptions than non-trauma clients, because they experienced too many "exceptions" to the usual rules while growing up. The trauma survivor early in recovery expects a perpetrator to emerge from the kindly figure making the exception, based on past experience. This fear damages the treatment alliance.

26

THE PROBLEM OF ATTACHMENT TO THE PERPETRATOR

The problem of attachment to the perpetrator is the core of trauma therapy. I defined the problem in the mid-1990's, in the context of the false memory war and concerns I had about the abreactive model of therapy. I thought that to be clinically, scientifically, politically and medico-legally defensible, a model should be grounded in science. Also, I thought, if you are grounded in science, you are more likely to be grounded in reality, and therefore are more likely to be able to help your client. I then cast my mind back through my scientific training, searching for a relevant body of knowledge and data. I arrived at fifth grade.

In fifth grade I learned about Darwin and the theory of evolution. In order to defend myself against attacks by hostile colleagues, I sought solid ground on which to build fortifications. It seemed like the theory of evolution offered a good starting point. What is the basic goal of all organisms according to the theory of evolution? To survive and reproduce. This is true from amoeba on up to mammals. Who will dispute that all organisms want to survive and replicate? This seemed like safe ground.

I made the drive to survival and reproduction the opening assumption of my treatment model. If one is a newborn alligator, the first imperative is to swim away as fast as possible, otherwise your mother might eat you. Dragonflies, grasshoppers, salamanders and alligators do not have families. They do not send cards on Mother's Day.

Things are different if you are a bird or mammal. Birds and mammals are absolutely dependent on adult caretakers for their survival for a period after birth, which ranges from weeks to decades depending on the species. For human parents, it seems like the period of dependency lasts over thirty years. In some species, if the nursing mother dies, the child dies. But in others, including elephants, if the nursing mother dies, a female relative takes over the care of the young one, and the child survives. In elephants there is a built in Child Protective Services, and there is a sociology of attachment.

Attachment is like the migration of birds. It is built in, deep in our brain stems and DNA. The infant bird or mammal does not engage in a cognitive, analytical process to assess the cost-benefit of attachment. It just happens. It's biology. The fundamental developmental task of the human infant is attachment. You will and you must attach. This is true at all levels of the organism. You must attach in order to survive biologically, but also in order to thrive and grow at emotional, intellectual, spiritual, interpersonal and at all possible levels.

We know the consequences of failure to attach from several sources. The first is the third world orphanage. Orphan babies may have an adequate intake of protein, carbohydrate and fat, and may have their diapers changed regularly, but if they are starved for love, stimulation, attention, and affection, they are damaged developmentally. Their growth is stunted at all levels, including basic pediatric developmental norms.

There is a large body of experimental evidence about the effects of child abuse and neglect on mammals. The Harlow monkey experiments, for instance, are systematic studies of abuse and neglect. Little monkeys cling desperately to their unresponsive wire-and-cloth mothers because they are trying to solve the problem of attachment to the perpetrator, in this case the perpetrator of neglect.

We also know from experimental evidence that profound neglect, deprivation and sensory isolation during early childhood physically damages the brain in a measurable fashion. The mammal raised in such an environment has fewer dendritic connections between the nerve cells in its brain than the mammal which grew up in a "culturally rich" environment. It is developmental suicide to fail to attach. At all costs, under the highest imperative, the young mammal must attach.

In a normal human family, attachment is secure, and things work out OK. I call the product of this environment an average neurotic mess. In a normal family, thankfully, the child's every whim and wish are not met. This toughens the child up for the real world. By age thirteen, the child has accumulated a long list of grievances against the parents: my allowance was too small, I had to share my bedroom, you're not going to give me a car when I turn sixteen, and my curfew is unreasonable. These grievances help fuel normal separation and individuation.

In a sense, we all have the problem of attachment to the perpetrator.

None of us have absolutely secure attachment. We all hate our parents for some reason, but love them at the same time. This is the normal human condition. But there is a large group of children who have the problem of attachment to the perpetrator to a huge degree. They have it to such a large degree, it is really a qualitatively different problem, I think. These are the children in chronic trauma families.

The trauma is a variable mix of emotional, verbal, physical and sexual abuse; neglect; absent parents through divorce, death, drug abuse, imprisonment or mental illness; family violence and chaos; urban violence; cultural disintegration; medical and surgical trauma; and sick family dynamics, rules, expectations and double binds. These cause the problem of attachment to the perpetrator.

The number one imperative is to attach. But there is another reflex built into human beings, deep in the brain stem and DNA. This is the recoil from pain. When you touch a hot stove, you do not engage in an analytical process in your cerebral cortex about the toxic effect of excess thermal stimulation on the integrity of the human epidermis, then, after the requisite cost-benefit analysis, elect to withdraw your finger. Your brain stem and arm pull your finger away almost before you realize it is getting hot. It is a reflex recoil.

Who will dispute that humans have a built-in recoil from emotional hurt and abuse? Is anyone going to attack this postulate as unreasonable or unscientific? In the trauma family, the child pulls away from the abuse and neglect and shuts down emotionally. But going into shutdown mode as a pervasive strategy would be developmental suicide. At all costs, you must attach.

The trauma model assumes that there is a built-in over-ride of the withdrawal reflex by the attachment systems. The child must solve the problem of attachment to the perpetrator. From the perspective of the child's attachment systems, it must be true that the perpetrator is safe to attach to, that the parent is good. That is why the child must split, fragment, fracture or dissociate. The bad events, bad feelings and bad reality must be put to the side.

The problem, fundamentally, is not the child's personal feelings, thoughts or conflicts about the abuse. The child doesn't fragment for personal psychological reasons. The problem is how to attach. There are two things going on in the child's psyche at the same time. There is approach, attachment, and connection. The child wants to love and be loved by the parent, and be special in the eyes of the parent.

At the same time, there is detachment, disconnection and avoidance. The child fears and hates the parent, and wants to flee. I liken this to the shear forces studied in physics. If you glue two pieces of wood together and pull one towards you, and one away from you, your action sets up a shear force at the interface between the two pieces of wood. Shear forces are very ripping, tearing, destructive forces in physics. Wind shear can cause plane crashes at airports.

The simultaneous approach and avoidance sets up a shear force deep in the child's soul. The conflict between the attachment and disconnection is the deepest conflict, the deepest source of pain, and the fundamental driver of the symptoms. The fundamental splitting of the psyche is necessary to solve the problem of attachment to the perpetrator. This split psychological organization is called borderline personality disorder in DSM-IV-TR. Bleuler, in his classical psychiatric writings, called it *schizophrenia*.

Mammalian attachment systems have a number of properties illustrated well by the letdown reflex of the nursing mother. When the mother is sitting in the living room, and the baby cries out from the nursery, she gets up and goes to fetch the infant. There is a bustle of helloes, changing of diapers, and carrying the infant back to the living room for feeding. While this is going on, the mother's brain does something very clever and adaptive.

The mother's hypothalamus tells her pituitary gland to secrete oxytocin, which it does. The oxytocin circulates around in her blood, where it is of no benefit in her elbows or toes. However, in her breast tissue the oxytocin stimulates the letdown reflex. It causes the milk to move from high up in the ducts to right down at the nipples. When mom and baby get set up to feed, breasts and baby are ready for action. This is a typical clever, adaptive mechanism built into evolution like countless others.

It is clear that the letdown reflex does not require conscious effort by the mother. She does not have to give her pituitary gland a pep talk. It just happens. It's biology. The letdown reflex is part of the biology of mammalian attachment. There are countless such attachment mechanisms, and they are reciprocal between the parents and the child.

Two women attended workshops of mine, one in Austin and one in

Albuquerque, in which I talked about the problem of attachment to the perpetrator and the letdown reflex. From each of them I learned something about the letdown reflex I hadn't known previously. The woman in Austin had brought her baby to the workshop, and it was lying on a blanket on the floor at the back of the hall when I stopped and talked to her at the break.

She explained to me that organizations which give assistance to nursing mothers, teach their clientele about the letdown reflex. If you are a working nursing mother, you have to pump your breasts at work and store the milk in bottles. This is a nuisance because of the time and sterile technique required, but also because it's hard to get the milk to flow. There has been no letdown.

The working mother is taught to look at a picture of her baby, and fantasize about her baby before starting to pump. The result? Through conscious effort the mother is able to stimulate the letdown reflex, and provide herself some practical assistance. From this fact I learned a general principle concerning the biology of mammalian attachment. It isn't just fixed and automatic.

The second woman told me that for several months after she stopped nursing, she still had the letdown reflex in response to her baby, and even to thinking about her baby. She would leak a little milk on those occasions. From her I learned that specific biological attachment mechanisms can remain active long after the developmental phase for which they were designed. If this can happen in the mother, it can happen in the child. If it can happen to normal attachment biology, it can happen to damaged attachment systems. If it can persist for months, it can persist for years.

From the woman in Austin, I learned that it is possible to reach down from the cerebral cortex into the depths of the brain, and influence the biological function of the attachment systems. This means that, in principle, it could be possible to repair damage to the attachment systems caused by trauma with verbal psychotherapy. In fact, if psychotherapy works, that must be the case. When I consider the profound healing I have seen in dissociative identity disorder patients treated to stable integration (Ellason and Ross, 1997), I realize that there must be healing in the brain.

The successfully treated DID patient experiences a massive reduction in symptoms, from two standard deviations above the mean to within the normal range for the general population, on measures of anxiety, depression, psychosis, dissociation, substance abuse and personality disorder. The self-mutilation and auditory hallucinations disappear. Utilization of psychiatric health care services, measured in dollars, drops by over 90%. Occupational and social function improve dramatically, as do self esteem and overall life satisfaction. For this to occur without a profound change in brain biology would be possible only under conditions of complete Cartesian dualism, a view I reject.

Like the working nursing mother who takes out a picture of her baby at work, therapy must reach down into the biology of attachment. This hypothesis leads directly to one of the predictions of the trauma model, namely that PET scans should function as a psychotherapy treatment outcome measure for dissociative identity disorder, or any of the trauma disorders characterized by hippocampal hypofunction.

I came to the attachment model of trauma by my usual route – listening to the patients. In terms of colleagues, by far the biggest influence on my thinking in this regard is Jennifer Freyd's (1996) book, *Betrayal Trauma*. She taught me the idea that the primary motive for amnesia is protection of the attachment systems. She showed me the logic by which cognitive psychology, social psychology and biology could be integrated.

I learned about attachment from the patients because they showed me the pain and suffering of disorganized attachment patterns. They also taught me the order and symmetry hidden in the chaos, for which the relevant chaos theory is the trauma model. The trauma model reveals the strategic and adaptive functions of the apparent chaos and disorganization, which are in fact governed by specifiable rules and logic. The patients are not crazy, they just came from crazy families.

The fundamental work of therapy is the attunement of opposites. The fundamental opposites are the good and bad mother, and the good and bad father. It is the contrast and conflict between the two which is the deepest source of pain. All the defenses are roads leading back to Rome, and the work of therapy is always grieving the loss of the parents you never actually had.

There are two defensive ways to solve the conflict: make the world all black or all white. Then the conflict between the two polar opposites disappears. One patient will come into the Trauma Program stating that she has no use for her parents. They never did anything for her, she hasn't seen them for ten years, and she would be glad to hear they are dead. This patient is in touch with her anger, and the disconnect, detach, avoid, recoil, withdraw, flee half of her conflict.

The anger and disconnection are serving the function of reaction formation. Reaction formation occurs when you take on the opposite set of feelings to what you really feel as a defense against the feelings you cannot tolerate. In the Republic of Texas, we see reaction formation commonly. We see big guys with big trucks, big belt buckles, and big rifles mounted in their rear windows, who drink a lot of beer. The Dallas Cowboys have a very big offensive line. According to Freud, this is reaction formation – the Texas he-men feel inadequate underneath.

The Trauma Program patient who has not seen her parents for ten years is likely using reaction formation. I know that her conflict has not been resolved. How do I know that? Because she is an inpatient in a mental hospital. The stance of "I don't need them," is a defense against the intolerable underlying truth. In truth, she wishes deeply that dad would come back, apologize, say it was his fault, say he loves her, and make everything OK again. There is zero chance that will ever happen, but the intolerable wish is still there. Really feeling the wish and hope will make reality really hit home, which will lead to the grief.

The patient is following the teachings of the great twentieth century philosopher, Alfred E. Newman, whose motto was, "What, me worry?"

She is not worried cause she doesn't need dad one little bit.

A second woman comes into the Trauma Program depressed, passive, helpless and enmeshed with her parents in the present. Not much out of the ordinary happened in her childhood, she claims. This woman has buried her anger and is exclusively in the attach, connect, love and be loved mode. Both women meet criteria for over ten DSM-IV-TR disorders lifetime and are actively suicidal, which is a clue that their defenses are not working very well.

For both, the work of therapy is feeling both poles of the ambivalent attachment simultaneously, tolerating both without acting out, getting stuck in neither, and using neither as a defense against the other. Both must mourn the loss of the parents they never actually had.

The logical structure of the problem of attachment to the perpetrator is exactly the same as Freud's 1917 theory of mourning and melancholia (Freud, 1963). It is no coincidence that both are structural models of unresolved grief. In the Freudian scenario, a woman is widowed at age 65 after forty years of marriage. Difficult as it may be to believe, her husband was a real jerk some of the time. But much of the time he was a really decent guy. As a result of his character foibles, his wife built up a lot of positive feelings towards him, and a lot of negative ones.

Now that her husband is dead, she has only her internal memories and feelings about him. In Freudian jargon, the husband now exists only as an introject. The introject has two poles, a positive and a negative, towards which she directs her positive and negative feelings. What happens in the outside world?

She cries at the funeral, the groom from her wedding gives a glowing euology, and her friends and relatives console her.

"It's such a tragedy. He worked so hard all his life. And he had just retired, and wanted so much to see his grandchildren grow up. It's such a loss. He was such a good man."

The widow's positive feelings about her husband are expressed, vented, supported, and validated. What about the negative feelings? They don't exist. There is no social ritual to validate them, they are not expressed, and no-one comments on them.

No girlfriend comes up to say, "The old crab-ass is dead. Let's party!"

But the negative feelings do exist. In Freudian jargon, the negative feelings are turned inwards and cathected to the negative pole of the ambivalently held introject of the deceased husband. Since the introject of the husband is actually an element of the self, all the negative energy is turned on the self, resulting in depression. The depression cannot lift because the negative feelings about the husband must be disavowed and repressed.

Freud's theory of mourning and melancholia is structurally identical to the problem of attachment to the perpetrator. One might say that the husband was the perpetrator during the widow's adult years.

People often ask me whether the problem of attachment to the perpetrator applies when the perpetrator is not a family member. The answer is 'Yes' for a number of reasons.

If the abuse occurred during childhood, a theory of its causation was constructed in the mind of the magical child. From the child's perspective, the abuse by the dirty old man down the street became absolute proof of mom's willful neglect. Mom, being omnipotent and omniscient, actively failed in her duty to protect her child, and thereby betrayed her. The betrayal trauma has taken place, not in objective reality, but in the mind of the child.

There will be ambivalent attachment to the non-offending parents due to the cognitive developmental level of the child. Similarly, in intrafamilial incest, the non-offending parent has always betrayed the child victim, in the child's mind.

"If mom loved me, she wouldn't let this happen," the child thinks to herself.

In adulthood, the problem of attachment to the perpetrator can occur under circumstances in which the traumatized adult is dependent for his or her survival on the perpetrator. Interrogation, hostage situations, abduction by a serial killer who does not kill right away, and extreme spousal battery or stalking situations can create the absolute dependency required for the problem of attachment to the perpetrator. It is a recognized element of Stockholm Syndrome that the captive victim perceives her captor as her protector, and the SWAT team as persecutors of her captor.

This mechanism, also called *identification with the aggressor*, is deliberately exploited in brainwashing and interrogation situations (Lifton, 1961; Sargant, 1957). In Pavlovian terms, the interrogated individual enters a state of *transmarginal inhibition* and identifies with the interrogator. He then perceives his comrades in his underground political cell as his enemies, and betrays them, following which he is imprisoned or executed.

The problem of attachment to the perpetrator is explained in didactic groups in my Trauma Programs, and in writing in the Patient Packet. I have explained it in survivor newsletters, professional workshops, books, a video I produced, cognitive therapy groups and other settings. I always use the same language and examples, whether the audience is lay people, professionals or patients.

The problem of attachment to the perpetrator is everywhere in the patients' speech, conflicts, defenses, acting out and current relationships. It is re-enacted over and over. In the classical transference triad, the structural pattern is present in the recollected early relationship with the parents, the relationship with the treatment team, and relationships outside therapy in the present. The pattern is called *splitting*.

It is not surprising that splitting is a hallmark of borderline personality, since borderline personality organization is the logical outcome of the problem of attachment to the perpetrator.

27

A TRAUMA THERAPY SESSION ON AMBIVALENT ATTACHMENT

A typical group trauma therapy session in my Trauma Program might go as follows. The group is called cognitive therapy because referring therapists and managed care companies are familiar with the term. Actually, what I do in it is trauma therapy.

"Good afternoon. For those of you who don't know me, I'm Dr. Ross. This is cognitive therapy group. The format of this group is it's not a process group. In a process group you look at the interactions among the group members. Here one person at a time will do some work."

"The idea is that while one person is working, everyone else is processing along in parallel, because what that person's working on probably has a lot to do with what you're working on. Then we have group comments and feedback thrown in as we go along."

"The subject matter we deal with in cognitive therapy group is anything at all. The only thing we don't get into is details of any trauma or abuse, or any acting out behavior. The reason for this is that the details would be too triggering for everyone else. So we leave the details for individual therapy, and here we refer to the trauma in general, overall terms."

"And the basic idea of cognitive therapy is that I focus on how your thought patterns are affecting your feelings and behavior. So the question is, who would like to start?"

Someone will then volunteer, "I'd like to work."

My reply is always, "OK. First I'd like to know a little background. How old are you?"

"Thirty-six."

"And what's your name?"

"Mary."

"Mary. And where do you live?"

"New Jersey."

"Do you live alone or with someone else?"

"With my husband and two children."

"And how old are they?"

"A girl twelve and a boy fourteen."

"How are the two children doing overall in life?"

"Good. They're great kids."

"No serious problems? They're doing well in school?"

"Yes, they're both A students."

"And how would you describe the marriage?"

At this point I am wondering what the current stresses are that drove her into the hospital. The likely candidates are the therapy, which has been too focused on abreaction and memory recovery, or the marriage. Because of her positive account of family life so far, I am looking for either reaction formation about the marriage or a problem outside the family.

She responds, "It's good. My husband is very supportive."

One of the other patients looks angry at this point. This could be something about her own life, or Mary could have told her negative things about the marriage.

"What is the main reason you are in the hospital?"

"Suicide."

"If your marriage is good and the kids are doing fine, why do you want to die?" I am implicitly raising the possibility that the picture of family life is incomplete, while asking about factors outside the family.

"I can't stand the memories."

"How long have memories been a problem?"

"My entire life."

"Did the problem with memories get worse recently?"

I now remind myself that the problem is not the problem. Starting to have flashbacks was the solution to some other problem, which must have arisen shortly before the memories worsened. I am also wondering about her home therapist's model and methods.

"About four months ago."

"Was there anything major that happened around that time that might have triggered the memories, or the worsening of the memories?"

"My husband had an affair with his secretary."

"Oh. How long had that been going on?"

"Two years."

"When did you find out?"

"Four months ago."

"How did you find out?"

"A friend of mine saw them checking into a motel and told me."

"Did you confront your husband right away, or how did you handle it?" I am now looking for both sides of her ambivalent attachment to her husband. It is clear that she is in reaction formation against her anger, and therefore it's likely that she is talking a passive victim role in the marriage.

"No, I took an overdose. My friend confronted him when I was in the hospital. Then he came to the hospital and told me about it. We've been in marital therapy twice a week since then."

I now suspect that Mary takes the role of victim and mentally ill patient to avoid her problems, manipulate her husband and express her anger. I ask, "Is the marital therapist any good?"

"Yes, she's excellent. She doesn't let either of us get away with anything."

"Has your husband stopped having sex with his secretary?"

"I think so."

"You think so? You don't know for sure?"

"He says he has. I believe him."

"Does she still work for him?"

"Yes. She's worked for him for fifteen years. She would be hard to replace. She really knows the business."

"Hmm. Who did you say you feel like killing? Your husband's secretary, or yourself?"

Mary smiles, the other patients guffaw, and then Mary says, "You're saying I'm angry at her?"

"I'm saying two things. One, you're a human being. Two, therefore you must be angry at both of them."

"My husband is really trying hard to make it better."

"How many times have you been sexually intimate with him in the last four months?"

"None. I can't because of the memories."

I postulate that one of the functions of the bad memories is to make sexual relations impossible. This provides a mental illness, victim-role cover for Mary's punitive withholding of sex from her husband. She has passive-aggressive dynamics. My goal is to get her to be more directly aggressive in a healthy manner. In a two-week admission, she can only begin to build the necessary skills. The inpatient treatment goal is to create a foundation for her post-discharge therapy.

"Why are you planning to murder your husband's wife?"

"What do you mean?"

I am going for her anger at her husband. I know that every suicide is also a murder. There are three simultaneous murders: the self is killing the self; the other is killing the self; and the self is killing the other. The first of these is literally true in suicide. The second and third are dynamically true.

For Mary, one of the motives of suicide is revenge on her husband. She will kill herself for several different reasons: to end her suffering; to deprive her husband of his wife, thereby getting revenge on him (she is going to kill him); to show everyone how much her husband hurt her (he is killing her); to rid the world of the worthless wife who drove her husband to infidelity; as a gift to her husband, so he can be free to marry his secretary, and finally find the happiness he deserves; and to put her husband on a guilt trip. The children are probably bystanders in the dynamics.

All of the above are hypotheses. I will have time to pursue only a few of them. My main goal is to get Mary to feel and acknowledge her anger, rather than acting it out. If she can be angry, she can be more assertive with her husband, get out of the martyr role, and either fix her marriage or get a divorce. Right now she is not in the marriage, because she is threatening to get out through suicide, but she is not committed to death either, otherwise she would not be a voluntary patient in the Trauma Program and would not have volunteered to work in cognitive therapy group.

"If your husband's secretary broke into your home and murdered you, would that be a friendly thing for her to do?"

"My husband might think so."

Great! A breakthrough! She has made a sarcastic statement about her husband.

"Your husband would be happy if his wife was murdered?"

"I'm very hard to live with. The memories..."

"Wait a minute. Are you saying that a healthy, happily married man would be happy if his wife was murdered?"

"Well, no, not if you put it that way."

"So, if you were murdered, and your husband was happy about it, he would have to be either really sick, or really unhappily married, or more than likely both."

"My husband isn't sick."

"Now you're getting angry at me for insulting your husband. But you just insulted him hugely. You said he would be happy if his wife was murdered. Why is it OK for you to insult your husband, but not me?"

"Because he's *my* husband."

"I see. I'll come back to that. But I want to ask you about the secretary's motive, the feeling that would be behind her killing you. Wouldn't it have to be anger?"

"I guess."

"You guess? What else might it be?"

"She might just want me out of the way."

"Sure, that's true, but I'm asking about the energy, the feeling behind the murder. Murder is a violent, hostile, destructive act towards another human being."

"That's true. I guess you're right. She'd have to be mad at me."

At this point, I am half way to where I want to be. My job now is to get her to see that suicide is murder of the self, motivated by anger. I take a didactic approach.

"The thing about suicide is, it is also murder. Murder of a human being. It is an angry, violent act towards the self."

"But I just want the pain to end."

"That's normal. Everyone wants to be free of pain. But murder is not an acceptable strategy for getting out of a painful marriage."

"But I have a right to kill myself if I want. It's my life."

"This is not about rights. It's about anger. I heard some sarcasm in your voice when you said your husband might think your secretary murdering you was a friendly act."

"If she did kill you, and you were looking down from heaven afterwards, and your husband was happy about it, how would you feel towards him?"

"I love my husband. I think he would be better off without me."

"That's not a feeling, that's an opinion. So, you're telling me that if the man you love, the man with whom you have had two children, is glad you have been killed by his girlfriend, that's fine with you?"

"She's not his girlfriend, she's his secretary."

"She's both. He has been having sex with her for two years. During those two years, he hasn't been having sex with you. And he's been lying to you about it, while you've been making his bed, doing his laundry, vacuuming his floors, and cooking his meals."

"OK. OK. Enough already."

"Enough of what? Being a domestic slave for your unfaithful husband?"

"You're making me feel worse."

"I'm trying to. Are you sure your husband having sex with his secretary is OK with you?"

"No, it's not OK with me!"

"How do you feel about it?"

"I hate it!" Tears begin to come to Mary's eyes.

"You hate it, but what are you doing about it?"

"What do you want me to do?" she shouts at me. "I'm depressed, I've got flashbacks, I've got two kids to take care of, what do you want me to do?"

"I want you to keep doing the dishes while your husband is having sex with his secretary."

"You're a real bastard."

"Good. You're angry at me. If you can get angry at me, you can get angry at your husband. When I make a mean, cruel statement like the one I just made, which I don't really believe – it isn't my real opinion - you get angry at me. When your husband says the same thing to you, through his actions, you have a flashback. You hide in the memories and the victim role."

"Well I'm sick of it."

"Are you angry at him."

"Yeah, I am."

" Are you angry enough that you might say to him, 'Heck, dear, I think it is somewhat inconsiderate of you to be boffing your secretary while I'm at home doing your dishes."

"No, I'm madder than that."

"Good, I'm glad to hear it. You need to get a lot more angry. You've been turning all your anger on yourself, and punishing yourself with depression, memories and threats of suicide. If your husband isn't going to treat you decently, at least you should."

"No-one has ever treated me decently. My father molested me from the time I was six years old, and my mother was too depressed to notice."

"I think you are re-enacting the problem of attachment to the perpetrator. And I think you're behaving towards yourself the way your mother behaved towards you when you were a child. Let me tell you why."

At this point, I would explain the problem of attachment to the perpetrator and how it must apply to Mary if she was a victim of chronic childhood abuse and neglect. It is virtually universal for patients in my Trauma Programs to treat themselves in adulthood they way their parents treated them in childhood. This is due to identification with the aggressor. The identification is an expression of positive attachment and loyalty to the parents, and adherence to the rules of the family of origin.

Mary comments, "I don't need my parents. I haven't talked to them for ten years."

"Right. The problem is, that can't be true for one simple reason: you are a mammal. Like I explained. Do you see the pattern here? You are angry at your parents, but you've buried your love for them. You love your husband, but you've buried your anger at him. Each time, you're only operating out of half of reality. There is no balance."

"I'm a mess. I should just kill myself."

"OK. Now I have to explain something else I call the locus of control shift."

That would be a typical cognitive therapy group session. It would end with feedback from the other patients, who would tell Mary that they have been in the same mess themselves, that she needs to stand up for herself, and that she can make it. They would affirm that she is a good person and point out to her all the positive character traits she has shown them on the Unit.

I would then conclude with, "Thanks. That's excellent feedback. And Mary, you did first class work today. You actually got angry at your husband, and you didn't go insane, commit suicide, or turn into a serial killer. When you were angry, you looked a lot less depressed. Remember, anger is the best antidepressant on the market. See you on Wednesday."

I just pointed out to Mary that her lifelong catastrophizing about what would happen if she ever got angry is a cognitive error. Her experience in the session proves that to her. She has taken a few steps up the anger desensitization hierarchy. If I was her individual therapist, I would have generated numerous hypotheses to test in later sessions. The session has illustrated many general principles of trauma therapy including collaborative empiricism, humor, use of paradox, direct teaching about the problem of attachment to the perpetrator, and the blending of systems, cognitive and dynamic approaches.

Trauma therapy differs from classical Beckian cognitive therapy in one important feature. In classical cognitive therapy, the errors of thinking are simply errors. Therapy consists of correcting them, following which the symptoms they have been causing spontaneously remit. In trauma therapy, the cognitive errors have defensive functions which must be taken into account. Mary's cognitive error of worthlessness proves to her that she has no right to be angry, which justifies her anger phobia and her plan for suicide, both of which serve the fundamental purpose of grief avoidance.

Mary has to feel her anger for her husband and her love for her parents before she can begin her grief work.

28

THE LOCUS OF CONTROL SHIFT

The scientific foundation of the locus of control shift is Piaget and developmental psychology. We know several things about the cognition of children age two to seven. I summarize this as, *kids think like kids*. Young children are self-centered. They are at the center of the world, and everything revolves around them. They cause everything in their world and they do so through magical causality. They do not use rational, analytical, adult cognitive strategies or vocabulary.

Imagine a relatively normal family with a four year-old daughter. One day, the parents decide to split up and dad moves out. What is true for this little girl? She is overwhelmed, sad, lonely, powerless, and helpless. She has experienced a major trauma, and there is nothing she can do about it. So she feels the feelings that correspond to this reality.

At the same time, the little girl is working on a Ph.D. in sociology. Like all graduate students in sociology, she is walking around making field observations about the social system under study. And she is recording her observations in her field notes. However, you can't get a Ph.D. in sociology with just field observations. You need a theory.

Using normal childhood cognition, the little girl constructs a theory to explain her field observation: "Daddy doesn't live here anymore because I didn't keep my bedroom tidy."

This is a really dumb theory. It is wrong, incorrect, inaccurate, mistaken and preposterous. What do we say to ourselves? Do we conclude that the little girl is mentally retarded? Do we say to ourselves, "Now there's a borderline little brat"?

No, we know that this is a developmentally normal cognitive error. This is how normal kids think. But there is more to it than that. The little girl was engulfed by a tidal wave of sadness, hopelessness, powerlessness, and despair. Or, no she wasn't.

The little girl thinks to herself, "I'm OK. I'm not powerless, helpless and overwhelmed. I'm in charge here. I'm in control. And I have hope for the future. Why? Because I have a plan. All I have to do is tidy up my bedroom and daddy will move back in. I feel OK now."

The little girl has shifted the locus of control from inside her parents, where it really is, to inside herself. She has thereby created an illusion of power, control and mastery which is developmentally protective. She is no longer engulfed by the tidal wave. She can carry on with her other developmental tasks, and feels autonomy and mastery in her life.

The locus of control shift is a normal and inevitable outcome of childhood cognition. It is also tactically brilliant.

Now consider another four year-old girl living in a major trauma family. She has the problem of attachment to the perpetrator big time. What is true for this little girl?

This other little girl is powerless, helpless, trapped, and overwhelmed. She can't stop the abuse, she can't escape it, and she can't predict it. She is trapped in her family by societal denial, her age, threats, physical violence, and family rules and double binds. A typical rule is: *good girls don't get angry*.

How does the little girl cope? She shifts the locus of control.

The child says to herself, "I'm not powerless, helpless and overwhelmed. I'm in charge here. I'm making the abuse happen. The reason I'm being abused is because I'm bad. How do I know this is true? Because only a bad little girl would be abused by her parents."

"The fact I am being abused proves I am bad. Also, I have bad feelings about the abuse. Only a bad girl would have bad feelings like that. Which proves I'm bad. I'm bad because I'm being abused and I'm being abused because I'm bad."

A small network of cognitions is set up which proves itself over and over. The ultimate proof of the locus of control, and the depravity and evil of the self, is any sexual arousal experienced during incest, especially if the child ever wanted, enjoyed or provoked the incest. The body has betrayed the self. The self retaliates by hating the body, and inserting a steel plate between the body and the head.

It is good to be bad, because only by being bad, by causing and deserving the abuse, can you create an illusion of power, control and mastery. One of the symptoms of DSM-IV-TR posttraumatic stress disorder is loss of a future. The child who has shifted the locus of control has a future:

"All I have to do is decide to be good, and the abuse will stop. I have to figure out how to do that. If the abuse doesn't stop, it's because I am bad and haven't decided to be good. It's good to know that."

The badness of the self is part of the package. You have to be bad in order to maintain the illusion of power, control and mastery. That is why it is good to be bad.

How did I figure out the locus of control shift? Not by reading textbooks or listening to my colleagues. I learned by listening to the patients in my Trauma Program. I noticed that not 60%, not 80% but 100% of the patients believed absolutely that they had caused and deserved the abuse, and that they were fundamentally bad. They stated this clearly and explicitly. They also demonstrated their self-hatred over and over in their self-destructive behavior, especially their self-mutilation.

Also, I noticed, 100% of patients knew that no-one else in the Program, and no other little girls anywhere on the planet deserved or caused their abuse. Why were they all endorsing the depravity of their selves, then?

My residency training provided an answer: "What else do you expect from a bunch of borderlines?"

It occurred to me that this is the locus of control shift. Trauma, I realized, hurts all aspects of a person's being. It hurts feelings, attachment patterns, hippocampal neurons, and memories, making them fragmented and frightening. It also hurts thinking. Abuse bends, breaks and damages cognition. We call these effects of trauma cognitive errors. The locus of control shift, when it is endorsed by a thirty-five year old woman, is evidence of unresolved trauma.

I also realized, yet again, that the problem is not the problem. Why, I asked myself, do the patients hold on so tightly to the locus of control shift, which should spontaneously reverse over time to some degree?

The answer lay in figuring out what happens when you reverse the locus of control shift, which, again, I learned from the patients. When you really get it, not just in your head, but in your heart and guts, that you didn't deserve or cause the abuse, then you get it that you were an innocent child like all other children. You deserved to be loved, protected and treated decently.

The locus of control shift is like an evil transfusion. All the evil inside the perpetrator has been transfused into the self, making the perpetrator good and safe to attach to – the locus of control shift helps solve the problem of attachment to the perpetrator. The two are intertwined with each other.

When you really reverse the locus of control shift, then you really get it that mom and dad weren't there for you, and didn't protect you. This throws you into the fundamental work of therapy: mourning the loss of the parents you never actually had. The locus of control is one of the fundamental grief-avoidance strategies.

If a person is early in recovery, and has many different symptoms, diagnoses, addictions, and self-destructive behaviors, the odds that the locus of control shift is in place are 100%. I have never seen an exception to this rule and have never met a mental health professional who claimed to have seen an exception to the rule.

The locus of control shift cannot be allowed to spontaneously reverse itself. It must be reinforced daily. This is done through negative self-talk, self-destructive and self-abusive behavior, denial of happiness and success to the self, and contracting with outside people to treat the self badly. The locus of control shift and the problem of attachment to the perpetrator are core problems at battered spouse shelters, prisons, mental hospitals, homeless shelters, and any other locations in our culture where symptom-ridden, self-destructive people gather, or are gathered together.

29

A TRAUMA THERAPY SESSION ON THE LOCUS OF CONTROL SHIFT

After my standard introduction to cognitive therapy group, a woman volunteers to do some work. I say, "Sorry, I forget your name."

"Heather."

"Right. You were here about two years ago, weren't you?" Our Trauma Programs have about a 40% readmission rate over three years.

"About that, yeah, but my hair was different then."

"I thought so. What would you like to work on?"

"I'm still having trouble with the locus of control."

"At least you know how to pronounce it, that's a good sign."

"I can't let go of the belief that I'm bad."

"Why not?"

"I don't know, I just can't."

"What does it do for you to hold onto the false belief that you are bad?"

"It makes my life miserable. It keeps me in bad relationships and it makes me feel bad about myself."

"Why do you hold onto it then?" I am defining the locus of control shift as a choice which has tactical functions.

"I want to let go, I just can't."

"Can't or won't?"

"I knew you were going to say it's a choice. I hate this Program."

"Good. The sooner you reverse the locus of control shift, the sooner you can get out of here, then."

"Can you help me do that?"

"Only if I'm in a good mood."

"Are you in a good mood?"

"No, really bad. Looks like you're going to have to reverse it yourself."

"I don't know how."

"You are one step ahead in the process. We're at the first step, which is deciding to let go. You have to say 'No' to drugs. Your drug is the locus of control shift. You're asking me for technical advice on how to reverse the locus of control shift, but you haven't done the first step. You haven't made a serious commitment to dropping the belief that you are bad. Asking to be told how to do that helps you avoid having to make the decision. You can always postpone it forever on the grounds that no-one has told you how to do it."

"But you must know something, with all these books you've written, and all the people who've been through your Program."

"Yeah, I've learned that no-one can decide for you. When do you think you might be ready to make this decision, sometime this year?"

"OK. I've heard you do this before. I could decide now... There, I've decided."

"And who do you think you fooled with that statement?"

"Not you, apparently."

"Did you fool yourself?"

"Not really, but I thought it sounded good."

"Didn't sound good to me."

"But if I didn't deserve the abuse, then I don't deserve the abuse I do to myself. If I believed that, I'd have to give up cutting and I'd have to kick my roommate out."

"Why?"

"Because my roommate treats me like shit."

"That's helpful if you want to feel bad about yourself."

"I'm sick of living like that."

"Good. There is one thing you really need to do the work of therapy. You have to be really fed up. Being fed up is a major motivator for recovery. Wanting things to be better is great, but it's being fed up that keeps you going. Because it's hard, painful work. Are you fed up enough to get serious about recovery?"

"Yes, I am."

"Good. Is it true that you deserved to be abused as a child?"

"No."

"What is true?"

"I deserved to be loved and cared for like any other child."

"You don't sound like you really believe that."

"I can say the words, but it isn't true here," says Heather, pointing to her heart.

"But you've done the first step. You have to get it in your head and say it out loud as the first step. If you can't do that, you can't work on making it true in your heart."

"I don't know why I can't get it in my heart. I must be stupid."

"Alert, alert! Cognitive error, cognitive error! You just did the locus of control shift again. You explained to me how stupid you are."

"Sorry."

"Instead of being sorry, you should stop trash talking yourself."

"It's a hard habit to break."

"True. But it's do-able."

"Thanks. I'll work on it."

I look around at the group and ask, "Anybody with a comment or feedback for Heather?"

A three hundred and fifty pound woman with fresh self-mutilation cuts on both forearms sits forward and says, "Heather, you're a really special person, and you deserve to be treated like the special person you are. You are a child of God. Don't ever forget that."

I know this woman well. She has acted out a great deal on the Unit, but has improved with strict behavioral management and a lot of direct confrontation. She typically acts helpless when she isn't, and she is highly skilled at getting other people to take care of her.
I ask, "Tell me, Sandra, do children of God deserve to have their forearms mutilated with knives and razor blades?"

Sandra looks horrified, and answers, "No. God loves all his little children."

I ask, "Are you a child of God?"

"No. I'm evil."

"I think you hold onto that belief, because if you drop it, you won't be able to self-mutilate anymore. If you can't self-mutilate anymore, or bury your feelings with food, you will have to feel them. It's your feelings you're avoiding. Everyone else in the room knows you aren't actually evil. You're unhappy, but not evil."

"You don't understand. I grew up in the cult. I was trained to be the Bride of Satan."

"But you're not in the cult now. The question isn't how did you get into this way of thinking, it's why do you hold onto it now."

"You don't understand. It's cult programming."

"Then the question is, why do you hold onto the false belief that you are programmed? We worked on that during your last admission, remember? Remember, you said you were going to let go of being programmed. When you did, you felt a lot less hopeless."

"It's true, I am programmed. "

"If you are programmed, then you are untreatable, and the situation is hopeless. You might as well go home."

"Why are you telling me I'm hopeless? I came here for help. I thought you helped people here. Now you're telling me I'm hopeless. I might as well kill myself, then." Sandra starts to look little and starts crying.

"We do help people here, every day, but they have to be willing to accept the help. It isn't me who's telling you you're hopeless, it's you. I'm telling you that you in fact aren't hopeless, that you could begin to recover if you dropped the belief you are bad and programmed, and started to work on tolerating your feelings."

Sandra puts her thumb in her mouth, takes it out, looks at the other group members, and says in a childish voice, "Is he the bad man?"

Instead of looking empathic, the other group members look exasperated and annoyed. The dissociative identity disorder, which is probably factitious, is the least of this woman's problems. She is entrenched in infantile defenses. That doesn't make her bad, but it does make her severely impaired.

"Sandra, if you can't stay grounded, you can't get any work done in cognitive therapy. This is a group for adult cognitive functions. Child parts can work in this group, but they have to be able to talk at least a little bit like grownups. Asking if I'm the bad man doesn't qualify. So you take it easy, I'm going to see if anyone else wants to work. Anyone?"

Heather raises her hand and says, "Me. I want to work on this some more. I don't want to be mentally ill for the rest of my life."

I ask, "How much fun is it being mentally ill?"

Everyone in the group makes a face. I have bumped everyone out of their investment in the patient role, at least temporarily, except Sandra, who is now asleep. I let her sleep because I decline to engage in her dance. In her dance, the next step is Dr. Ross trying to wake her up and get the adult Sandra back. This would keep the attention on her and ensure that neither her nor anyone else got any work done. None of the other patients try to wake her up.

"Heather, tell me about your roommate. How does she treat you badly?"

"She's completely irresponsible around the apartment. I do all the shopping, cooking and cleaning. Half the time, she never even pays her half of the rent."

"So there is no financial need to keep her there. Why don't you kick her out?"

"I feel sorry for her."

"Why? What's pitiful about her?"

"She was abused. She hasn't got any friends."

"Why hasn't she got any friends?"

"She treats everyone like shit."

"Including you, you said. How does it help you to have a roommate who is abusive towards you?"

"It doesn't."

"It must in some way, otherwise she wouldn't be there. What would happen if she moved out?"

"I'd get some peace and quiet, finally."

"And after a week of peace and quiet, how would you feel?"

"Lonely."

"And if the loneliness got too intense for too long, what would you do?"

"Cut."

"So that's it. You keep an abusive roommate in your apartment to prevent being lonely, which in turn prevents cutting. That's good. It proves you are working hard at taking better care of yourself."

"Yeah, but my life sucks."

"For that to change, you're going to have to work even harder. What would happen if you felt really, really lonely but didn't self-mutilate?"

"I'd have to drink."

"What if you didn't drink or act out in any other way? What if you just let yourself feel lonely?"

"I'd have to kill myself."

"What if you cancelled all forms of acting out and addiction, including suicide?"

"Then I'd have to come into the hospital."

"What if you didn't come into the hospital?"

"I'd die. It would be too much. I'd get lost in it. I don't know. It's just too much. There's too much pain. I can't stand it."

I switch into didactic mode.

"People do not die from feeling their feelings. In fact, the opposite is true. People die from the things they do in order not to feel their feelings. There is something important about feelings you need to know. They don't last forever. Look at anger. Is anyone ever rip-roaring angry every day for ten days in a row from the moment they wake up each day, full tilt angry? No. Does anyone ever bawl her head off every minute non-stop for days in a row? No. There is a natural curve to it. The feelings get real intense, they stay there for a while, then they ease off."

"You're telling me I wouldn't get lost. I could stand it. It wouldn't last forever?"

"Right. And don't forget how good you are at dissociating. You are highly skilled at stuffing your feelings. If they get too much, just stuff them again. Then take them out later and try again."

I am teaching the procedure of systematic desensitization.

"You hold onto the belief that you are bad because it gives you permission to treat yourself badly, or contract with someone else to treat you badly, which reminds you that you are bad. By being bad, you hold onto the illusion of power, control and mastery. Specifically, you can control your loneliness."

"Problem is, having an abusive roommate and feeling bad drives other people away. You end up more lonely than ever. It's very hard to be close to someone who hates herself, probably impossible. Your self-hatred is a shield that keeps other people out. It does so very effectively. This may keep you safe in a way, in that other people can't get close and can't hurt or disappoint you. But the price you pay is loneliness."

"So I have to be ready to take the risk of being vulnerable, is what you're saying?"

"You don't have to do anything. It's your choice. But if you don't want to be buried behind a wall of negativity, yeah, you have to reverse the locus of control shift, open up, and take a few risks. You also need to work on choosing better people to take risks with. Your roommate isn't on the list."

"So I have to take the risk."

"Yeah."

Another group member pipes up with, "You can do it, Heather. You've let some of us in here. I know you can do it."

"Thanks. But it's safe here. I don't know if I can do it out there."

To which I comment, "One step at a time. Practice in here, practice more in Day Hospital, and get used to it."

"I'll do that. Thanks, Dr. Ross."

"You're welcome. Good work."

Another woman asks, "Can I work next week?"

"You're on for Monday."

30

THE VICTIM-RESCUER-PERPETRATOR TRIANGLE

The problem of attachment to the perpetrator and the locus of control shift are the two major foundations of the treatment model. But there are several other schemes I use all the time. One is the victim-rescuer-perpetrator triangle, which is shown in Figure 30.1.

Figure 30.1. Victim - Rescuer - Perpetrator Triangle

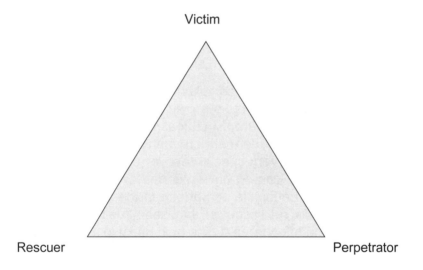

Victim

Rescuer   Perpetrator

In psychoanalytical terms, the triangle is one way to analyze the transference. I like the triangle vocabulary because it is tagged directly to observable behavior and fits in well with trauma. Whenever there has been trauma, there has been a victim, a rescuer and a perpetrator. This is true even if the trauma is a tornado. Then the perpetrator is God, at least in the mind of the magical child.

There is always a rescuer, even if it is only the Absent Rescuer. The Absent Rescuer is a recurrent figure in trauma therapy. In the mind of the magical child, one or both parents willfully failed to intervene and stop the abuse. Though the rescuer did not show up, a rescuer was still wished, hoped and longed for. This is true whether the abuse occurred inside or outside the family. There is always ambivalent attachment to the non-offending parent because that parent willfully adopted the role of the Absent Rescuer, not in objective reality but in the child's developmentally normal cognition.

The therapist is always under transference pressure to adopt a position on the triangle, including perpetrator, rescuer, absent rescuer and victim.

The tactical challenge to the therapist is to stay off the triangle, to maintain therapeutic neutrality. In family therapy, the therapist must be careful not to get drawn inside the family system. If you are inside the family system, you are part of the problem, and have lost your therapeutic leverage. Most commonly, in individual trauma therapy, the therapist's error is to adopt the rescuer position. Unless the problem is a simple technical mistake, such as all therapists make, in virtue of being human and fallible, there is likely to be a triangle dynamic at work. Often, the therapist has recruited the client into the therapist's re-enactment and undoing.

The rescuer therapist needs a compliant victim to rescue, not to help the client, but to undo the therapist's own past. By being the Present Rescuer for the client, the therapist undoes her own trauma caused by her own Absent Rescuer. There are too many ghosts in the therapist's office. In order to be a very special rescuer of a very special victim, it is necessary for the victim to have extreme symptoms and extreme memories. A regular pedophile perpetrator in the victim's past will not do. For the victim to be really special, it must be true that the perpetrator was a really extreme offender (e.g., the high priest in a Satanic cult).

The triangle dynamic is in place whether the extreme memories are accurate or inaccurate. Confabulated and accurate memories can serve the same dynamic functions. Whatever assumption the therapist makes about the accuracy of the memories, the same rescuer-perpetrator-victim triad is being re-enacted. It is the re-enactment in the present which is the target of treatment. The triangle dynamic is not a theory - the pattern is directly observable in present-day behavior and cognition.

With borderline clients (equals severe trauma clients) the triangle is unstable. There can be several triangles in operation at the same time. The client was a good, grateful compliant client, and the therapist was a much valued rescuer, until the Great Catastrophe struck. A call was not returned quickly enough, or a look was not empathic enough, and suddenly the therapist is a perpetrator, and the client is a victim of the therapist. This dynamic is referred to as splitting, denial and projective identification in the psychoanalytic literature.

Actually, the client is the perpetrator. She is projecting her anger into the therapist, which is an attack on the therapist. The therapist may experience the projected anger and act it out back on the client. The therapist is hurt and wounded by the false accusation, when she has worked so hard and cared so much. She tries to persuade the client that she in fact cares a great deal. The client doesn't buy it and demands more extravagant proofs of good intentions. The boundaries loosen and the hugs start to get very special.

The number of sessions starts to increase. There are more phone calls and more crises. The therapist has to go over to the client's home one evening because no-one else is available, no-one else really understands, and no-one else feels safe to the client. The therapist starts to share her own trauma history with the client in order to persuade the client that she really understands and really cares.

Once the therapy dyad has escalated to this degree of specialness, special rules and exceptions are required. Other colleagues might not understand all these special rules, but that just proves how special the therapy has become. It is all right for the hugs to become erotic. The therapist's hands begin to wander, and the client begins to feel really good and special. Now the incest secret has been re-created in the therapy, and the therapy is no longer therapy. The therapy has become a traumatic re-enactment, and a cause of pain, complications and medico-legal damages.

Plaintiff's lawyers and their expert witnesses usually focus on what they conclude are false memories in such cases. From my perspective, the memories, "true" or "false," are a minor component of the overall problem. The damages I attribute to the memories in such cases are only one element of the overall damages, and not even the most important one. Much more harm is caused by the boundary violations, the deviations from therapeutic neutrality, the sexual misconduct, and the betrayal trauma. In every serious malpractice case I have seen, there have been numerous different types of boundary problems, and major trouble in the victim-rescuer-perpetrator triangle. When these types of problems are absent, usually there has been no serious malpractice, and any memories alleged to be false have not caused significant damages.

For example, hostile confrontation sessions with falsely accused fathers require triangle errors by the therapist. Why? Because even if the accusations are accurate, therapist hostility and identification with the victim are countertransference errors. Destructive confrontation sessions with accused perpetrators are harmful to all parties even when the accusation is historically accurate. The therapist is always on the triangle and always stuck in a re-enactment.

Sometimes I call the geometrical structure under scrutiny the victim-perpetrator- mental health professional triangle. No-one would become a mental health professional without rescuer tendencies. Rescuing, however, is not a bad thing in and of itself – we don't criticize the Coast Guard for rescuing sailors. It is always a matter of balance and moderation, if I remember my Aristotle accurately.

I see serious triangle errors on a routine basis in the therapies conducted in North America. A number of times, during cognitive therapy group, a patient has described victimization by a prior therapist, and I have asked everyone in the group who considers herself to be a victim of previous professional misconduct by a therapist to put up his or her hand. Usually at least one third of the people in the group raise a hand. Sexual victimization by a prior therapist is a common part of the trauma history among Trauma Program patients. As a group, they are particularly vulnerable to such victimization because of their poor boundaries, locus of control shift, and unresolved ambivalent attachment to the perpetrator. All of these are set up for re-enactment and exploitation.

The conversation in cognitive therapy group might go like this:

A woman in her late twenties raises her hand and says, "I'd like to work."

"OK, Susan, what would you like to work on?"

"Memories."

"You mean memories of past trauma, or what?"

"Yeah, cult abuse. I grew up in a cult."

"Uh huh. What trouble are these memories causing you in the present? Remember, in this group we don't get into any graphic details that would trigger other people."

"I can't sleep. Can't study for school. I can't stand it when my partner touches me."

"Is your partner male or female?"

"Female. Does it make a difference?"

"No, I just wanted to get the facts straight. What are you studying in school?"

"I'm working on my Master's in Social Work. I want to work with abused teenagers."

At this point, I sigh to myself. I hope Susan resolves her trauma before she enters the workplace. I predict that she is planning to work with abused teenagers in order to get into the rescuer position and undo her own trauma. From this it follows that she is likely in the victim position in her current therapy, with her referring therapist acting as the Present Rescuer. As well, I note, the woman is in the active phase of PTSD with ritual abuse content. That information alone tells me to look for a rescuer therapist who has violated therapeutic neutrality and adopted a rescuer position on the triangle.

"I always tell people to be sure they have resolved their own trauma before they begin work as a mental health professional. You should keep that in mind. How long have you been in therapy with your current therapist at home?"

"Five years."

This tells me that one of two things is going on, or both at the same time. Either the client is very low trajectory and treatment resistant, or the therapist is reinforcing PTSD and dependency. I look for the enmeshed, rescuer therapist.

"And how many hours a week of therapy have you been getting?"

"You mean recently?"

"Yeah, recently, and average over the last year. How many hours a week?"

"About six. Sometimes eight, not counting phone calls."

"And how many phone calls are there per week, on average?"

"It depends on how I'm doing. Three or four."

I have never seen an example of a therapy with four or more hours a week of direct contact, on a sustained basis, which was not regressive and harmful. Once you get to six or eight hours a week, you always, without exception have an over-involved Rescuer Therapist and a regressed, dependent client. Without exception. A large number of hours can be fine on a short-term crisis basis, but once the pattern has been going on for a couple of months, there is always serious trouble.

"How long does the average phone call last?"

"About half an hour. Sometimes an hour."

"So if there are three or four phone calls a week averaging 30 – 60 minutes each, you are in the ballpark of two hours a week on the phone. How long are your therapy sessions?"

"An hour and a half."

"What are the rules in your therapy concerning physical contact between you and your therapist?"

"I don't want to talk about that."

"Why not?"

"Because you're going to say my therapist is bad."

"Actually, I wouldn't say that your therapist is bad as a person, bad to the core. I might conclude that some of her practices are bad practices, but that wouldn't mean I was condemning her all cross the board as a person. Remember about black and white thinking?"

"Yeah," the client answers, wishing she hadn't gotten into the conversation.

"What physical contact is going on that you are worried will make me think badly about your therapist?"

"Hugs and stuff."

"Hugs and stuff. There are two kinds of hugs. There are A-frame hugs which are asexual and OK. Then there are more intimate hugs with full body contact. Which kind does your therapist do?"

"The second kind."

"How long do the hugs last?"

"Sometimes a couple of minutes."

"How do you feel while the hug is going on?"

"Good. I feel she really cares about me."

"Any other feelings?"

"Dirty."

"Dirty. Why?"

"Because I feel sexual. It makes me feel dirty."

"Does your therapist know you feel this way?"

"No. I couldn't tell her."

"Why not?"

"Because she might stop seeing me."

"Your therapist might stop seeing you if she knows how you feel?"

"Yeah. I think she'd be embarrassed."

The client is taking care of the therapist, but feels bad and dirty about it. The odds are very high that she shifted the locus of control in childhood and felt dirty while sexually servicing one or both of her parents. The therapy is not therapy, it is re-enactment. This is true no matter how much distortion there is in the woman's account. If the trauma dynamic has not been re-created by objective behavior on the therapist's part, it certainly is active in the client's mind. The objective reality will be pursued by a Trauma Program therapist in a subsequent phone call, and the woman's case will be brought up by me at the next team meeting.

I ask, "Have the hugs ever involved your therapist putting her hands on your buttocks, breasts or genital area?"

The client puts her face in her hands, starts crying, and answers, "I know you think I'm dirty."

I respond, "Actually, that's not true. It's you who thinks you're dirty, not me. Remember about the locus of control shift? If what you are describing is an accurate account, then your therapist is having serious boundary problems. But you didn't answer my question. Has your therapist ever touched you on your buttocks, breasts or genital area?"

"Yes. Is that what you want to hear?"

"This isn't about what I want to hear. It's about what is actually going on. Can you tell me?"

"She came over to my house and had sex with me."

"When did that happen?"

"Two weeks ago."

"Has it happened before?"

"Yes."

"How many times?"

"Maybe ten, fifteen times."

"Has it involved both of you having your clothes off?"

"Yes."

"OK. I want to tell you something. I don't know objectively what is actually going on with you and your therapist. But I have no reason to disbelieve you. What you are describing is very serious. It is professional misconduct and in Texas we have mandatory reporting. But I would report your therapist to her Board even if it wasn't mandatory."

"When a therapist is having sexual contact with a client, it is always the therapist's fault and the therapist's responsibility. It doesn't matter if you participated willingly. Even if you took off all your clothes in your therapist's office and offered her sex, it would be her responsibility not to touch you. There are no exceptions. The professional has total responsibility. And such contact is never helpful. It is always harmful."

"But it makes me feel special."

"That's part of the harm. Feeling special because you are being sexually victimized by your therapist puts you right back in the position you were in in childhood. The therapy has become a re-enactment of the incest situation."

I already know that Susan has described childhood incest repeatedly in her therapy, and while in the Trauma Program.

"But I don't have anybody else. If you report my therapist, I won't be able to see her anymore. I'll have to kill myself."

"That's not true. You might *choose* to kill yourself, but you won't *have* to do so. Other people have disconnected from abusive therapists, found new, healthy therapists and eventually done well. We will work with you to find a new therapist."

"I can't do it."

"Oh, oh, you've been reading that book again."

"What book?"

"The Little Engine Who Couldn't. The Little Engine said, 'I know I can't, I know I can't.' It became a self-fulfilling prophecy, and the engine didn't make it up the hill."

"So I have to be the Little Engine That Could?"

"You don't have to be anything. It's a choice, which only you can make for you. We encourage you to make a healthy choice, but it's up to you."

"I really like my therapist."

"I know you do. Just like you loved your parents. But your parents abused you, and you felt dirty, at the same time as you loved them. Both feelings were real and true. And that's what hurts so much, having both feelings at once. Your therapy has re-created this conflict, and you are blaming yourself just like you blamed yourself as a child. The thing is, you aren't a child. Today, you are grown up. You are big, you are strong, you almost have your Master's Degree, you have a supportive roommate, and you have the support of this Program. You can do something about the present situation with your therapist. You're not trapped in it, like you were as a child. Now things are different."

"I think I can, I think I can."

"Good!"

"My therapist isn't all bad. She has done a lot to help me."

"I agree. Nobody is saying she is all bad. Unless you are. Are you telling me that?"

"Part of me is."

"What about the other parts of you."

"I guess I can see it in a balanced way. I guess I can see the good and the bad at the same time."

"That's important, because if you can hold onto the good, you won't have to kill yourself. If what you describe is true, then you need to stop seeing your therapist. But that doesn't mean you will lose her completely. You can take the memory and the good work you've done with her forward into the future. That can be the foundation for further recovery. Getting well is the best 'Thank You' you can give your therapist, in thanks for the good things she has done for you."

I have just linked non-suicide to not losing the therapist. Recovery can be a love letter to the therapist, in part. At the same time, Susan has to really get it how she was betrayed by her therapist, and how much her therapist set her back. She will have to mourn the loss of the therapist she never actually had, which was a therapist with good boundaries.

The therapist has added more grief on top of what already existed, which was already almost more than Susan could bear.

I track all of this in the language of the victim-rescuer-perpetrator triangle. In later sessions, Susan's individual therapist in the Trauma Program might explicitly use triangle vocabulary to help her reverse the locus of control shift and acknowledge her ambivalent attachment to her referring therapist. The negative side of the ambivalence was demonstrated by her disclosure to me in cognitive therapy. Susan already knew, even if she couldn't quite admit it to herself, that something was seriously wrong. The shame and dirtiness she felt were evidence that there was a triangle problem.

Even if the sexual misconduct was confabulated, there is something seriously wrong in the therapy. The Trauma Program staff will need to get confirmation from the referring therapist about the number of hours per week of contact, the duration of therapy and other factual details. The referring therapist may or may not be advised of the client's allegations, depending on our clinical judgment, and Susan's ability to tolerate our doing that without serious self-harm. Reporting will occur immediately.

I have assumed in this example that I have prior knowledge of outside corroboration of Susan's childhood sexual abuse. Usually, such corroboration is not available, so the childhood allegations will be treated as allegations, not established fact. Fact or fiction, there is definitely ambivalent attachment to the parents. Susan is definitely in the victim role in her speech and behavior, and there are definitely a Rescuer and a Perpetrator at the two other points of her triangle.

31

RE-ENACTMENT AND UNDOING

Re-enactment and undoing are universal in trauma survivors with extensive comorbidity. Undoing is an ego defense mechanism in which the original trauma or conflict is "undone" through some present behavior. Commonly, the person was in the victim position in childhood, and now gets out of the victim position in adulthood by adopting the rescuer or perpetrator position. The problem with undoing, like any ego defense, is that it provides no long-term solution. Undoing is a band-aid and must be re-applied every day, year in and year out. The ego defenses are treadmills.

I learned about undoing in the mid-1980's from a woman who was working as a prostitute. She explained to me that now she had sex when she wanted to, and she got paid for it. She felt she had power and was in control. She saw her customers as objects. The prostitution was in fact a symptom of unresolved trauma, and it exposed her to many risks including infection, rape and beatings

This woman had dissociative identity disorder. When I asked her whether her child alter personalities participated in the prostitution she was horrified, and said that she kept them hidden in order to protect them. This proved to me that the prostitution was traumatic to her as a whole person, and could be tolerated only with the defensive illusion that the vulnerable aspects of her were unaffected.

Every sexual offender I have talked to in my inpatient work has had dissociative disorder not otherwise specified. There are adult offender, child victim and adult non-offender ego states. The sexual acting out is usually an undoing of childhood victimization, which need not necessarily be sexual. The sexual acting out always serves the purpose of mood state regulation in the present, like any addiction.

One man grew up in a violent, chaotic home. Both parents drank heavily and they got into big fights with each other, with much yelling, hitting and throwing of objects. As a boy, he would escape to a tree fort. There, in solitude, he would smoke his mother's cigarettes, look at the nude pinups lining the wall of the fort, and masturbate. As an adult, his sexual addiction had destroyed several marriages, gotten him into legal trouble, and ruined him financially. Many of his sexual activities were highly ritualized and involved smoking a specific long, thin woman's cigarette, just like his mother's.

This man had many solitary sexual activities that consumed hours per day, including spending hours in sex chat rooms in the internet, while smoking and masturbating. I pointed out to him that all this behavior took him back to the fort, back to the cocoon of sexual arousal, safety, solitude, and connection with mother. He escaped back to the fort over and over, but just as in childhood, the solution was never permanent. Another bad, lonely, scary or conflicted feeling would come up, and off he went to the fort again. The addiction had also taken on a compulsive, autonomous quality, so that he did it independently of current context or problems.

Once the undoing function of the behavior is clear, it is addressed using the techniques described in other chapters. There is no specific treatment technique for undoing, other than educating the person about what is going on, and asking for a commitment to stop the undoing.

Re-enactment can take several forms, and can occur at several levels. It can be combined with undoing and reaction formation. Sometimes, especially in sexual compulsions, the original sexual abuse is re-enacted in great detail. The person may wear clothing similar or identical to that worn during childhood sexual victimization while engaged in adult sex, or may stage specific dramas during sex that are copies of childhood trauma scenes. The behavior can be highly ritualized and consistent from episode to episode, much like the obsessive-compulsive person who checks every lock three times before going to bed, or counts all jewelry in the house three times.

Re-enactment commonly occurs at the level of transactional patterns with other people. The person will go through the same sequence of steps in relationship to a battering spouse that she did with her physically abusive father. She may re-enact her childhood attempts to placate the perpetrator by trying to please, distract, or otherwise calm down her husband. The next day she may irritate her husband in an effort to provoke violent behavior.

I remember when I lived in the Canadian Arctic in the early 1970's, a woman had her jaw wired shut because her husband had broken it. When she returned from the hospital down south, one night she was at the local hotel, drunk, and annoying, irritating and provoking him unmercifully. You could see the man struggling to contain his irritation. Later, when drunk, he broke her jaw again. She got it wired again, but did not leave him.

Not uncommonly, the victim spouse in the re-enactment will deliberately provoke violence in order to get into the refractory period. In epilepsy, usually there is a refractory period after a seizure during which another seizure will not occur. The same is true in spousal abuse. The tension escalates, the abuser starts to look, move and talk in an escalating fashion, and anxiety mounts as the inevitability of another beating increases. The powerlessness of the victim spouse is undone by provoking the violence, getting it over with, and being at least partially in control of the cycle. The abusive spouse often behaves pleasantly during the refractory period.

Controlling the perpetrator by provoking him is an undoing of the powerlessness of the present. It is also a re-enactment of the undoing strategies of childhood.

Re-enactment can occur at the level of emotions. The person has an emotional reaction to a minor current event or stimulus which is far out of proportion to current reality. This is one of the DSM-IV-TR criteria for PTSD. There is no specific behavior and no undoing, but the person is re-enacting the feeling she had in the past, which has been provoked by the trigger in the present.

Flashbacks are a form of re-enactment. They can involve visual pictures, feelings, cognitions, sensations and behavior in all possible combinations. One could say that a purely emotional re-enactment is a flashback at the level of emotion. Usually, we think of re-enactment as behavioral because of the word *act*, but it can occur at all levels. The Vietnam Vet who is outside barbecuing hears a news helicopter fly by overhead. He dives under the hedge and starts hallucinating a combat scene. This is re-enactment simultaneously at all possible levels.

From the perspective of the trauma model, rage attacks, impulse control disorders, pathological timidity, and most of the Axis II personality disorder criteria are re-enactments in one way or another.

Re-enactment often gives the impression that the brain is stuck. There seems to be a neural network that has gotten stuck in a self-perpetuating feedback loop. But often, on inquiry, I will discover that the person is actively holding onto the traumatic scene, either as self-punishment, as a testimonial to the reality of the abuse, or as a core component of identity.

Many people believe that if they get well, it will mean the abuse never happened. Their sickness is their personal Vietnam Memorial.

One man told me in cognitive therapy group that without his anger he would be nothing. He had driven everyone in his life away with his constant anger, but he was able to state that he was a good father and loved his daughter, whom he could not see because of a restraining order. I pointed out that he had described many qualities of himself other than his anger, and said that if he continued to hold onto the false belief that he was nothing without his anger, then he would continue to turn his life into nothingness. I defined this as an anger addiction, explained the possibility of desensitization of his grief, and told him he had experienced more loss and tragedy in his life, than any other person in his mid-twenties I had ever met.

His answer was, "Nobody's going to take my anger away from me."

I agreed with him on this point. But I think he got what I was saying. Certainly, everyone else in the group did.

32

DEALING WITH EGO STATES: TALKING TO THE VOICES

Talking to the voices is a core intervention in the psychotherapy of dissociative schizophrenia. No matter what the diagnosis, whenever there are voices, there is the possibility of a therapeutic conversation with them. Talking to the voices may be the most radical contribution of the trauma model to general psychiatry. A paradigm shift must occur for voices to be patients. In conventional psychiatry, the patient is afflicted with voices, which are symptoms of brain disease, just like the symptoms of multiple sclerosis or stroke.

Within the trauma model, the therapist forms a treatment alliance with the voices. They too are the patient, and should not be chemically suppressed if they can be engaged in productive therapy. Even if a non-sedating antipsychotic medication is used, and the person does not appear "drugged," the voices have been chemically suppressed. It is perfectly acceptable to suppress the voices with medication if they cannot participate in therapy, but there will always be medication nonresponders, even when adequate trials of numerous classes of neuroleptic have been undertaken.

There are several different possible sequences for trials of psychotherapy and medication in schizophrenia and schizoaffective disorder. The first approach would be to treat all cases with medication and add psychotherapy only for nonresponders. This is the most conservative approach from the perspective of mainstream psychiatry. However, in principle, it assigns some people to chemical suppression of voices who could benefit from trauma therapy. Once the voices are suppressed, they are not available for therapy.

The alternative approach would be to institute a trial of trauma therapy in all cases and add medication to nonresponders. This sequence would cause prolonged symptoms among individuals who could not participate in therapy. The solution to the dilemma is to identify a profile which predicts both medication and therapy responsiveness. This, according to the trauma model, is the dissociative subtype of schizophrenia. Subjects with dissociative schizophrenia could receive therapy first, those with other subtypes could receive medication first, and nonresponders in both groups could then be crossed over to the opposite treatment.

Looking at the problem from a purely methodological perspective, the best design would be to randomize dissociative schizophrenia and non-dissociative schizophrenia subjects to both medication and therapy-first sequences. From an ethical perspective, however, this could be a questionable plan. The argument in favor of full randomization is the fact that hundreds of thousands of people with schizophrenia have been randomized to placebo in drug studies conducted around the world. The counter-argument to this argument is the possibility that talking to the voices might be harmful to people with schizophrenia, and not just an inert placebo intervention.

In response, one could assert that if talking to voices has the potential for harm, then, properly managed, it should have the potential for benefit. In the end, trials of psychotherapy for dissociative schizophrenia will be resisted for ideological reasons, and the arguments marshaled in favor of the resistance will not be balanced or dispassionate. I am in favor of such trials being conducted.

In the dissociative identity disorder literature, voices can assume executive control and can be engaged in conversation directly. When the voice is not in executive control, the therapeutic procedure is called *talking through*. Often, in dissociative identity disorder, a series of four or five questions to the voice not in executive control provokes a switch. This will happen in dissociative schizophrenia too, in the more clearly structured cases, but the conversation can be continued uninterrupted. It is not necessary to explicitly acknowledge the switch in executive control or to change the content of the questions in response.

A typical conversation with the voices might go as follows:

I would say, "Liz, I'd like to find out a little bit more about the voices you hear. How long have you been hearing them?"

"Since I was a kid."

"Did you first hear them before age ten, or between age ten and twenty?"

"I don't remember much before age ten, but my mom said I used to talk out loud to my voices when we lived in Seattle. We moved away from there when I was eleven."

"What would be the longest stretch of time you have gone without hearing voices since you were ten? By the way, how old are you now?"

"Thirty-four. There was quite a while in my early twenties when I didn't hear them."

"About how long?"

"Well, everything was pretty good after I got married. That was when I was twenty-one. Then when my husband got killed, the voices came back right away. That was when I was twenty-six."

"I'll come back to your husband's death in a bit, but I'd like to finish asking about the voices first."

"OK."

At this point, I predict that Liz re-activated the locus of control shift in response to her husband's death, in order to suppress her grief. I predict that the voices reinforced the locus of control shift by telling her that she was bad, that she never deserved a decent husband, and that he was killed by God in order to inflict punishment on her. I assume that she has been actively suicidal, in part, because if she died she would be reunited with her husband in heaven, where she would finally find permanent peace. At the same time, she is suicidal as a punishment for the crime of causing her husband's death. She is her own judge, jury and executioner. The only reason she has not actually killed herself is because she deserves lengthy pain, suffering, loss and loneliness on earth before she is allowed to escape into death.

The treatment of the auditory hallucinations, then, is fundamentally grief work. Liz has unresolved grief about her husband's death, layered on top of unresolved grief about her childhood. Her ambivalent attachment to her parents is re-enacted in her ambivalent attachment to her husband: she wants to be with him in heaven, but will not allow herself to die because she does not deserve the idealized reunion. She is with her idealized husband all the time in her imagination, but might kill herself in order to consign herself to Hell, thereby causing eternal loss of the one good person in her life, the husband she caused to die through her malevolent hatred of him. His love for her threatened to reverse the locus of control shift, so he had to be killed off.

I make these predictions based on my experience with the several thousand people who have gone through my Trauma Program before Liz. At this point, though, I want more background information on the voices, so I steer away from the dynamics to the phenomenology. Later, I will engage the voices in therapy because they will express the forbidden half of Liz's ambivalence, which she has disavowed.

I ask, "The voices that you hear, do they seem like you talking to yourself, or do they seem like someone else talking?"

"Sometimes it's just me talking to myself, but other times it really isn't me. The voices say things I'm not even thinking about, and I can't make them stop."

"And are the voices out loud, or are they quiet, more like thoughts?"

"No, they're out loud, just like your voice. Sometimes, I hear their thoughts too, when they're just thinking. But I can tell the difference between thoughts and voices."

The two main dimensions of the initial mental status examination of voices are volume and how ego-alien the voices are. To be full voices, they must be out loud, and must be experienced as not coming from the self. The quieter the volume, the more the voices are like thoughts. The less ego-alien they are, the more one is dealing with normal inner monologue and dialogue. For talking through to work, the voices must be ego-alien and must have at least some increased volume above regular thinking. Otherwise, one is simply inquiring about the person's thoughts.

"OK. How many different voices are there? Is there one, or more than one?"

"There are three voices, an angry one that says bad things about me, a voice that's a little girl, and one that's nice. The nice one and the bad one get into arguments with each other."

According to DSM-IV-TR, Liz meets the symptom criteria for schizophrenia based on her description of her voices. However, the mental status examination of the voices has only just begun. I have not yet gathered enough information to make a triaging decision about psychotherapy versus medication. Liz is not currently manic.

"How long have you been hearing each of these three voices?"

"Since I was a kid."

"All three of them?"

"Yup."

"What percentage of the time, over the years, have you heard the voices?"

"Sometimes I don't hear them for a day or two, sometimes it's non-stop."

"Do you hear the voices more when you're really depressed, compared to when you're feeling OK?"

"No, about the same amount. But when I'm really depressed, I hear the angry voice a lot more, and it gets a lot more ugly. Sometimes when I'm really down, I don't hear the nice voice for weeks. That's usually when I take an overdose."

"What would you say is the longest period you've gone, since age eighteen, without being seriously depressed?"

"From the time I met my husband when I was eighteen until he died. I felt pretty good most of those years. I was down some, but never bad. I was never suicidal, I never lost weight or had trouble sleeping or anything. I slept great when I slept with my husband."

"I notice you always call him 'my husband.' What was his name?"

"I don't like to say his name. It was Jim."

"Does it make you sad when you say his name?"

"Yeah."

"Do any of the voices have an opinion about your saying his name?"

"Yeah, the angry voice tells me I don't have a right to say his name. He was too good for me."

"Is that true?"

"I don't know. Sometimes I think so. But I was good for him, too. We were good for each other."

"Would you mind if I asked the angry voice a question about Jim?"

"What do you mean?"

"I mean I would ask the voice a question, the angry voice; the voice would answer inside your head, and you would tell me the voice's answer."

"You can do that?"

"Sometimes it works. It's just another way to gather information."

"I thought I was crazy. Now my shrink is talking to my voices. Do you talk to garbage cans too, Dr. Ross?"

"Only if they talk to me first."

"You shouldn't let garbage cans control your life like that, Dr. Ross."

"Thanks for the advice, Liz. Can we get back to your voices?"

"Aren't we out of time?"

"Unfortunately, we're not."

"OK. I guess so. Go ahead then. This is kind of weird."

"Thanks. Angry voice, I'd like to ask you a couple of questions, if you don't mind. Like I explained, I'll ask you a question, you'll answer inside Liz's head, and Liz will tell me what you answered. The first question I have is, 'Angry voice, can you hear me?'"

Liz looks a little tranced out for a second, then says, "Yeah, he said he can hear you."

This reminds me that I forgot to ask whether the voices have genders, ages or names. I say, "Good. Angry voice, Liz referred to you as 'he.'

Do you feel that you are male?"

"He says he sure isn't a girl."

"And are you a certain age, or do you not have any particular age?"

"He didn't answer."

From this response I don't know whether he has an age but doesn't want to say, has no specific age, feels awkward for some reason, or what is going on. I say, in an effort to form a treatment alliance, "Voice, if you don't want to answer a certain question, feel free to say so. I'm not looking to nose in where I don't belong or cause any trouble."

"He says that's good."

"Voice, what is the relationship between you and Liz?"

"He says, 'What do you mean?'"

"I mean, where are you in relation to Liz?"

"I'm inside her head. Where do you think I am, in the garbage can?"

"I wasn't sure. That's why I asked."

"He says you should get your own shrink."

"I seem to be getting the same advice from both of you. That's one point you're agreed on, anyway. Which is good, that you agree on something."

"He said, 'Yeah, we're real pals.'"

"I'm interested in knowing what else you have in common. Liz was obviously in love with Jim. Voice, what did you think of Jim?"

"He was a jerk."

"Why do you say that?"

"He screwed around on her."

"He did. How do you know that?"

"He's a guy."

"I understand, but do you know for a fact that he was unfaithful to her, or do you conclude he must have been because he was a guy?"

"Why don't you ask her?"

"Good idea. Liz."

"Jim had an affair just after we were married. It only happened twice. He told me about it. We talked about it with our preacher. We went for counseling with our preacher for three or four months. I forgave him. Not right away. It was hard. It took time. I told him if he ever did that again, I would leave him."

"Did you in any way blame yourself for Jim's affair?"

"I was having trouble with sex, lots of flashbacks. But he took full responsibility."

Suddenly, Liz's voice deepens a bit and becomes more angry and assertive, and she says, "It was her fault. Her and her stupid flashbacks. I don't know why she doesn't get over it."

"Over what?" I ask.

"What her father did to her. The incest."

"How could you help her get over it?"

"It's not my problem."

"Yeah, but when Liz has the flashbacks, how do they affect you?"

"I just tell her she's a bitch and she deserved it."

"Well then, I'll change my question. How does calling her a bitch help you deal with the flashbacks?"

"I don't need any help."

"OK, thanks for clarifying that. What would happen to you, do you think, if she was having a flashback and you didn't say bad things about her?"

"Nothing. They don't bother me."

"That I understand. I'm thinking maybe, this is just a theory, I'm thinking that trash talking Liz helps to create a gap between you and her, helps push the flashbacks away and make them be not your business. It's just a theory."

Liz replies, in her usual voice, "He said that's enough for today. He's bored."

I respond, "OK. Good. Thanks for talking, angry voice. I'd be angry too, if I were you, and had to watch all the stuff Liz has gone through. I'm thinking that in some ways it's been a big help to her, having you on board. For one thing, it seems like you've held a lot of anger and other feelings for her."

"What do you mean?" Liz asks with a quizzical expression. "I was always told my voices were symptoms. Other doctors always wanted to get rid of them. I thought hearing voices meant you were psychotic?"

"Not necessarily, not psychotic in the sense of being crazy, disorganized and out of touch with reality. Tell me, is it true that you hear voices?"

"Yes."

"Do you believe the voices come from people outside you?"

"No."

"Martians?"

"Dr. Ross!"

"Communist agents that have infiltrated your mind through the drinking water?"

"I'm not that crazy."

"Would you accept that your voices could be different thoughts and feelings of your own that you're having a hard time accepting?"

"Could be."

"OK. Then when I'm talking to your voices, I'm just talking to feelings and thoughts you're having a hard time accepting. What's crazy about that?"

"Nothing, I guess. But it still feels weird."

"Sure it does, but after a while you get used to it. Then it becomes just another part of therapy. If it is true that your voices are your own thoughts and feelings, then they need to be listened to and respected, like any other thoughts and feelings."

"That makes sense."

This is typical of how such therapy sessions go. From this point, I could branch off in a number of different directions. I decide to pick up where I digressed earlier, and gather more history. I decide to refer to her husband as 'Jim,' to make him more real, thereby bringing her closer to her unresolved grief, and in order to begin desensitizing her to this specific traumatic trigger, her deceased husband's name.

"How did Jim die?"

" A car wreck."

"Was he driving?"

"Yeah, he was alone in the car."

"Was there another car involved?"

"No. It was a single car accident."

"How did it happen?"

"He was out at the bar with his friends. It was raining. He spun out on a curve and hit a tree.
He was doing eighty."

"What was his blood alcohol?"

"It was just under the legal limit."

"I'm sorry that happened to you. And to him. Did you cry at the funeral?"

"No. I was strong. His mother fell apart, but I was strong."

"You were strong. So only weaklings cry at funerals, when a loved one is being buried?"

"Well, no."

"But you said you didn't cry because you were strong."

"I *was* strong."

"I know you were. You were very strong. You just weren't strong enough to cry."

"Strong enough to cry?"

"Yeah, it takes a lot of strength and courage to cry. To really feel the loss and the grief, and not to bury it. That takes real guts."

"Are you serious?"

"One hundred per cent. Maybe that little girl voice inside has been crying for you. Maybe she's the strong one."

"But I've had her since way before I met Jim."

"Maybe you've had a lot to cry about in your life."

"I was never allowed to cry in my family."

"What would happen if you did cry?"

"I never did."

"But how did you learn it was important not to cry?"

"My older sister got hit for crying. I decided never to be dumb like her."

"So it's both weak and dumb to cry?"

"In my family it was."

"I see. Was your family healthy?"

"Are you kidding? My mom was depressed all the time. They both drank and fought all the time. My dad molested me and my sister and beat the hell out of us."

"So your family did not have healthy rules, then?"

"That's right."

"Then if you are following your family's rules today, you are choosing to live by unhealthy rules. I understand how you learned those rules as a kid. I'm talking about the rules you choose to live by as an adult. Your choosing to live by the rule, 'It's weak and dumb to cry,' is an expression of loyalty to your parents. You're still living within the unhealthy family rules, which means you haven't really left yet. I'm not talking about abandoning your parents, I'm just talking about growing up and moving out of the house, and having your own home and rules. It seems you did that with Jim, at least partly."

"You mean I can just decide to change the rules. It's that simple?"

"Yes and no. It's a simple decision, but it's hard to make and hard to follow through on. Maybe if you did decide to change the rules, your voices could help with that. It seems like your little girl voice lives by the rule, 'It's OK to cry.' Maybe you could learn how to cry from her."

"But she never stops. I don't want to be like her, crying and sniveling all the time."

"Sniveling is not a very kind way to talk about a little girl who's in a lot of pain, and who has suffered a lot of loss."

"Sorry."

"Don't tell me. Tell her."

"I'm sorry I've been mean to you."

I ask, "What did she say?"

"She said she loves me."

"You're lucky to have her, then. It's hard to get too much love in life."

"That's true."

"If you did some of the crying for her, I bet she wouldn't have to cry all the time. Also, if you took better care of her, she might not be so sad. You could help her not to cry so much. It would be a two-way street."

"The nice voice said you're pretty smart, Dr. Ross."

"I wouldn't even consider questioning that voice's judgment."

"Thanks, Dr. Ross. I'm ready to stop now."

"OK. That was first class work, for someone who's crazy and hears voices."

"The angry voice says he's not crazy."

"He's right. I was just kidding. Sorry if the joke was in bad taste, angry voice."

"He says you're forgiven. He says if you can help stop the little girl from crying all the time, he's on your side."

"Deal. Actually, it won't be me, it'll be you. By the way, did you notice that the angry voice has other feelings and attitudes besides anger?"

"I never realized that before. I guess you're right. Can I stop now?"

"Sure. Anybody with a comment or feedback?"

Several other members of the group now provide feedback about the benefits they've received from making friends with their voices, and how difficult it was to do so at first.

This is typical of how such sessions go. Talking through to the voices requires desensitization on the part of the therapist. It goes against standard training and provokes angry statements by the therapist's internalized critical peers. Once the 'boggle barrier' has been overcome, however, no new techniques are required. One does conventional therapy focused on the cognitive errors, or defenses and conflicts, depending on one's preferred school of thought. Talking to the voices can be done within any model of therapy, once ideological resistance to the procedure is overcome.

Voices which can be engaged in rational and productive conversation are a diagnostic criterion for dissociative schizophrenia.

33

OTHER SPECIFIC TECHNIQUES

There are a number of other specific techniques I use on a regular basis. Since 1991, I have been running a specialty inpatient and day hospital program in Dallas. The initial name of the program was the Dissociative Disorders Unit. It is currently called The Trauma Program. The reason for the name change was the broadening of the clinical model to include borderline personality disorder, posttraumatic stress disorder, depression and many other forms of trauma comorbidity. I am ready for another name change.

Trauma psychiatry is really general adult psychiatry. Clinically and conceptually, I am ready to drop the specialty name of my program altogether. What I would really like to do is call my program, The Ross Institute (www.rossinst.com), and not specify any specialty function of the program. This step doesn't involve any further refinement of the trauma model; it is a financial and business problem only. I have to figure out how to make The Ross Institute, as a program name, work from a financial, contractual and business perspective. The techniques I describe in this chapter are suitable for general adult psychiatry, which, according to the trauma model, is the same thing as trauma psychiatry.

The What If Cascade

In medical school I learned about biochemical cascades. For example, the amino acid, tyrosine, is converted into dopa by the enzyme tyrosine hydroxylase. Dopa is in turn converted into dopamine by the enzyme dopa decarboxylase. In the next step, dopamine is converted into noradrenalin by dopamine beta-hydroxylase. Finally, noradrenalin is converted to adrenalin by phenylethanolamine N-methyltransferase. This is a biochemical cascade. It is a step-by-step process.

I frequently ask a series of questions designed to take the patient through a cognitive cascade, which I call *the what if cascade*, because each step involves a "what if" question. The purpose of the cascade is to get around the defenses and cognitive errors to the core conflict or feelings that are being avoided, which always turn out to be unresolved ambivalent attachment and grief.

A typical what if cascade looks like this:

I ask, "What would you like to work on today?"

The thirty-six year old woman who has volunteered, Janice, says, "I want to stop cutting."

I reply, "Good. Why don't you just stop?"

Janice looks puzzled and a bit astonished, and says, "What do you mean, just stop?"

"I mean, hypothetically speaking, let's say you just stopped cutting, what would happen?"

"Well, them I'd have to start drinking again."

"What if you didn't drink either?"

"Then I'd cut."

"But what if you didn't cut or drink, or act out in any other way?"

"Then I'd have to kill myself."

At this point, Janice has confirmed that she is a rational adult, operating in problem-solving mode, and dedicated to self-preservation and mood state management. Her acting out is designed to prevent her suicide. She is accepting the consequences of lesser evils, her acting out, in order to prevent a greater evil, suicide. My task is first to find out why she would have to kill herself, then to help her create a viable plan for not acting out and not having to die.

I ask, "What if you didn't act out and didn't kill yourself? What would happen?"

"I'd go crazy."

"What if you decided not to go crazy?"

"I couldn't help it."

"Yes you could. Going crazy would be another form of acting out. What if you didn't act out in any way at all?"

"Then I'd get lost in the feelings?"

"What feelings?"

"Loneliness, sadness, it's just too big."

"What would happen if you just stayed in the feelings, and didn't get lost?"

"I'd explode."

"Hmm. Do you mind if I get a video camera? I'd like to get this on tape, a person actually exploding into pieces from feeling her feelings. How many pieces do you think there would be?"

"Well, I wouldn't really explode."

"What would actually happen, if you just sat with the feelings, and didn't get lost, didn't explode, didn't act out in any way?"

"It would last forever. I couldn't stand it."

"If it was actually true that the feelings would last at peak intensity forever, that would in fact be intolerable. You are smart to avoid that. The thing is, that's not how feelings work. Take laughter. How many people wake up in the morning laughing uproariously, and laugh full tilt all day, then go to sleep, get up and laugh non-stop another day, and do so day after day without stopping?"

"None."

"What about anger? How many people are full tilt angry every second of every day, days on end?"

"I see what you mean. It wouldn't last forever."

"Right. That's the way it is with feelings, they come on, they reach peak intensity, they stay at peak intensity for a while, then they ease off. Don't forget how good you are at dissociation and avoidance. You are a highly skilled expert at avoidance. Stay with the feelings a while, then when you've had enough, do something else. Distract yourself, call a friend, watch TV, go out for a walk, whatever. You already have a long list of strategies. Or just zone out for a while."

"You mean I could just sit with the feelings?"

"Yeah, why not?"

"I thought they would last forever and I couldn't stand it. Thanks"

"You're welcome. It turns out you aren't a helpless victim of your own feelings after all, which is good."

The what if cascade always involves several steps. It follows the principle that the problem is not the problem. First comes the primary form of acting out, which may be self-mutilation, substance abuse, psychological dissociation, vomiting, internet sex, or any of countless behaviors. In the hypothetical, one says no to the drug of choice. Then come several steps in which alternative addictions are mobilized. Once these are canceled, the person is left with her feelings.

The next step in the cascade is to block suicide and stay with the feelings. At this point a classical cognitive error of catastrophization will be encountered. This is rebutted with education and explanation and a desensitization hierarchy is constructed. Scores on scales of hopelessness, depression and suicidal ideation drop and a constructive plan is formulated.

I use the what if cascade all the time. Often the first step in the cascade is to ask what would happen if the locus of control shift was reversed, not just intellectually but in the heart and soul as well.

Factitious And Iatrogenic Problems

In 1995, I formulated a testable scheme for differentiating childhood abuse, childhood neglect, factitious and iatrogenic pathways to dissociative identity disorder and dissociative disorder not otherwise specified (Ross, 1997). Although I have not done formal research to test the pathway predictions, they continue to fit with my clinical experience, with one exception. The more experience I accumulate, the more I am convinced that the modal case in my Trauma Programs is a mix of all four pathways in ratios that vary from case to case. Pure pathway cases are uncommon.

The more time goes by, the more I am convinced that treatment for cases judged to be predominantly iatrogenic or factitious does not differ much from cases judged to be due to trauma. This is so for several reasons. First, people with factitious disorders are never well individuals. In my experience, they always come from backgrounds of serious trauma and neglect. Factitious disorders are trauma disorders and require trauma therapy. They always involve profound damage to attachment systems. The factitious disorder is basically a pathological attachment strategy.

As well, the factitious disorder is always accompanied by extensive "legitimate" comorbidity, at least among psychiatric inpatients. The problem of attachment to the perpetrator and the locus of control shift are sure to be active, as is the victim-rescuer-perpetrator triangle. The doctor of the factitious patient is always unwittingly in the rescuer role, until the factitious disorder is diagnosed, then he flips into the perpetrator role, if he exhibits the counter-transference response sanctioned by modern medicine.

Pure iatrogenic trauma cases with extensive iatrogenic comorbidity are rare. I have seen only one or two relatively pure iatrogenic cases of dissociative identity disorder arising after the early 1990's. This is because of managed care, which has reduced inpatient lengths of stay below the threshold required for full thought reform and indoctrination into the new identity of DID. Restructuring of a person's identity and history into polyfragmented multiple personality with intrafamilial Satanic ritual abuse requires a lot of control and time. It can't be done in an hour a week of outpatient psychotherapy. If such a picture arises for the first time in a well-bounded outpatient therapy, it is highly likely to be factitious rather than iatrogenic.

More common are cases with considerable iatrogenic components. These people still fit the trauma model and require trauma therapy. Indeed, part of their trauma is their previous therapy, which has created more symptoms, dependency, regression and entrenchment in the victim role. In the year 2000, such a cases are still a regular part of the caseload in my Trauma Programs.

Confrontation

I heard quite a lot about confrontation during my residency training, but I never could grasp what it meant. Confrontation seemed to mean rudely pointing out to a person that you didn't like their behavior and were going to punish them for it. Or, alternatively, it seemed to mean psychoanalytical interpretation delivered in a more active and blunt manner than usual.

Mental health professionals would sometimes ask me, "Why don't you confront that behavior?"
The professionals, usually nurses, seemed to want me to get angry with the patient, to tell her off, throw her out, threaten her with consequences, or otherwise beat her up in some fashion. In these situations, the patient's behavior had usually been classified as "inappropriate" by the mental health professional.

In fact, trauma therapy as I do it is highly confrontational, but patients rarely feel confronted. It's all a question of delivery. In cognitive therapy group I analyze defenses and cognitive errors in an active fashion, and do so quickly. But I am not blaming or belittling the person. If the person feels attacked or blamed, I define this as a misinterpretation and explain what is really going on. Change is difficult and requires prodding. The point is to help the person live a happier, healthier life.

A typical confrontation might go as follows:

"You are holding onto the false belief that you are bad for a reason. How does it help you to believe you're bad?"

"I am bad."

"No you're not. That's a false belief you're holding onto because it helps you avoid something else."

This statement by me leads into a what if cascade.

Another example of a confrontation, this time with a woman in the Day Program, is:

"If you self-mutilate one more time, you will not be able to come back to the Program for six months. This is a choice. It is under your conscious control. I can't stop you from choosing to cut yourself again, but I can tell you what the consequences will be. They are non-negotiable."

"But I can't help it."

"You are telling yourself you can't help it in order to keep the option of cutting open. It isn't true that you can't help it. Cutting is not a symptom of a seizure disorder. It is a controlled, conscious action chosen from a range of options because it does its job effectively, which is to make your feelings go away."

"Until you make a serious commitment to not cutting, we can't work with you productively. Cutting drives people away, in treatment and in life. It's self-destructive to your skin and your relationships and your recovery. But it's up to you. If you think the risk of cutting is too high, then you need to be re-admitted briefly. If you go home and cut, you are out of the Program for six months."

Although the second confrontation has more of the "in your face" stereotype of confrontation, it is delivered in the same manner, and is based on the same principles as the rest of trauma therapy. I am not angry during such a confrontation. I am just stating the facts. The person has to decide what to do with those facts.

Paradox

There is endless paradox in trauma work. The core logical bind is loving the person who hurt you and being hurt by the person you loved, which is the problem of attachment to the perpetrator. Neurotransmitter systems are probably also stuck in feedback loops which have the logical structure of double binds, in the brains of highly comorbid patients. For instance, according to the serotonin tolerance hypothesis, self-soothing can be attained only through activation of pain and alarm systems.

The locus of control shift is a paradox: it is good to be bad, because only by being bad can I be in control, which is good, although I am bad precisely because I was in control in childhood, and caused my abuse, according to the logic of the magical child. In therapy in adulthood, it is good to reverse the locus of control shift and realize you are intrinsically good, because then you can feel all the bad feelings you have been avoiding.

Similarly, protection from perpetrators can be obtained by being fifty pounds underweight or two hundred pounds overweight. Alternatively, one can be normal weight and promiscuous to achieve the same goal, because then you always want, initiate, control and enjoy any sexual contact you have; in reality, the promiscuity is a trauma-driven compulsion which ensures you are a victim of ongoing self-imposed re-enactment.

On the other hand, a person can be underweight, obese or a normal weight for reasons which have nothing to do with trauma.

While in my psychiatry residency I became briefly enamored with the paradoxical interventions prescribed by some schools of family therapy. Mainly, I liked the logical structure of the interventions as sculptures in psychological space. I wasn't so interested in their clinical utility. The glow on paradoxical interventions dulled for me when I saw the unnecessary trickery in them. That element reminded me of the stance of psychoanalytical psychotherapists who did not share their insights with their patients because the patients weren't ready, weren't "prepared" yet. I prefer to be much more up front.

By far the most common paradoxical intervention I make is to adopt the stance of the impotent therapist, which is a powerful therapeutic stance. This is the basic stance of AA. Until the addict makes a serious commitment to recovery, I am impotent. I too am powerless over the addiction. This could be regarded as a clever paradoxical intervention. I prefer to look at it as a straight forward statement of the facts.

I also construct logic boxes for patients using the method of a Socratic dialogue. I set up a series of questions which will force them to a conclusion they are trying to avoid. A question about whether the addictive behavior is caused by a seizure disorder locks the patient into the response I am seeking. There is a humorous *reductio ad absurdum* inherent in the question. I take the patient's experience of the involuntary or irresistible nature of the symptom to its absurd extreme, namely that it is a symptom of epilepsy.

Since it is obviously absurd to claim that the alcohol consumption, cutting, burning, vomiting or other behavior is a symptom of epilepsy, the person is stuck with the admission that it is voluntary. If the behavior is voluntary, it is a conscious choice and a decision. If it is a conscious decision, the person can choose to stop the behavior. If they choose to continue the behavior, that is fine, but they are deciding against recovery, and are not committed to sobriety. This conclusion is unacceptable for self-esteem and peer-pressure reasons, so the person is locked into a serious attempt to stop the behavior.

None of these strategies are fool-proof, and I have heard a million out-clauses for each one. An example of such a line of questioning is:

"OK. So you are confused about whether what your father did was sexual abuse."

"Right. Was it?"

To which I reply, "Let's get clear on what we are talking about. You were sixteen years old, right?"

"You were asleep in your bed at 7:00 AM on your birthday, right?"

"You had told your father the previous night that you wanted a neck rub for your birthday, right?"

"Right."

"And according to your description, your dad came into your room, got into your bed under the sheets wearing only his boxers and started rubbing your neck, which woke you up, and you felt uncomfortable, right?"

"Right. But I thought maybe it was just me. All he was doing was giving me what I asked for."

"And you're also telling me that your dad molested you sexually including intercourse starting when you were ten, correct?"

"Right."

"OK. Let's assume your account is accurate. Let me ask you this. By the way, how old are you now?"

"Twenty-one."

"OK. What if your dad came into your roommate's bed at 6:00 AM and started rubbing her neck while she was asleep without her permission, wearing only his boxers?"

"That would be awful."

"And what if a guy you had dated a few times climbed in your bed in his boxers while you were asleep?"

"That wouldn't be right."

"Tell me, from your knowledge of males in their early twenties, how many males in their early twenties climb into the beds of sleeping twenty-one year old women wearing only their boxers, without having sex on their minds?"

"Well, none."

"Do you think sometimes those men are just being friendly?"

"No."

"Doing a good deed for the Boy Scouts?"

"No.

"Completing a homework assignment for a sociology class?"

"No."

At this point, most of the other group members are smiling but one has her face in her hands and is very upset. The upset woman has seen the absurdity of her own pleadings on behalf of her own perpetrator.

"But you are telling me that your dad getting into your bed in his boxers without your permission while you are asleep at age sixteen could be normal dad behavior and have no sexual motive?"

"I don't know. I don't think he meant to hurt me?"

"OK. Was your dad a pedophile?"

"I don't like that word."

"I know, it's an ugly word, but according to what you have told me, your dad was a pedophile. Do you think sometimes pedophiles are being kind to the children they molest?"

"No."

"Is it sometimes OK to molest little girls if you're nice about it?"

"No."

"Do you think people sometimes drop children out of airplanes to help them?"

"No."

"Shoot them with machine guns?"

"No."

"Molest them sexually?"

"No."

"But your dad might have been molesting you in order to be nice to you?"

"But I thought I wanted it. I did at the time."

"So if you wanted attention from your dad, that made it OK for him to molest you?"

"No."

"So what are you confused about, then? Your dad was a pedophile who sexually molested you. He did big things like intercourse and smaller things like getting into bed in his boxers and rubbing your neck. It's all part of a pattern of sexual abuse. It's like the battered spouse. Sometimes she gets one whack on the head, sometimes she gets a broken rib. That doesn't mean the whack on the head is OK or no big deal."

"But I don't think he meant to hurt me."

"Oh. What was his IQ?"

"He was very bright. He was a Professor."

"So we can rule out stupidity as an explanation for why he didn't realize he was hurting you. Was he so delirious and out of it that he couldn't tell right from wrong?"

"No. He was the Chairman if his Department."

"OK, we can rule out being out of it. What other explanation is left besides just being mean?"

"He had to know somewhere inside himself that it was wrong."

"Right. You just answered your own question. Did he ever stand up in church and say, 'I'm molesting my daughter. Praise the Lord'?"

"No."

"Why? Why did he keep it a secret? If he didn't realize it was wrong and didn't realize he was hurting you, why would he have to keep it a secret? Are you telling me that he never read newspapers, never watched TV, never knew that incest is wrong?"

"No, he had to have known that."

"OK. So what are you confused about?"

"I loved him."

"That's the problem. You are hiding in confusion about how to classify his behavior in order to avoid the conflict. To avoid feeling the love and the anger at the same time, about the same person. It is crystal clear, beyond a shadow of a doubt, that getting into bed with your sleeping sixteen year-old daughter in your boxers and starting to rub her neck is not good parenting."

As always, we are back to the problem of attachment to the perpetrator and the locus of control shift. The purpose of paradox is to get there.

Humor

I joke around a lot in therapy. I do so to take care of myself, and to provide comic relief from the tragedy. Humor helps form a treatment alliance, disrupts negative transference, has an antidepressant effect and may even benefit the immune system. I have only told set jokes a few times.

For example, one day I started a group by asking, "There are two questions I would like an answer to before we continue. First, if the police arrest a mime, do they advise him that he has the right to remain silent? Second, if a person with multiple personalities threatens to commit suicide, is this considered a hostage situation?"

I was posing the questions to a group of twenty women, over half of whom had multiple personality disorder, and most of whom had been actively suicidal within the previous two weeks. They thought both questions were hilarious. Thank you, George Carlin. The questions lightened the mood and shattered a lot of transference distortions about me. We joked around for a minute then got down to work. One thing I really like about working with the worst of the worst of bad borderlines, is they get my sense of humor.

Art Therapy

In medical school and psychiatry residency I was taught that art therapy is "basket weaving", which was an insult to both basket weaving and art therapy. We send patients to art therapy, I was taught, to fill in time. No psychiatrist ever took art therapy seriously, went to an art therapy group, or had anything to say about patient artwork, with one exception. It was acceptable to make psychoanalytical comments about the phallic symbols in patient drawings. Such comments demonstrated the sagacity of the psychiatrist, but had zero impact on the treatment plan.

Art therapy is in fact a powerful treatment modality with trauma survivors. In my Trauma Programs we do not use art therapy for describing childhood events, "expressing feelings" or "surfacing memories." Any of those things may happen in art therapy, but they are incidental to its primary purpose.

Art therapy works with the magical child, who is alive and well in every patient in my Trauma Program, even if there is no dissociative disorder. There is always lots of magical thinking. It can be found in the locus of control shift, the behavior of running down the hall to get away from your feelings, the belief that you are safe because you are at home with your battering spouse, the countless attempts at undoing, and the magical belief that recovering memories will by itself make you better.

Art therapy is a tunnel through the defenses, resistance, avoidance and cognitive errors to the underlying conflicts and phobically avoided emotions. The problem is not the emotions themselves, it is the self-destructive gymnastics the patient uses to avoid them. The purpose of a magical exercise with colors, scissors and paper is to correct cognitive errors, and reverse hopelessness and powerlessness. The art therapy works because of the powerful imaginations and vivid inner worlds of the patients.

The inner absorption, fantasy-proneness and imaginative involvement of Trauma Program clients is a great asset. It is one of the core attributes that makes them treatable. But it is a two-edged sword. In a mis-managed therapy with poor boundaries, tons of "memory work" and lots of victim-rescuer dyadic enmeshment, the same qualities of mind can lead to extravagant false memories, regression, dependency and deterioration.

Suggestibility is not a bad thing. I am very glad that when I suggest to a borderline or dissociative client that her involuntary symptoms are in fact choices, she can absorb that suggestion and make it part of her reality. Dissociative identity disorder patients can use their talents to create false memories and get lost in an internal video game, or they can use them to unlearn the past and become well. Art therapy has an especially powerful ability to push the clients in either direction, depending on how it is done.

In 1992 in Dallas, I saw art therapy productions full of Satanic symbols, blood and gore, drawn by women with multiple personality disorder. I saw exactly the same content, style and colors in the artwork of a person diagnosed with schizophrenia on display at a conference in Norway in June, 2000. The "schizophrenic" drawing including a lot of black and red, upside down crosses, pentagrams, many faces and eyes looking out from many locations, and a scene of figures in black robes roasting a baby on a spit. The content does not always come from the therapist, but it can be massively reinforced by the therapist.

Good art therapy involves structured drawing exercises in which the core conflicts are depicted, discussed and restructured. A typical exercise would involve drawing both the self and a person who hurt you badly in your childhood. The self will be a small, helpless child and the perpetrator a big powerful adult. This leads into a discussion of the victim role, re-enactment and the realistic differences between past and present, which are absent in the drawing.

The exercise continues with the patient instructed to write down beside the picture of herself, everything about her that is similar to her perpetrator, and everything that is different. The purpose of the exercise is to tighten up boundaries and reduce the identity diffusion universal in Trauma Program clients. The activity also helps the client recognize her ambivalent attachment to and identification with the perpetrator. This recognition is the first step in resolving the conflict, rather than acting it out. As well, the smallness of the child and the immensity of the perpetrator lead into a discussion of how the client is re-enacting the victim-rescuer-perpetrator triangle in the present.

Art therapy is a separate modality within the Trauma Program, but it is integrated into the trauma model. The same basic work is done in art therapy that I do in my cognitive therapy group. The overall Program has more power because of the wide range of channels though which the basic information is delivered, which includes cognitive, didactic and experiential groups.

Anger Management

In the early 1990's, managed care reviewers sitting in their offices over a thousand miles away gave us a lot of grief over the telephone about anger management group, which they insisted was regressive. This objection had melted away by 1998. Anger management can indeed be highly regressive, and isolated video clips of Anger Management Group can make it look ridiculous. In fact, the group may be our single most powerful intervention.

The patients throw balls of clay at a board. The board is painted with oil-based paint so that the balls of clay do not stick to it too hard, and can be pealed off and re-used. While one person is throwing clay, the other patients in the group watch, provide support and feedback, and process along in parallel, since they all both avoid and act out their anger. Several patients help retrieve the clay balls and give them back to the therapist, who rolls them into nice spheres again and hands them to the person who is throwing. The balls make a very hyper-alerting rifle crack sound when they hit the board.

The anger group has several components. First, in order not to be an arid, intellectualized discussion of skills for use outside the hospital, the anger must be up and running. Actually experiencing the anger is vital for three reasons. First, in order to do the work of desensitization, the phobic stimulus, in this case anger, must actually be present. Second, in order to really practice anger management skills in the structured environment of the group, the anger must be present. And third, it is always good to blow off steam.

By getting in touch with their anger, feeling it, expressing it, and not losing control or acting out, the patients correct a catastrophizing cognitive error. The anger phobia is based on the cognitive error that letting the anger out leads inevitably to enraged violent, out-of-control behavior. This lesson was learned many times over by observation of parents who either catastrophized about anger and avoided it or acted it out violently themselves. In either environment, there were severe consequences for any expression of anger by the child.

The patients are taught didactically that their anger is a biologically normal response to abuse and neglect, whether actual or perceived. The anger is normalized and de-pathologized. It is redefined as positive energy that can be channeled into healthy assertiveness. The patients are taught by example that anger is tolerable when they watch other patients do anger work, and they are taught in a powerful, concrete way that other people, especially the therapist authority figure, will not retaliate if the anger is expressed.

Additionally, while the anger is up and running, the person gets to practice modulating and reducing it back to baseline, which creates mastery and reverses hopelessness, and thereby reduces depression and suicidal ideation. Actually experiencing the anger has a direct benefit, because the angry energy is a powerful antidepressant, in the mind, and probably also in the brain. The anger turns off responses of flight, freeze and learned helplessness, and thereby fosters autonomy, independence and adult problem solving.

In an outpatient setting, throwing clay at a board is not feasible. The structure of the anger management has to be modified. There has to be more emphasis on the didactic and cognitive components of the work, and less on the experiential. However, this does not mean that no anger can be felt at all. An outpatient client can get angry without having to shout or throw things. The same principles apply, but the ascent through the desensitization hierarchy has to be slower and more cautious.

Anger management group is a powerful weapon against angry, destructive acting out, whether the target of the anger is self or others. It de-escalates the drives to both homicide and suicide.

As always, the flip side of the anger is the grief. We could re-title Anger Management Group, Covert Grief Group. The person who is grief-phobic, who is often an angry, entitled "borderline," is delighted to throw balls of clay while hurling expletives at her perpetrators.

When this person is almost at the point of rage, the therapist makes a simple statement, "Now say, 'I couldn't make you love me'."

This simple statement often brings forth a river of tears, instantaneously.

Anger management can teach a person how she uses anger to avoid grief in a concrete, compelling way unapproachable by any other method. The cognitive error that the client is not sad is refuted at a deep level, technically, at the level of schema, by the experiential lesson. General principles and theories are important, but we always learn most deeply by experience.

Couple and Family Therapy

We do quite a lot of couple therapy in the Trauma Programs and a little bit of family therapy. Our main problem is that most of the families live far away and cannot attend, plus they are often pretty dysfunctional, if not outright abusive. We do talk to parents and spouses long distance on the phone, and within a few years we will be able to video conferences conveniently with most people.

The purposes of couple and family therapy are generic and no different from conventional non-trauma work. The same systems and communications principles apply. The spouse is very often placed in both the rescuer and perpetrator roles, and not uncommonly the spouse has a childhood trauma history, which he or she is trying to undo by being a therapist for the identified patient. There are life cycle problems with aging parents, and not uncommonly there is reconciliation work required when false memories have been retracted.

Patients further along in their recovery, who are in their last hospitalization often are starting to outgrow friends and family members, and are ready to move on to healthier relationships. This growth provokes anxiety about entering the new life and guilt about abandoning the people left behind. One purpose of couple work is to help the spouse move to a higher level of health. Other purposes include support and education for the spouse, gathering of collateral history, and giving the spouse a heads up on substance abuse or other secret acting out. Sometimes we act on a duty to warn about threatened assault, homicide or suicide.

Family members may benefit from explanations about the usual course of recovery. For instance, three children were grateful to hear that the "progress" reported by their mother and therapist was real, even though it wasn't visible to them. In the initial stage of therapy, one expects symptom reduction and internal restructuring before the visible payoffs of recovery seen in the pre-integration phase have occurred. I advised the children that if they were still hearing about all the wonderful progress in three years, but seeing none of it outside therapy, then the conclusion that the progress was illusory would be overdue. Besides being factual and educational, the explanation set high expectations for the mother's work, which I thought she could meet.

I have learned over and over that trauma patients rise or sink to the level of expectations others have for them. This is true in treatment and at home. High expectations are helpful and humane. They are based on empathy, but they have a tough behavioral edge. I recommend them to all partners and family members, and to myself.

Confronting the Perpetrator

Confronting the perpetrator is a good plan if you want to get sued. It is also an effective way to break up families and provoke acting out by all family members. Otherwise, it doesn't have much to offer.

Underneath the plan to confront the perpetrator, always, is the magical hope for reconciliation. The problem is, an angry, accusatory confrontation reduces the likelihood of real reconciliation. It is actually an acting out device to seal over the unfulfilled hope, thereby reducing the grief and conflict.

Meetings with accused perpetrators must be based on therapeutic neutrality and must include education about the problem of attachment to the perpetrator, delivered during the meeting. Dispute about whether the "perpetrator" is accurately or falsely accused does not change the fact that ambivalent, conflicted attachment patterns are dominating the relationship between accuser and accused.

There is always a victim inside every perpetrator, so it is never true that one party has exclusive claim to victim status. I have never met a victim-patient who has not perpetrated against herself on numerous occasions, based on identification with the aggressor. Black-and-white role definitions and battle lines are based on cognitive errors and are a form of acting out, whether they occur on television, in the professional literature, or in a therapy session.

There must be a clear goal whenever an accused perpetrator is brought into a session. The goal must be stated at the beginning of the session, and the first task is to negotiate the goals of the session. The "victim" will usually have at least some unrealistic goals, and will often be pumping the victim role for secondary gain. When the accused perpetrator denies the allegations, there may be a fight to see who has the right to victim status. The accused perpetrator's therapist may be aligned with the victim status of his client, and may be present as a ghost even if he is not physically present.

My opening assumption in such sessions, which I state out loud, is based on the fact that both parties are physically present. Both want something. Both are invested enough in the future of the relationship to arrive at the session. The goal is to define and negotiate what kind of a relationship is mutually feasible in the future, which could range from estrangement to reconciliation. There are many points on this continuum, not simply two black-and-white options, one at each extreme.

Medication

There isn't much to say about medication as a component of trauma therapy. There is zero scientific literature on the psychopharmacology of the complex, comorbid patient, if we limit ourselves to randomized, prospective, placebo controlled, double blind studies. Everything is based on anecdote or inference from the drug literature on simple, clean cases.

Generally, most trauma patients are on a selective serotonin reuptake inhibitor, which often seems to be very helpful for depression, obsessive-compulsive, panic, bulimia, PTSD and other symptoms. Many are on a benzodiazepine, which though helpful, carries the risk of dependency and abuse. Anecdotally, the novel neuroleptics seem to help a subgroup of patients. The anticonvulsants have not impressed me so far, mainly because the target symptoms are so polymorphous and there are usually many other psychotropic medications prescribed concurrently.

Overall, trying to reach scientific conclusions about the psychopharmacology of the complex, comorbid patient is impossible. Until this problem is taken seriously by drug companies, and until hundreds of millions of dollars are invested in it, we are doomed to anecdotal prescribing practices. Such prescribing is within the standard of care given the present state of the art. The principles of psychopharmacology are available in the mainstream psychiatric literature.

Hypnosis

I don't do hypnosis. In reality, hypnosis is a highly useful and interesting treatment modality with a large supporting scientific literature. But reality doesn't count for much in the courtroom. Psychiatric expert witnesses for plaintiffs in malpractice cases produce a tidal wave of unscientific propaganda against hypnosis. The cost of countering this propaganda is tens or hundreds of thousands of dollars in expert witness and lawyer fees, and even then one must overcome the jury's difficulty believing that so many "authorities" on the plaintiff's side could be simply propaganda merchants.

These financial and legal conditions make formal inductions of hypnosis way too high a medico-legal liability for me. I just don't do hypnosis, or guided imagery, or dream interpretation, or sodium amytal interviews, or "memory work," and haven't since 1992.

Fortunately, I don't need any of those modalities. There is nothing that I want to accomplish in trauma therapy that requires hypnosis, or even quasi-hypnotic procedures like guided imagery. Since I don't use hypnosis, there is no reason for me to write about it in this book.

This does not mean that I am against hypnosis. I believe that use of hypnosis with complex, comorbid patients can be within the standard of care. I fully endorse experimental research on hypnosis, and it is clear to me that, loosely defined, hypnotic trance is an element of countless activities in cultures all around the world. A flurry of malpractice lawsuits in North America for a decade or two is not going to remove hypnotic trance from human history.

Hospitalization

Since I manage hospital-based Trauma Programs, I can't be against hospitalization. But in a way, I am. Mental hospitals are not good places to be. It is much healthier to be in the outside world. The same is true of medical-surgical hospitals. They are very dangerous places, from an infectious disease perspective. Also, hospitals are negative energy vortices. What do you find in a hospital? Death, disease, dying, pus, blood, amputation of limbs, tragedy and loss. In mental hospitals, insanity, despair, self-mutilation, drug addiction, suicide and homicide.

The idea that you would go to a mental hospital to get healthy is preposterous. Stays in psychiatric hospitals should be few and far between and as short as possible. You should never go to a mental hospital unless you really need to be there. Which raises the question, what are the admission criteria to the Trauma Program?

The admission criteria to the Trauma Program are the same as those for general psychiatry. Trauma Program patients meet managed care acuity criteria, and over half the patients have managed insurance policies, the rest having medicare, with only a trickle of self-pay. To be a psychiatric inpatient you have to be acutely suicidal or homicidal, or else so disorganized you cannot take care of yourself. There are no "health spa" admissions anymore, which is a good thing. The biggest favor managed care has done is to eliminate long inpatient stays at psychiatric hospitals.

Patients are not admitted on an elective basis or simply to get more work done. The goal of every admission is discharge. The treatment model is short-term acute care stabilization. The average length of stay in the year 2000 is about 12 days, down from an average of 17 days in 1992. I would say two weeks is just about right for an average inpatient length of stay.

I recently reviewed a transcript of a telephone conversation between inpatient clinicians and an M.D. managed care reviewer that took place in 1993. I was most amused to note that the managed care definition of an admission for acute stabilization in 1993 was thirty days. Now, often, it is three days. Three days is absurd. No meaningful work or change can be accomplished in three days, except for the most straightforward acute crisis situation. Acute detoxification from alcohol or street drugs is possible in three days, but that's it. Psychiatric drugs don't start working for longer than three days.

The financial, documentation and length of stay pressures on inpatient psychiatry have gotten so extreme that major hospital systems are going out of business. There just isn't the money to do a decent job, or any job at all. Hospital-based Trauma Programs are held together with baling wire in North America in the year 2000, at great cost to staff. Staff burnout and turnover are extremely high. In this environment, I am amazed that I am still able to run three Trauma Programs. Amazed, and tired.

34

HOW NOT TO BE SUED

I'm not sure the figure is accurate, but I believe that at one time in Dade County, Florida annual malpractice premiums for neurosurgeons reached $135,000.00. The United States is an extremely litigious place. If someone slips and falls on your driveway, and sprains an ankle, they can probably collect $10,000.00 in a settlement if they are obnoxious and dishonest enough. This is called a *cost of defense settlement*.

The lawsuit industry in the United States serves several different social functions. First and foremost, it is a lottery system operated through the courts. Everyone knows they might get lucky someday, so everyone tolerates the inhumanity and perversity of the system. Second, lawsuits are used as a mechanism of social reform to a far greater degree in the United States than they are in Canada, or anywhere else in the world. Third, lawsuits are another form of interpersonal violence in an extremely violent society, another way to act out the anger of the populace. Fourth, they are a cash cow for lawyers. At the bottom of the list, lawsuits are a social mechanism for the fair compensation of true victims of misfortune or others' malevolence.

I moved from Canada to the United States because the move had a positive cost-benefit. The benefits of living in the United States have far outweighed the costs over the last nine years. This does not mean there have been no costs, however.

Getting sued is a cost of doing business as a trauma therapist in the United States. Anyone who hasn't been sued is just lucky, or doesn't deal with seriously disturbed, highly comorbid patients. It's just like practicing for thirty years and never having a patient commit suicide. All that proves is that you were lucky, that you had a small caseload, or that you dealt only with easy cases.

If you are sued, the first thing you have to forget about is justice. The next thing to eliminate from consideration is fairness. The third is objective reality. The purpose of a lawsuit is not to find out what really happened. The plaintiff's lawyer is a business person. It is all about business. The goal is to make money.

Your goal as a defendant is not to prove your innocence. Your goal is not to show the world that you are a good person and good therapist. Your goal is survival and survival only. The number one priority is to protect your personal assets. Unless you are guilty of major league malpractice, this can always be achieved through settlement. It is all a poker game run by businessmen.

The depositions, petitions, motions, expert opinions and other moves in the poker game are all designed to establish a range within which settlement negotiations will take place. The purpose of the insurance policy is to protect your personal assets. Except in the most extreme cases, the plaintiff's lawyer will always settle below your insurance cap.

Your job as a defendant is to co-operate with your lawyer to generate the smallest settlement possible. Only in the extremely frivolous lawsuit should you go to trial, and even then it's better to settle for ten, twenty or thirty thousand dollars, most of the time. You have to totally divorce your identity, self-esteem and personal feelings from your decision-making as a defendant. It's a business transaction.

This is hard to swallow as a defendant, but it's the truth. The insurance companies, the defendant's lawyers and the plaintiff's lawyers are all part of the same social system, the same micro-economy. Without lawsuits, the insurance companies would have nothing to insure, no clients and no income. Auto insurance companies couldn't survive without car accidents and litigious car occupants. The same is true for medical malpractice insurance companies. There have to be lawsuits for the industry wheels to keep turning. Lawsuits are not a bad thing for insurance companies, unless there are too many of them or a small number of awards are enormous.

The threat of an enormous award is also a good thing for the insurance company. The top guns get to come in, do their thing, and rescue the company from the big judgment. Big awards are the stick by which everyone measures their own performance at risk management. The big awards are big news, but they aren't actually what keeps the industry alive. The insurance company needs skilled lawyers with lots of experience in its panel, in case The Big One comes along. To maintain good lawyers in its panel it has to offer them cases and income. It is no good for the defense lawyers if the case settles too quickly, because they get paid by the hour.

The plaintiff's lawyer knows how this works and puts up with it. The jockeying back and forth has to do with two curves, one for the plaintiff's lawyer's costs, one for his recovery. His goal is to contain costs and maximize recovery. The defense lawyers are incentivized to increase costs and contain the plaintiff's recovery. But all parties are incentivized to keep the status quo in place, except the defendants themselves.

None of these facts mean that lawyers are bad people. The system is structured to reward certain behaviors by lawyers. The individual lawyer is just playing by the rules of the system, which he has not created and cannot control. If you are sued, you definitely want a skilled, experienced lawyer on your side.

If malpractice lawsuits were capped at actual material costs in terms of lost income and medical expenditures due to the malpractice, with nothing for pain and suffering and no punitive damages, insurance premiums would drop dramatically. The revenues of both the defense and plaintiff's lawyers would drop. Medical malpractice would become a boring area of the insurance industry to work in, and the best people would go elsewhere. The net revenue of the insurance company would drop.

As a defendant, you have to realize that you are a small actor in this large drama. The rules of the system are beyond your control. The most irritating aspect of the lawsuit is the testimony of the plaintiff's experts. You can expect it to contain lies, a great deal of stupidity, a lot of political sadism disguised as science, hypocrisy, and just plain evil. The jury will not be able to grasp that things are this bad in psychiatry, and will believe that all these experts must be at least partly right. They will testify with complete confidence and authority even when they are completely wrong.

It just isn't worth it putting yourself through the mill. Those things said, what steps can a trauma therapist take to prevent being sued? The only way to guarantee you will not be sued is not to practice. Otherwise, you are at risk and the risk is above negligible. In industry parlance, it boils down to risk management.

Fortunately there is nothing arcane about the procedures for lawsuit risk reduction, given that you are treating trauma model patients. Basically, you just have to practice ethical, sensible psychiatry, psychology, social work, or whatever discipline applies in your case. The things to do and not do are:

- Do not have sex with your client
- Do not have a personal relationship with your client outside therapy
- Do not adopt the rescuer position
- Keep good boundaries
- Maintain confidentiality
- Obtain informed consent
- Keep thorough records – consciously make notes on a regular basis that will protect you in a law suit
- Maintain therapeutic neutrality, especially for memory content
- Follow the principles and procedures of trauma therapy
- Obtain written consultation if necessary
- Stay current with the literature
- Obtain supervision if necessary

It is pretty hard to have a big lawsuit if there has been no sexual misconduct, no suicide and no hospitalizations.   Even a few short hospitalizations are not enough.   The reduction in inpatient lengths of stay imposed by managed care is the main reason why the major false memory lawsuits of the early 1990's have disappeared.   There just isn't enough for plaintiff's lawyers to sink their teeth into.

The more thorough, detailed and sensible your treatment records, the better. Skimpy notes are not a good defense, because you will not be able to rebut the plaintiff's experts' allegations effectively, which they will make with great certainty in the absence of an adequate foundation. They will make their inflammatory allegations no matter what the facts are – you are in a better position to refute them, the more documentation you have.

Concerning boundaries, tighter is better.   This doesn't mean so tight that you are suffering from gluteal ischemia, but many trauma therapists have way too loose boundaries. I see this regularly in the therapies that lead to inpatient admission. I also see a lot of excellent work by highly competent therapists. But a lot of the time, it is an embarrassment to be in the mental health field.

If you are considering a dual relationship with a client in the form of a joint book, art exhibition, film or speaking project, or some similar activity, the best procedure involves a series of steps. The first priority must be the therapy. Next, the project should be discussed repeatedly in the therapy over a period of time, not launched into on an impetuous basis. Third, both parties should have the project reviewed by their own independent counsel. Then there should be an assessment of the client by an independent mental health professional. This party should be contracted with by the client's lawyer. The consultant should provide a written report to both parties and should give an opinion as to whether the project is in the client's best interest, and whether undue influence has been exerted by the therapist. The client should be in the late stage of therapy or finished therapy, although this is not absolutely necessary.

This procedure was recommended to me by a lawyer who worked for many years as counsel for a State Board of Medical Examiners. There is nothing in any of the ethical codes governing psychiatry which prohibits such joint ventures.

This doesn't mean that boundaries can be stretched infinitely. In my opinion, once you have provided trauma therapy with someone for a prolonged period, he or she should never become your sexual partner. In theory, you could surrender your license and leave the profession prior to entering into a sexual relationship, and could follow a procedure such as I outlined above prior to the relationship, but in practical reality, therapists never do that. Even if you followed such a procedure, your client-sexual partner could later argue in favor of the statute of limitations being tolled on the grounds of coercive persuasion by you, and plaintiff's experts for the case would not be hard to find. Plus, the relationship is highly unlikely to be healthy in the long-term.

I have had a number of patients appear in documentaries in which I also appeared. I have obtained written informed consent in each case. A doctor and patient appearing in the same production is a common occurrence in all branches of medicine, and can be seen on cable television frequently, if not nightly. This, however, is not a joint business venture, so does not require the review procedure I outlined above.

Minor deviations from the usual therapeutic procedures are fine, such as planned therapeutic outings. However, they should have a clear purpose and should be documented as such. They carry a risk of engendering special status in the client's mind, which generates a later risk of revenge through Board Complaints or lawsuits when the special status fails to escalate, or fails to be permanent.

A thorough discussion of the legal and ethical dilemmas in trauma therapy can be found in the Fall-Winter 1999 issue of *The Journal of*

Psychiatry and the Law (Brown and Scheflin, 1999) and in *Memory, Trauma Treatment, And The Law* (Brown, Scheflin, and Hammond, 1998).

One of the negative consequences of the wave of lawsuits against trauma therapists in the 1990's, which has already peaked and declined, was the departure of grounded, sensible therapists from the field. From a risk analysis point of view, a substantial defense-oriented literature is available, cases have been won by the defense at trial, defense lawyers and experts are better educated and trained, Professional Association Guidelines and Position Statements are available, and there is a lot more scientific and clinical research on trauma available than there was ten years ago. Hopefully, therapists will not be as dissuaded from trauma work by the specter of lawsuits in the future as they have been in the past decade.

I have been involved in about fifty legal cases as an expert witness, most of which have not gone to trial. However, I have testified in court in three states and two provinces. My work is divided about two thirds defense and one third plaintiff. I considerate it an ethical and professional responsibility to help police the profession by acting as an expert witness for the plaintiff in cases where there has been serious malpractice. There is a political cost to be paid within the trauma field for such work, but it is bearable.

V. CONCLUSIONS

35

THE STRUCTURE OF SCIENTIFIC REVOLUTIONS

Thomas Kuhn (1962) wrote a very interesting book called *The Structure of Scientific Revolutions*. His thesis in the book is that scientific progress occurs by two distinct processes. One he calls *normal science*. In normal science, the basic model or philosophy is set. Scientists dedicate their careers to working out details within the model. This can be highly creative and challenging work, and includes most Nobel Prize-level research.

In normal science, there is linear progress as one discovery builds on the next.

The really interesting form of scientific advance is what Kuhn calls a *paradigm shift*. Paradigm shifts occur less than once a century in a given field, whether it be physics, biology, chemistry or astronomy. In a paradigm shift, the basic model governing normal science is changed. This doesn't involve tinkering with details or making a few adjustments. It involves a fundamental, discontinuous change, a gestalt switch from an old model to a new one.

Paradigm shifts have certain properties. They are discontinuous and occur in time intervals of centuries. They are accompanied by a characteristic sociology in which the old guard resists the new paradigm literally to the death, not through rational analysis, but through political attacks and other sociological mechanisms.

A paradigm shift is preceded by the accumulation of what Kuhn calls *anomalous data*. More and more observations build up which cannot be accounted for by the dominant paradigm. These are discredited or ignored by the dominant majority. Finally, the anomalous data reach a critical mass which forces a paradigm shift. A thinker or group of thinkers generates a new paradigm, a new set of basic rules and assumptions. This is fought tooth and nail by the old guard, which consists of the leading Professors and experts in the field, who have behind them the weight of authority, science, tradition and academia.

The relationship between the old and new paradigms is specific. The new paradigm can account for the anomalous data plus all the observations accounted for by the old paradigm. The old paradigm is a subset of the new one. The old paradigm isn't discredited; it is replaced by incorporation not elimination. The new paradigm stimulates generations worth of normal science and eventually becomes the dominant paradigm, awaiting its displacement during the next paradigm shift.

The classical example of a paradigm shift is the shift from Newtonian physics to relativity theory and quantum mechanics at the end of the nineteenth century and beginning of the twentieth century. When acceleration is set at zero, Einstein's equations yield the same results as Newton's. It is only under conditions of rapid acceleration that relativity theory can predict outcomes which are anomalous from a Newtonian perspective.

The trauma model represents a paradigm shift in psychiatry. Throughout the twentieth century, and still at the beginning of the twenty-first, psychiatry has been dominated by reductionism. All serious and fundamental causality has been endogenous and unidirectional. It is a cystic fibrosis model of serious mental illness. Psychiatry seems to be just about ready to drop the one gene-one illness model (Cook, 2000) but it is adopting instead a polygenetic reductionist model. This is a minor adjustment, not a paradigm shift.

There are preliminary signs that the environment is going to be allowed into the equation for the etiology of schizophrenia, but only in the form of viral infections and birth complications (Tsuang, Stone, and Faraone, 2000). The psychosocial environment is still fundamentally irrelevant. The search for a genetic test for schizophrenia is still on.

Within the trauma model, that is not how the biology works. The genome has no meaning or function in the absence of the environment. Without an environment, DNA is a biologically inert molecule. Put a strand of DNA in outer space, and it is meaningless and inert. It is dead.
Psychiatric disorders are part of life. They are a phenotype. The phenotype is the outcome of an interactive dance between the genome, the executive self, and the environment. Except perhaps in a tiny subset of pedigrees, the cystic fibrosis model does not apply. The genetic predisposition is to psychopathology in general, not to any of the DSM-IV-TR categories.

The psychosocial environment can turn genes on and off. So can decisions made by the executive self. A psychiatric disorder may be due to gene activation or deactivation, and its genetic treatment may involve either or both gene activation or deactivation. The genes manipulated in gene therapy for psychiatric disorders in the future may have no direct relationship with the genetic machinery involved in the illness. For instance, psychiatric gene therapy could involve turning off suppressor genes on one chromosome which have been activated by a step late in a biochemical pathway initiated by a gene on a different chromosome, which in turn was activated by the psychosocial environment through activation not of the gene itself, but of a normally suppressed promoter.

The trauma model predicts that the brain has the capacity for self-repair. The self-repair, however, does not occur in mammals without language. I was taught in medical school that skin can repair itself, within certain limits, as can other organs and tissues to varying degrees. But not the brain: all it can do is scar down. That was nineteen years ago. Twenty years from now, in the year 2020, it will be an established scientific fact that the brain has the capacity for self-repair.

What will the repair mechanism be? How will be it activated? Genetic engineering? Designer drugs? Who will the technician be on the outside, the person who activates and guides the brain's self-repair? A neurosurgeon? A pharmacologist? A geneticist?

Where will this significant event in the history of western medicine take place? At a medical school? A private biotech laboratory?

None of the above. Brain self-repair will be done by Master's level therapists in their private offices using psychotherapy. Trauma therapy will result in measurable normalization of hippocampal function on brain scan and this will be accompanied by hippocampal cellular regeneration at the microstructural level. This in turn may result in a measurable increase in hippocampal volume.

If these predictions are correct, Cartesian dualism will be refuted within the next twenty years. My medical training was based on fundamental and absolute Cartesian dualism, with all causality being unidirectional from brain to mind. Psychotherapy could cause changes in behavior, but not in the physical structure of the brain. Modifications in software could not cause changes in hardware, or so I was taught.

The trauma model states that Cartesian dualism is biologically incorrect.

There are psychiatric problems which are clearly pure software problems, like a specific phobia. It is also clear that massive damage to the brain causes irreversible software failure. But there is a gray zone in the middle, where schizophrenia resides. The trauma model pushes the boundary between brain and mind much further into the brain that I was taught in medical school.

Using psychotherapy, it is possible to readjust the quantum mechanics, harmonics and EEG printout of the human brain. These changes in harmonics are measurable using EEG technology, but also occur at energy levels that are too subtle to measure with twentieth century technology. The changes in harmonics reach down from the cortex into deeper levels of the brain, where they alter the electromagnetic fields in the white matter, thereby activating cellular gating and other mechanisms. These effects in turn cause alterations at the intracellular and synaptic biochemical levels, which lead to measurable dendritic growth and cellular regeneration, accompanied by measurable normalization of neuronal transport physiology. The only reason we can't measure all these things is because our science hasn't gotten there yet.

What we call the mind is the harmonic or subtle energy level of a unified brain-mind field. There are feedback and causal arrows going in countless directions in the field. Human beings are neither biological machines nor puppets of the environment. They have will and the capacity for choice. This is a fact in biology, according to the trauma model. Because we have language, we can initiate brain self-repair. That is what makes us human.

Within the Cartesian dualist model, biological psychiatrists attempt to scan the brain while it is making decisions. That is absurd, not just philosophically, but biologically. It is the mind that makes decisions: to do this, the mind needs its energy level activated by combustion of glucose in the brain. The brain cannot decide to repair the damage done to it by psychological trauma. Only the mind can do that.

In the psychiatry of the future, it might also be possible to do the work of psychotherapy using targeted electromagnetic fields. When the technology is subtle and directable to a sufficient degree, it might be possible to activate brain self-repair without words. I predict that in the end, language will prove to be the deeper and more subtle tool.

When one monozygotic twin has schizophrenia, the other twin gets it less than half the time. That fact is fundamental to my understanding of mental illness. We cannot understand or cure mental illness if we have a mistaken model of the brain-mind field. The psychosocial environment is a major player in the etiology of schizophrenia. Psychosocial trauma is a major form of noxious environmental input at the genome level. The trauma model leads to literally thousands of research projects which would never arise from the paradigm currently dominating psychiatry. It accounts for a broad range of anomalous data. In fact, most of clinical psychiatry is anomalous data.

Anyone interested in the logic or the sociology of paradigm shifts has a unique opportunity. One is knocking on the door in psychiatry.

VI. APPENDIX

36

ERRORS OF LOGIC AND SCHOLARSHIP CONCERNING DISSOCIATION

The purpose of this paper is to review and analyze a series of logical and scholarly errors concerning, dissociation, dissociative identity disorder, repression, and alleged false memories.

DEFINITION AND SCIENTIFIC STATUS OF DISSOCIATION

Equating Dissociative Amnesia, Dissociation, Repression And Traumatic Amnesia As Synonyms

This is a scholarly and logical error which has tactical functions (McHugh, 1997; Ofshe and Watters, 1994; Piper, 1997; Spanos, 1996). It is true that there is no scientific evidence for the intrapsychic defense mechanism of repression as defined by Freud. If repression is synonymous with dissociation, it follows that there is no scientific evidence for dissociation. It then follows that there is no scientific evidence for the dissociative disorders, in this series of false logical steps.

There are three meanings of repression in the professional literature.

1. *Primal repression*, an unconscious ego defense against unacceptable id impulses and wishes (Freud, 1915/1963). This meaning of repression has nothing to do with trauma, outside events or memory.
2. *Repression proper*, an unconscious defense mechanism used by the ego to push unacceptable thoughts, feelings and memories down into the id, or unconscious (Freud, 1915/1963).
3. A synonym for "suppression," which is consciously putting thoughts or problems on the back burner (Beardslee and Vaillant, 1997).

The claim is made that there is no scientific evidence for Freudian theory, therefore the theory of repressed memory is unscientific. A corollary is that recovered memories, if ever accurate, are more error-prone than continuous memories. This corollary claim is not supported by any clinical data or research. The authors cited above ignore or dismiss in an unscholarly fashion the existing literature and evidence on accurate recovery of traumatic memory (Brown, Scheflin, & Whitfield, 1999).

There are four meanings of dissociation.

1. The operationally defined meaning of dissociation in measures like the Dissociative Experiences Scale (DES) (Bernstein and Putnam, 1986), the Dissociative Disorders Interview Schedule (DDIS) (Ross, 1997), and the Structured Clinical Interview for DSM-IV Dissociative Disorders (SCID-D) (Steinberg, 1995). The operational meaning of dissociation is based on the same rules and procedures that are applied to measurement of anxiety, depression or psychosis and is supported by over 100 data-based peer-reviewed publications using the DES, and numerous publications using the DES, DDIS and SCID-D (Ross, 1997).

2. A general systems meaning of dissociation. Dissociations, or disconnections between variables are understood and measured mathematically in all areas of science, including general medicine (Ploghaus, Tracey, Gati, Clare, Menon, Matthews, & Rawlins, 1999).

3. A technical term in cognitive psychology (Cohen and Eichenbaum, 1993). Dissociations between procedural and declarative memory have been studied in cognitive psychology experiments for decades. Subjects have included normal college students, brain-damaged humans and experimental animals. Dissociation within long term memory is one of the most rigorously demonstrated phenomena in cognitive psychology. This is the literature relevant to the scientific status of dissociation. The authors cited above ignore it or are unaware of it. It is a proven scientific fact that real memory of real events can be present in procedural memory, and can affect verbal and behavioral output in a measurable fashion, in the complete absence of conscious memory of that information. Contrary to the authors' claims, this phenomenon does not depend on special mechanisms or assumptions like "robust repression" or "repression theory." It is a proven aspect of the psychological function of the normal human mind.

4. Dissociation is a defense mechanism postulated to be used to cope with traumatic events (Putnam, 1989; 1997).

It is possible that the fourth meaning of dissociation could be a synonym for the second meaning of repression, however it is not. As defined by Hilgard (1977), dissociation involves vertical splitting. Traumatic information is never pushed down into the unconscious mind. It is pushed across a vertical barrier into another compartment of the ego or conscious mind. It is never "repressed." Repression occurs when material is pushed downward across a horizontal split into the unconscious mind, where it is not available for conscious recall. Hilgard's use of the term "repression" corresponds to Freud's *repression proper*.

Initially, in his book *Studies on Hysteria* (Breuer and Freud, 1895; Ross, 1997), Freud subscribed to a trauma-dissociation theory. Women patients came to him with childhood sexual abuse memories and a wide variety of symptoms. He viewed the dissociated components of the abuse memories as the cause or drivers of the symptoms. He assumed the memories to be real. They were held in split-off compartments of the ego. This was the same theory espoused by Pierre Janet (1965; 1977) in the same time period. Freud called his theory The Seduction Theory. Treatment involved re-integrating the dissociated information and feelings.

In the late 1890's, as reflected in his letter to Wilhelm Fleiss of September 21, 1987, Freud repudiated the Seduction Theory (Masson, 1985). He decided that the sexual abuse memories were false memories. In order to explain why his women patients were presenting to him with false memories of childhood sexual abuse and myriad symptoms, he developed repression theory. It is when the memories are judged to be false that repression theory applies. The authors cited above have it backwards.

Freud broke with Janet. Dissociation theory and repression theory are separate, different things. That is why the word "repression" does not appear in DSM-IV. That is why there is no section called "Repression Disorders." It is why DSM-IV has a diagnosis of dissociative amnesia but not one of repressed memories or repressive amnesia. The difference between repression and dissociation is the reason why Freudian psychoanalysts do not diagnose DID, according to Spanos (1996).

Dissociative amnesia is based on conclusive findings in cognitive psychology. It assumes the scientifically proven memory processes of the normal human mind, not any special or unusual theory. When one makes a diagnosis of dissociative amnesia, one is making an observation. The phenomenon of dissociative amnesia, that is, a dissociation between procedural and declarative memory, is a fact of normal psychology. The diagnosis is based also on the judgment that this particular instance of dissociative amnesia is too extensive to be explained by ordinary forgetting. One explanation is ruled out by the DSM-IV criteria, but no other one is required, since the diagnosis is phenomenological, not mechanistic.

Recovery Of "Repressed Memory" Is A Scientifically Demonstrated Operation Of The Normal Human Mind

Several authors claim that there is no scientific evidence for the accurate recovery of repressed memory (Ofshe and Watters, 1994; Piper, 1997; Pope, Hudson, Bodkin and Oliva, 1998; Spanos, 1996). The logical error concerning repression reappears in this claim.

There is a large body of scientific literature in cognitive psychology demonstrating the reality of cued retrieval (Cohen and Eichenbaum, 1993). Subjects are given memorization tasks and later are asked to recall as much of the task information as possible. They have imperfect recall in this situation, which is called spontaneous recall, unassisted recall, or free recall. The subject is then given clues about information he has not remembered in the free recall situation. He now reports more accurate information for which, in clinical terms, he previously had amnesia. This is called *cued retrieval*.

The inability to recall the information prior to cueing of the retrieval is proof of the reality of dissociative amnesia. An amnesia, or inability to recall, was reversed by a simple verbal stimulus. The reversal requires a prior dissociation between procedural and declarative memory, accurate storage of the information in procedural memory, and successful transfer of the accurate information to declarative memory in response to the cue. These are operations of the normal human mind.

Calling these operations an example of the reversal of dissociative amnesia, does not require an assumption about the retrieval mechanism. Cued retrieval is a proven fact of normal human psychological function, not a theory or belief. Recovery of accurate memories is an inevitable outcome of any psychotherapy involving presentation of retrieval cues by the therapist or repeated recall effort by the patient (Erdelyi, 1996).

There is abundant experimental information about the conditions internal and external to the subject during a recall task which both augment and inhibit accurate retrieval (Erdelyi, 1996). There is also abundant data on the original stimulus variables that affect cued retrieval. These include duration of stimulus presentation, type of stimulus, clarity of the stimulus, emotional valence or meaning of the stimulus, and so on.

The phenomenon of recovery of memory in therapy is simply an example of cued retrieval. The accuracy and error rate of the recovered, cued material is an empirical question. There is abundant evidence that the simple repeated effort to recall results in the retrieval of more information than was previously available to conscious memory. There is evidence, summarized by Erdelyi (1996), that the procedure of hypnosis adds nothing to the effects of repeated recall effort.

There is no scientific evidence that sodium amytal affects the ratio of accurate to inaccurate memory recall in clinical situations. Yet, the authors cited above assert that sodium amytal and hypnosis increase the rate of memory error. The hypnosis literature is clear that hypnosis also increases the quantity of accurate recall. However, when the effect of simple effort to recall is controlled for experimentally, the procedure of hypnosis adds nothing to the subject's recall performance. Hypnosis in and of itself does not increase either the quantity of accurate nor the quantity of inaccurate memories recovered, independently of simple repeated recall effort (Erdelyi, 1996).

The Theory Of Robust Repression Is Irrelevant To The Scientific Status Of Dissociation

Robust repression is a term coined by Richard Ofshe (Ofshe and Watters, (1994). Robust repression requires complete amnesia for massive amounts of trauma until so-called "recovered memory therapy" begins. "Recovered memory therapy" is another coinage of Dr. Ofshe's.

I have never seen a case of dissociative identity disorder (DID) or dissociative disorder not otherwise specified (DDNOS) I judged to demonstrate real robust repression, out of over 2000 individuals with dissociative disorders admitted to my program over the last eight years. In fact, in my practice, a claim of robust repression is a red flag for false memories. Actual DID and DDNOS patients do not present for treatment with the extreme form of robust repression. They present with extensive continuous memory for trauma plus variable amounts of amnesia for details.

In a 1990 study (Ross, Miller, Reagor, Bjornson, Fraser and Anderson, 1990), DID patients reported as much trauma at the time of initial diagnosis as did comparison patients well into treatment. This was a study using the DDIS in 102 subjects in Ottawa, Winnipeg, Utah and California. Ellason and Ross (1997) showed that in two years of follow-up post-discharge from inpatient care, DID patients did not significantly increase the quantity of childhood physical and sexual abuse they reported, despite receiving ongoing therapy for DID.

Robust repression is one of many straw men set up by Ofshe and Watters (1994). It is not part of the clinical reality of DID or DDNOS, and is refuted by the research literature on DID. A corollary of the robust repression rhetorical strategy is the claim that there is no scientific evidence for robust repression. Brown, Scheflin and Whitfield (1999), in an exhaustive review of the literature, conclude, however, that there is in fact strong evidence for the existence of robust repression. My point here is that, whether or not it occurs in nature, robust repression is not characteristic of DID or DDNOS.

Repression Theory Is Not Relevant To The Scientific Status Of Dissociative Identity Disorder Or Dissociative Amnesia, Or Standards Of Care For Treatment Of Either

The studies by Herman and Schatzow (1987), Williams (1994), Briere and Conte (1993), Feldman-Summers and Pope (1994), and Loftus, Polonsky and Fullilove (1994), and other studies reviewed by Brown, Scheflin and Hammond (1998) and Brown, Scheflin and Whitfield (1999), deal with the phenomenon of recovered memory but do not address dissociation as such. Conclusive relevant science concerning dissociation is contained in the experimental cognitive psychology literature (Cohen and Eichenbaum, 1993; Ross, in press).

For instance, *repetition priming* is an example of the operation of dissociation in the normal human mind, as is *task interference*. A typical repetition priming experiment involves *homophonic word pairs*. These are words which sound the same, but are spelled differently and have different meanings, such as *bear-bare* and *reed-read*. Normal subjects are presented with lists of homophonic word pairs, which they memorize. Later, in a free recall situation, they are asked to write down as many word pairs as they can remember, but cannot remember *read-reed*. In clinical terminology, they have amnesia for the experience of memorizing *read-reed*.

The subjects are then asked to write down the answer to a question which invokes one word in the word pair, for example, "What is the name of a tall, thin, tubular aquatic plant that grows in marshes?"

Students who have been exposed to the *read-reed* word pair spell the answer incorrectly as *read* more often than control subjects who did not have the *read-reed* word pair in their lists.

Repetition priming demonstrates the proposition that accurately held information about real events can be stored in the unconscious mind and affect verbal and behavioral output in a scientifically measurable fashion, in the complete absence of conscious memory for that information. The experimental cognitive psychology literature on the reality of dissociation is voluminous and conclusive. The scientific status of dissociation is confirmed by clinical psychiatry and the DSM-IV, but is not dependent on it.

Dissociative amnesia in response to trauma does not require any special cognitive operations peculiar to traumatic memory, nor any neuropsychological mechanisms from outside normal human psychology. Non-traumatic, accurate memory of real events is routinely held in procedural memory, where it is unavailable to declarative memory without specific cueing. The name for this phenomenon in long term memory is *dissociation*.

Arguments about the theory of repression are relevant to the diagnosis and treatment of DID and DDNOS only if the disorders depend on repression theory, which they don't. There are Freudian, repression-based theories for almost every diagnosis in DSM-IV. Freudian psychoanalysts have tried to treat just about every disorder in DSM-IV using treatment methods based on repression theory. The reliability and validity of the dissociative disorders and the efficacy of their treatment are *empirical questions* which do not require Freud. Freud could be rejected completely and this would have no effect on the scientific status of the dissociative disorders or their treatments. This is true for the dissociative disorders, as it is for all disorders on Axis I and II.

The phenomena of dissociative amnesia and its reversal (recovered memory) do not depend for their scientific validity on the Freudian defense mechanism of repression. As formulated, the Freudian defense mechanism of repression is not scientifically testable.

Dissociation And Hypnosis Are Distinct Phenomena

The authors cited above frequently equate dissociation with hypnotizability. This is a tactical maneuver because it allows the experts to equate being highly dissociative with being highly suggestible. Being highly suggestible is then said to be a vulnerability for iatrogenic DID. There are several errors in these logical steps.

First, scores on the DES and standard measures of hypnotizability correlate at about r=0.10 in non-clinical populations (Whalen and Nash, 1996). Hypnotizability and dissociation are separate constructs. The existing science clearly refutes the dissociation=hypnotizability equation.

The authors claim that highly dissociative people are necessarily highly suggestible. This claim, though advanced with complete confidence as fact by Ofshe and Watters (1994) and Piper (1997), is not supported by any scientific evidence. The only empirical study on the question (Leavitt, 1997), shows a correlation between DES and suggestibility scores of r=0.17.

The authors attribute to hypnosis powers and correlations which it does not have. Their arguments about the relationship between hypnotizability, dissociation and suggestibility do not have a scientific foundation.

DIAGNOSIS AND TREATMENT OF DISSOCIATIVE IDENTITY DISORDER

The Claim That DID Cannot Be Diagnosed Reliably

Piper (1997) claims that the DSM-IV criteria for DID are vague and asks (p. 28), "That is, how do MPD theorists determine that the disorder is *not* present?"

There are abundant data on methods for determining that DID is not present using clinical interviews, the Dissociative Experiences Scale (DES), the Dissociative Disorders Interview Schedule (DDIS), or the Structured Clinical Interview for DSM-IV Dissociative Disorders (SCID-D) (Ross, 1997). None of this research is reviewed. Studies finding a prevalence of undiagnosed DID of 5% among general adult psychiatric inpatients are ignored - they show that DID is not present in 95% of cases, according to the DDIS, SCID-D and clinician (Ross, 1997).

Piper never discusses how depression or any other DSM-IV disorder is shown to be absent. The scientific rules for establishing the specificity, sensitivity, reliability and validity of psychiatric diagnoses are well defined, and apply to DID. Piper claims that the DSM-IV definition of DID is vague but never examines the actual reliability data. One could make the same critique of any DSM-IV criteria set, for instance Substance Abuse (DSM-IV, p. 182) which requires "clinically significant impairment or distress" (American Psychiatric Association, 1994). Who is to say what is "clinically significant?"

Depression (DSM-IV, p. 327) requires "depressed mood most of the day, nearly every day." How are "most" and "nearly" defined, and how depressed does "depressed" have to be?

Reliability is demonstrated by scientific studies of inter-rater reliability. These have defined rules and methodology which apply to all diagnoses. Virtually all criteria sets in DSM-IV could be made to look vague and subjective using the methods of Piper (1997). Piper's criticisms of the DSM-IV criteria for DID are semantic, not scientific or methodological. It is possible that a vaguely worded criterion set could result in poor reliability. This can only be determined if the necessary reliability research has been done. Otherwise, the claim that vague wording has caused poor reliability is simply an untested hypothesis.

Piper (1997) insists on his hypotheses, without subjecting them to a scientific test. He does not use the existing data to test them, and has never conducted any research himself. The claim that the DSM-IV criteria for DID generate false positives is a hypothesis worthy of study, but not a fact. The published reliability data on DID show that it has reliability as good or better than the average for Axis I (Ross, 1997).

Piper (1997) states that "Ross has written a 382-page book on MPD (Ross, 1989) without once explaining what an alter personality is." The index to Ross (1989) includes 16 sub-entries under "alter personalities," the first of which directs the reader to pages 103 - 108. On page 109, Ross defines alter personalities, devoting a full page to the definition.

There are numerous such errors of scholarship in Piper (1997). For instance, the Structured Clinical Interview for DSM-IV Dissociative Disorders (SCID-D) developed by Marlene Steinberg is not discussed and Dr. Steinberg is not referenced. The SCID-D was developed in the mid-1980's, data on it were first published in 1990 by Steinberg, Rounsaville and Cicchetti (1990), a book on it was published by the American Psychiatric Press in 1995 (Steinberg, 1995), and the SCID-D research was funded by the National Institutes of Mental Health. The SCID-D cannot be ignored in any scientific discussion of the reliability of dissociative identity disorder (DID).

Piper (1997) and other authors who reject the validity of DID (Ofshe and Watters, 1994; McHugh, 1997; Merskey, 1995; Simpson, 1995; Spanos, 1996) must account for the procedure of taxometric analysis and its application to the Dissociative Experiences Scale (DES). This procedure was used in papers by Waller, Putnam and Carlson (1996) and Waller and Ross (1997). It shows that DES scores divide general population and clinical samples into two discrete categories with little or no overlap: normal versus pathological dissociation. The taxometric data establish that pathological and normal dissociation can be differentiated with high levels of scientific reliability, and thereby provide a fundamental foundation for the reliability and validity of the dissociative disorders.

Failure To Understand The Rules Of The DSM System

Several authors state that DID is not a valid psychiatric disorder (McHugh, 1997; Merskey, 1995; Ofshe and Watters, 1994; Piper, 1997; Simpson, 1995; Spanos, 1996). This opinion is based in part on the above errors of logic about repression. The authors have failed to grasp the rules of the DSM system (DSM-III, DSM-III-R and DSM-IV have the same rules). The DSM-IV diagnostic criteria sets are phenomenological. They are not based on theories of causality. Theories of causality are irrelevant to the reliability and validity of DSM-IV disorders, as is the efficacy of treatment. This is true throughout medicine. For instance, cancer of the pancreas is a valid diagnosis, even though no-one knows its cause and there is no treatment.

Reliability is demonstrated through studies and data. The rules for these studies are standard for all disorders. These rules have been applied to the dissociative disorders using the DES, DDIS and SCID-D (Ross, 1997). The authors cited above cannot account adequately for this literature. Pope and Hudson (1992), however, stated that the DDIS has established reliability.

Disagreement about etiological theories of DID is irrelevant to discussion of the reliability of the disorder. DSM-IV does not differentiate iatrogenic from trauma-induced DID. Patients judged to have iatrogenic DID still meet DSM-IV criteria and receive the diagnosis by DSM-IV rules. These are the rules for making psychiatric diagnoses of the relevant scientific community, namely the American Psychiatric Association.

If an author argues that inclusion of a disorder in DSM-IV does not, by itself, prove the scientific validity of the disorder, he is correct. However, the inclusion of a disorder in DSM-IV represents the authoritative judgment of the relevant scientific community. It is therefore within the standard of care to make that diagnosis. Inclusion of a disorder in DSM-IV provides strong evidence in favor of the inverse proposition: for a disorder to appear in DSM-IV, there can be no conclusive scientific proof available in the literature that it lacks acceptable reliability and validity.

There Is No Scientific Evidence That Iatrogenic DID Can Be Differentiated From Childhood-Onset DID In A Reliable, Scientific Fashion

There are several paradoxes here. For there to be such a thing as iatrogenic DID, proponents of that disorder must demonstrate that they can diagnose iatrogenic cases in a reliable fashion. Reliability means a good level of agreement between clinicians as to who has or does not have the disorder. The only research demonstrating that DID can be diagnosed reliably is based on the DDIS and SCID-D (Ross, 1997; Steinberg, 1995). Without the DDIS or SCID-D, there could be no evidence that iatrogenic DID is a reliable diagnosis. In order to conclude that a given case is iatrogenic, an author must rely on the DDIS and SCID-D research, and must judge it to meet the standards of the relevant scientific community. Otherwise, the author has no scientific foundation for his conclusion.

If an author cannot determine scientifically that iatrogenic DID has occurred, then he cannot testify scientifically as an expert witness in a malpractice lawsuit that there has been a breach of the standard of care, proximate cause or damages. Therefore such an expert witness is absolutely dependent on the research by Ross (1997) and Steinberg (1995).

There is scientific evidence that DID can be diagnosed with good reliability. However, there is no evidence that iatrogenic DID can be differentiated from childhood-onset DID with reliability. The DDIS or SCID-D can be used scientifically to establish that a person has DID, thereby making it scientifically possible that the person could have iatrogenic DID, but there is no evidence that the etiological pathway can be identified in a reliable fashion. The DDIS and SCID-D can accomplish the first step of diagnosing DID, but not the second step of differentiating iatrogenic, factitious and childhood trauma etiologies.

The only published, scientifically testable scheme for differentiating iatrogenic, factitious and childhood-onset DID from each other is by

Ross (1997). The authors hostile to DID cited above have made no scientific contribution in this regard, and therefore must rely on Ross' scheme. To do so, they must accept his work as scientifically sound. Once this proposition is accepted, the reliability and validity of DID become unavoidable conclusions.

The paradox is that authors can conclude that a given case of DID is iatrogenic only if they accept the validity of the DSM-IV definition of DID, and the supporting scientific literature

Dr. Spanos' Experiments Do Not Provide Evidence In Support Of The Theory Of Iatrogenic Dissociative Identity Disorder

Spanos (1996) performed experiments in which normal college students acted like they had DID when he asked them to do so. He regarded this as evidence in favor of the iatrogenic theory of DID. Spanos himself differentiates between *simulation* and *role enactment*. Simulation is conscious and deliberate and corresponds to clinical factitious DID. Role enactment is not deliberate, is truly believed in by the person doing the enactment, and is unconscious. Role enactment corresponds to clinical iatrogenic DID

Spanos (1996) says that iatrogenic DID is based on role enactment. The therapist gives the cues and suggestions necessary for the iatrogenic patient to enact the role. Spanos states that iatrogenic DID is not based on simulation.

Spanos' college students simulated DID. They never believed they really had it, otherwise Spanos would have created iatrogenic DID on purpose, which would have been unethical, harmful, and grounds for a lawsuit. The college student data on simulation of DID are irrelevant to the claim that DID is role enacted in patients who develop it through iatrogenic causation.

If DID Is Caused By Role Enactment, Then DID Patients Have Never Repressed Any Memories

There is another paradox in the rhetorical strategies used to attack DID. DID is said to be iatrogenic and based on role enactment (Spanos, 1996). At the same time (Ofshe and Watters, 1994), it is said to be based on the theory of repressed memory and unscientific "recovered memory therapy." Both these propositions are examples of straw man argument.

If it is true that a given case, most cases, or all cases of DID are iatrogenic role enactments, then there has been no amnesia. There can therefore have been no memory recovery. Within the sociocognitive model (Lilienfeld, Lynn, Kirsch, Chaves, Sarbin, Ganaway, and Powell, 1999; Spanos, 1996), the alter personalities are not intrapsychic structures. They are play-acting. There are no real alter personalities. Therefore there can be no real amnesia barriers.

According to the sociocognitive model, there is no real amnesia in DID. The claim of amnesia is another element of the role enactment, according to the sociocognitive model. The unavoidable conclusion, within the sociocognitive model, is that no memories "recovered" in DID therapy have ever been repressed. Since there has been no repression and no recovered memories, there can be no damages due to recovered memories.

All "recovered memories" must be fantasies constructed during the process of therapy, or memories misinterpreted as "recovered" but actually explainable by cued retrieval, normal forgetting and remembering, or other memory processes besides repression, according to the sociocognitive model.

This logical problem has forced the authors cited above into an absolutist, all-or-nothing stance. They have had to adopt the position that one hundred per cent of recovered memories are false, because they have conceded that continuously held memories of childhood trauma are by and large accurate (Ofshe and Watters, 1994). They cannot afford to accept the logical outcome of the role enactment analysis of DID, namely that the "recovered memories" have been continuously held in normal memory, subject to normal forgetting, normal recall, cued retrieval and other scientifically valid memory processes.

The authors have adopted an untenable position because the scientific literature on memory shows that it is reconstructive and error-prone, even when defined as continuous (Cohen and Eichenbaum, 1993). In reality, continuous and recovered memory are not simple, dichotomous categories about which global pronouncements can be made. The arguments of Ofshe and Watters (1994) are fatally flawed for this reason alone.

The Claim That DID Therapy Makes Patients Worse

This claim is made by a number of authors (McHugh, 1997; Merskey, 1995; Ofshe and Watters, 1994; Piper, 1997; Simpson, 1995; Spanos, 1996). It is an anecdotal clinical impression. The authors state it as fact, but it is a hypothesis. The authors present no scientific data to support their hypothesis, nor even any detailed case studies. They over-generalize from the tiny minority of cases that result in malpractice lawsuits, as if that is a representative sample.

The authors cited above denigrate the treatment outcomes of the DID "theorists" but never provide any detailed description of the treatment they recommend for this population, or its outcomes. The population still exists, even if the DID diagnosis is not made. The authors ignore the outcome literature on borderline personality disorder provided by Stone (1989). Stone showed that hospitalized borderlines who also have clinical depression have an 18% rate of completed suicide in long term follow-up. Since 65% of DID inpatients meet criteria for both borderline personality disorder and major depressive disorder (Ross, 1997), one could postulate, in the absence of evidence to the contrary, that one in five DID patients would eventually kill themselves if treated as borderlines within mainstream psychiatry.

My point is this: authors hostile to the diagnosis and treatment of DID have not presented any data on the outcome of individuals who meet structured interview criteria for DID but receive a treatment protocol they endorse. They therefore have no scientific foundation for their denigration of treatment methods they dislike. The outcome of these cases in their hands could be as poor as the prognosis for borderline personality disorder defined by Stone.

Piper (1997) claims that the voluntary-involuntary distinction concerning personality switching is confused and unscientific in the DID literature. How does this ambiguity in DID differ from that in alcoholics, who can control but can't control their drinking, who have periods of sobriety then relapse? Patients with numerous diagnoses experience their symptoms as involuntary and out of control but nevertheless respond to behavioral management and can learn to control the previously uncontrollable. This is routine in psychiatry.

The authors cited above state that there are no adequate outcome data to demonstrate the efficacy of DID treatment. However, they claim to know that the treatment is harmful. If inadequate data exist to demonstrate the efficacy of the treatment, then inadequate data exist to demonstrate its harmfulness.

A pervasive rhetorical strategy used by the authors, is raising and lowering the bar depending on the viewpoint. If the claim is that DID therapy is harmful, the bar for proof of that proposition is lowered to anecdotal impression. If the opposing claim is made, namely that the treatment is helpful, the authors raise the bar very high and demand a high standard of proof for the proposition they oppose.

The Term "Recovered Memory Therapy" Mischaracterizes The Treatment

"Recovered memory therapy" is a coinage of Dr. Ofshe's (Ofshe and Watters, 1994). Prior to his coining it, the term never appeared in the professional literature. No professional has ever claimed to practice recovered memory therapy or described using it in the professional literature. The recovery of memory is clearly defined as a minor component of DID therapy in all authoritative writings in the dissociative disorders field (Putnam, 1989; 1997). The strategy is to take this minor component of well-conducted therapy, and make it the predominant intervention. Another straw man is thereby set up to bolster the argument against the validity of DID.

GENERAL ERRORS OF LOGIC AND SCHOLARSHIP

Using An Observation To Prove A Hypothesis

This logical error is pervasive in the scholarly attack on DID. For instance, it is an agreed-upon fact that more cases of DID are diagnosed inside North America than outside, by far. Similarly, more cases have been diagnosed in the 1980's and 1990's than previously, by far (Merskey, 1995; Piper, 1997; Simpson, 1995; Spanos, 1996).

In science, one makes an observation, then forms a hypothesis, then conducts an experiment or some form of research to test the hypothesis. The two competing hypotheses, in this instance, are: 1) DID is iatrogenic, versus 2) DID is naturally occurring. If DID is iatrogenic, the epidemic is limited primarily to North America. If DID is regarded as naturally occurring, the prediction is that DID is equally common outside North America, but under-diagnosed.

The authors cited above use the observation that DID is diagnosed less often outside North America as proof of their hypothesis that it is iatrogenic. In fact, the observation is neutral and equally compatible with both hypotheses. The only way to tell which hypothesis is correct is with science. The authors cited above provide no data of their own and ignore or distort the existing data (Akyuz, Dogan, Sar, Yargic, and Tutkun, 1999), or simply dismiss it without analysis.

The question of the prevalence of DID in other countries, clinical populations and the general population is epidemiological. The scientific rules and procedures for answering such questions are well established.

Confusing Phenomenon With Mechanism

When dissociative amnesia and repression are equated, there has been a confusion of logical categories. Dissociative amnesia is not a theory. It is an observation. The doctor observes the patient report inability to remember important personal information, usually of a traumatic or stressful nature, that is too extensive to be explained by ordinary forgetfulness. Thousands of patients have made this claim to thousands of psychiatrists throughout the twentieth century, for numerous kinds of trauma including verified events (Loewenstein, 1993).

The DSM-IV criteria do not assume any cause or mechanism. When the phenomenon of dissociative amnesia is observed, the defense mechanism of repression is only one possible cause.

The Many Studies Of Trauma Survivors That Do Not Report Amnesia Do Not Provide Evidence Against The Validity Of Dissociative Amnesia

Ofshe and Watters (1994) refer vaguely to numerous studies of trauma survivors in which none reported amnesia. Such studies are relevant only if they employed reliable, valid measures of amnesia or dissociation, or made a systematic, scientific effort to inquire about or document amnesia. Studies which found no amnesia because they did not inquire about it cannot provide scientific evidence about the prevalence or validity of dissociative amnesia.

Contradictions Between Experts' Views of Freud

A number of authors hostile to dissociation and DID cite each other as authorities and attempt to present a united front on Freud, however they contradict each other. Piper (1997), McHugh (1997), and Ofshe and Watters (1994) attack Freud and his theories. They characterize recovered memory therapy as based on unscientific Freudian repression theory. They also endorse Spanos' college student experiments as evidence against the validity of DID, and regard Spanos as authoritative in his analysis of DID.

Spanos (1996), however, states that adherence to Freudian theory protects the therapist against creation of iatrogenic DID. He states that trauma-dissociation theory was rejected by Freud and argues that repression theory steers the therapist away from personification of ego states or a belief in dissociation within the ego.

The Data In The February 1999 American Journal of Psychiatry Article Contradict Dr. Pope's Conclusions In That Article

Pope, Oliva, Hudson, Bodkin and Gruber (1999) claim that their paper proves that there is no consensus about DID and dissociative amnesia in American psychiatry. Their own data refute that conclusion.

In the abstract, the authors state that "Only about one-third of respondents replied that dissociative amnesia and dissociative identity disorder should be included without reservations in DSM-IV; a larger proportion replied that these categories should be included only as proposed diagnoses."

This is a distortion of the methodology and data. For one thing, 35% of respondents endorsed inclusion in DSM-IV without reservation, while only 43% endorsed the other option. These two response rates would not have differed significantly using a chi square test if a statistical analysis had been done. In Table 1 the authors state that the full text of the second response option was, "Should be included only with reservations (e.g., only as a 'proposed diagnosis')."

A respondent who endorsed inclusion with reservation was not necessarily endorsing the 'proposed diagnosis' option. Shifting these disorders to the proposed diagnoses section of DSM-IV-R would be a radical change and far beyond the usual modifications in criteria one sees throughout the various editions from DSM-III to DSM-III-R to DSM-IV.

Pope et al. (1999) did not review the changes in the criteria for depression and eating disorders from DSM-I to DSM-IV. There have been what Pope et al. (1999), referring to the dissociative disorders, call "sharp shifts in the features of these disorders as described in successive editions of

DSM." For example, dysthymic personality disorder was shifted from the personality disorders section on Axis II to the affective disorders section on Axis I between DSM-II and DSM-III. DSM-IV (American Psychiatric Association, 1994, p. 732) retains Depressive Personality Disorder under Criteria Sets and Axes Provided for Further Study, demonstrating that the status of this form of depression in the diagnostic system is unresolved. The criteria for eating disorders have changed between DSM-III and DSM-IV.

The changes in dissociative disorder criteria are no greater than the norm for the rest of the manual. The Affective Disorders section of DSM-III was renamed the Mood Disorders section in DSM-III-R. Bipolar affective disorder became bipolar mood disorder.

Table 1 in Pope et al. (1999) shows that only 15% of psychiatrists believe DID should not be included in a revision of DSM-IV, and only 20% believe there is little or no evidence of its scientific validity. It's a safe assumption that these respondents do not know the empirical literature, and cannot name the DES, DDIS and SCID-D, or their authors. Table 1 shows that 78% of respondents believe DID should be included in future editions, and 72% believe there is partial or strong evidence of its validity. In politics this would be called a landslide victory. Pope and coauthors belong to a small minority in psychiatry, according to their own data.

A number of authors cited above attack repression theory as based on unscientific Freudian ideas. Yet 40% of respondents in the Pope survey rated their theoretical orientation as psychodynamic-psychoanalytic, which means Freudian. When DID is supposedly being supported by Freudian theory, Freud is attacked. When the responses of Freudians are being used to oppose DID and dissociation, their opinions are suddenly of value.

The authors cited above attack Freudian and "recovered memory" therapy as unscientific and point out that only cognitive-behavioral therapy has a real scientific proof of its efficacy, plus perhaps interpersonal therapy. Yet only 3% of psychiatrist respondents in the Pope survey are cognitive-behavioral in their primary orientation. This must call the validity of the respondents' opinions into question, according to the logic of the attack on Freud.

The final paragraph of the paper includes false arguments and conclusions not supported by the data. The authors reference themselves as authorities supporting their own conclusions. The recent closure of several dissociative disorders units, referred to in the final paragraph of Pope et al (1990), is irrelevant to the scientific status of the dissociative disorders. Many specialty units for eating disorders and other disorders have closed under managed care pressure. Yet the authors argue that closure of dissociative disorders units is evidence against the scientific validity of the DSM-IV dissociative disorders.

This is an example of a pervasive rhetorical strategy (Braude, 1995). Arguments are mounted against DID which apply equally to other disorders, but are never used against them. Pope et al. (1999) would never conclude that closure of eating disorders units is relevant to the nosological validity of the eating disorders.

Pope et al. (1999) claim that DID and dissociative amnesia lack empirical support but do not reference or discuss any of the large empirical literature.

The purpose of this Appendix has been to review and analyze some of the most common errors of logic and scholarship concerning dissociation, dissociative identity disorder, repression, and alleged false memories. Additional analysis of these and related errors is contained in other sources (Barton, 1994a; 1994b; Braude, 1995; Brown, Scheflin, and Hammond, 1998; Brown, Scheflin, and Whitfield, 1999; Dickstein, Riba, and Oldham, 1997; Gleaves, 1996; Kluft, 1998; Martinez-Taboas, 1995; Pezdek and Banks, 1996; Pope, 1996; 1997; Putnam, 1995; Ross, 1990; Ross, 1997). Together with the present paper, these sources provide a substantial and scholarly counter-argument to attacks on dissociation, the dissociative disorders and psychotherapy for them.

REFERENCES

Akyuz, G., Dogan, O., Sar, V., Yargic, L.I., & Tutkun, H. (1999). Frequency of dissociative identity disorder in the general population in Turkey. *Comprehensive Psychiatry*, 40, 151-159.

American Psychiatric Association. (1980). *Diagnostic and Statistical Manual of Mental Disorders (3rd ed.).* Washington, DC: American Psychiatric Association.

American Psychiatric Association. (1987). *Diagnostic and Statistical Manual of Mental Disorders (3rd ed., Revised).* Washington, DC: American Psychiatric Association.

American Psychiatric Association. (1994). *Diagnostic and Statistical Manual of Mental Disorders. (4th ed.).* Washington, DC: American Psychiatric Association.

American Psychiatric Association. (2000). *Diagnostic and Statistical Manual of Mental Disorders (4th ed., Text Revision).* Washington, DC: American Psychiatric Association.

Barton, C. (1994a). Backstage in psychiatry: The multiple personality disorder controversy. *Dissociation*, 7, 167-172.

Barton, C. (1994b). More from backstage: A rejoinder to Merskey. *Dissociation*, 7, 176-177.

Beck, A.T., & Emery, G. (1985). *Anxiety Disorders and Phobias: A Cognitive Perspective.* New York: Basic Books.

Beck, A.T., Rush, A.J., Shaw, B.F., & Emery, G. (1979). *Cognitive Therapy of Depression.* New York: Guilford.

Bernstein, E.M., Putnam, F.W. (1986). Development, reliability, and validity of a dissociation scale. *Journal of Nervous and Mental Disease*, 174, 727-735.

Beardslee, W.R., Vaillant, G. (1997). Adult development. In A. Tasman, J. Kay, J.A. Lieberman (Eds.), *Psychiatry.* Philadelphia: W.B. Saunders.

Blazer, D.G., Kessler, R.C., McGonagle, K.A., & Swartz, M.S. (1994).

The prevalence and distribution of major depression in a national community sample: The National Comorbidity Survey. *American Journal of Psychiatry*, 151, 979-986.

Braude, S. E. (1995). *First Person Plural. Multiple Personality and the Philosophy of Mind (Rev. Ed.)*. London: Rowman & Littlefield.

Bremner, J.D., & Marmer, C.R. (1998). *Trauma, Memory, and Dissociation*. Washington, DC: American Psychiatric Press.

Breuer, J., & Freud, S. (1986). *Studies on Hysteria*. New York: Pelican Books. (Original work published in 1895).

Briere, J., & Conte, J. (1993). Self-reported amnesia for abuse in adults molested as children. *Journal of Traumatic Stress*, 6, 21-31.

Brown, D., & Scheflin, A.W. (1999). Editor's page. *Journal of Psychiatry and the Law*, 27, 367-372.

Brown, D., Scheflin, A.W., & Hammond, D.C. (1998). *Memory, Trauma Treatment, and the Law*. New York: W.W. Norton.

Brown, D., Scheflin, A.W., Whitfield, C.L. (1999). Recovered memories: The current weight of the evidence in science and the courts. *Journal of Psychiatry and the Law*, 27, 5-156.

Cannon, T.D., Kaprio, J., Lonnqvist, J., Huttunen, M., & Koskenvuo, M. (1998). The genetic epidemiology of schizophrenia in a Finnish twin cohort. *Archives of General Psychiatry*, 55, 67-74.

Cohen, N.J., & Eichenbaum, H. (1993). *Memory, Amnesia, and the Hippocampal System*. Cambridge: MIT Press.

Cook, E.H. (2000). Genetics of psychiatric disorders: Where have we been and where are we going? *American Journal of Psychiatry*, 157, 1039-1040.

Courtois, C.A. (1999). *Recollections of Sexual Abuse: Treatment Principles and Guidelines*. New York: W.W. Norton.

Dickstein, L.J., Riba, M.B., & Oldham, J.M. (197). *Repressed Memories*. Washington, DC: American Psychiatric Press.

Ellason, J.W., & Ross, C.A. (1997). Two-year follow-up of inpatients with dissociative identity disorder. *American Journal of Psychiatry*, 154, 832-839.

Ellason, J.W., Ross, C.A., & Fuchs, D.L. (1996). Lifetime Axis I and II comorbidity and childhood trauma history in dissociative identity disorder. *Psychiatry*, 59, 255-266.

Engdahl, B., Dikel, T.N., Eberly, R., & Blank, A. (1998). Comorbidity and course of psychiatric disorders in a community sample of former prisoners of war. *American Journal of Psychiatry*, 155, 1740-1745.

Erdelyi, M. H. (1996). *The Recovery of Unconscious Memories. Hypermnesia and Reminiscence.* Chicago: University of Chicago Press.

Feldman-Summers, S., & Pope, K.S. (1994). The experience of "forgetting" childhood abuse: A national survey of psychologists. *Journal of Consulting and Clinical Psychology*, 62, 636-639.

Follette, V.M., Ruzek, J.I., & Abueg, F.R. (1998). *Cognitive-Behavioral Therapies for Trauma.* New York: Guilford.

Freud, S. (1963). Repression (1915). In P. Rief (Ed.), *Freud: General Psychological Theory.* New York: Touchstone Books.

Freud, S. (1963). Mourning and Melancholia (1917). In P. Rief (Ed.), *Freud: General Psychological Theory.* New York: Touchstone Books.

Freyd, J.J. (1996). *Betrayal Trauma: The Forgetting of Childhood Abuse.* Cambridge, MA: Harvard University Press.

Gainer, K. (1994). Dissociation and schizophrenia: An historical review of conceptual development and relevant treatment approaches. *Dissociation*, 7, 261-271.

Gleaves, D.H. (1996). The sociocognitive model of dissociative identity disorder: A reexamination of the evidence. *Psychological Bulletin*, 120, 42-59.

Herman, J.L., & Schatzow, E. (1987). Recovery and verification of memories of childhood sexual trauma. *Psychoanalytic Psychology*, 4, 1-14.

Hilgard, E.R. (1977). *Divided Consciousness. Multiple Controls in Human Thought and Action.* New York: John Wiley & Sons.

Hudson, R.G., & Cain, M.P. (1998). Risperidone associated with hemorrhagic cystitis. *Journal of Urology*, 160, 159.

Janet, P. (1965). *The Major Symptoms of Hysteria.* New York: Hafner. (Original work published in 1907).

Janet, P. (1977). *The Mental State of Hystericals.* Washington, DC: University Publications of America. (Original work published in 1901).

Kessler, R.C., McGonagle, K.A., Zhao, S., Nelson, C.B., Hughes, M., Eshelman, S., Wittchen, H., & Kendler, K.S. (1994). Lifetime and 12-month prevalence of DSM-III-R psychiatric disorders in the United States. *Archives of General Psychiatry*, 51, 8-19.

Kessler, R.C., Zhoa, S., Katz, S.J., Kouzis, A.C., Frank, R.G., Edlund, M., & Leaf, P. (1999). Past-year use of outpatient services for psychiatric problems in the National Comorbidity Survey. *American Journal of Psychiatry*, 156, 115-123.

Kluft, R.P. (1998). Reflections on the traumatic memories of dissociative identity disorder patients. In Lynn, S.J., & McConkey, K.M. (eds). *Truth in Memory.* New York: Guilford.

Kuhn, T. (1962). *The Structure of Scientific Revolutions.* Chicago: University of Chicago Press.

Leavitt, F. (1997). False attribution of suggestibility to explain recovered memory of childhood sexual abuse following extended amnesia. *Child Abuse and Neglect*, 21, 265-272.

Levitan, R.D., Parikh, S.V., Lesage, A.D., Hegadoren, K.M., Adams, M., Kennedy, S.H., & Goering, P.N. (1998). Major depression in individuals with a history of childhood physical or sexual abuse: Relationship to neurovegetative features, mania, and gender. *American Journal of Psychiatry*, 155, 1746-1752.

Lifton, R.J. (1961). *Thought Reform and the Psychology of Totalism: A Study of "Brainwashing" in Red China.* New York: W.W. Norton.

Lilienfeld, S.O., Lynn, S.J., Kirsch, I., Chaves, J.F., Sarbin, T.R., Ganaway, G.K., Powell, R.A. (1999). Dissociative identity disorder and the sociocognitive model: Recalling the lessons of the past. *Psychological Bulletin*, 125, 507-523.

Linehan, M. (1993). *Cognitive Behavioral Treatment For Borderline Personality Disorder*. New York: Guilford.

Loewenstein, R.J. (1993). Psychogenic amnesia and psychogenic fugue: A comprehensive review. In Spiegel, D. (ed.). *Dissociative Disorders: A Clinical Review*. Lutherville, MD: Sidran Press.

Loftus, E.F. (1993). The reality of repressed memories. *American Psychologist*, 48, 518-537.

Loftus, E.F., Polonsky, S., & Fullilove, M.T. (1994). Memories of childhood sexual abuse: Remembering and repressing. *Psychology of Women Quarterly*, 18, 67-84.

Lynn, S.J., & McConkey, K.M. (1998). *Truth In Memory*. New York: Guilford.

March, J.S., Biederman, J., Wolkow, R., Safferman, A., Mardekian, J., Cook, E.H., Cutler, N.R., Dominguez, R., Ferguson, J., Muller, B., Riesenberg, R., Rosenthal, M., Sallee, F.R., & Wagner, K.D. (1998). Sertraline in children and adolescents with obsessive-compulsive disorder. *Journal of the American Medical Association*, 280, 1752-1756.

Martinez-Taboas, A. (1995). A sociocultural analysis of Merskey's approach. In Cohen, L., Berzoff, J., & Elin, M. (eds). *Dissociative Identity Disorder. Theoretical and Treatment Controversies*. Northvale, NJ: Jason Aronson.

Masson, J.M. (1985). *The Complete Letters of Sigmund Freud to Wilhelm Fleiss 1887-1904*. Cambridge, MA, Belknap Press.

McHugh, P.R. (1997). Foreword. In Piper, A. *Hoax and Reality. The Bizarre World of Multiple Personality Disorder*. Northvale, NJ: Jason Aronson.

Merskey, H. (1995). The manufacture of personalities: The production of multiple personality disorder. In Cohen, L., Berzoff, J., & Elin, M. (eds.).

Dissociative Identity Disorder: Theoretical and Treatment Controversies. Northvale, NJ: Jason Aronson.

Michelson, L.K., & Ray, W.J. (1996). *Handbook of Dissociation.* New York: Plenum.

Morrison, J. (1989). Childhood sexual histories of women with somatization disorder. *American Journal of Psychiatry*, 146, 239-241.

Ofshe, R., & Watters, E. (1994). *Making Monsters: False Memories, Psychotherapy, and Sexual Hysteria.* New York: Charles Scribner's.

Pam, A., Kemker, S.S., Ross, C.A., & Golden, R. (1996). The "equal environments assumption" in MZ-DZ twin comparisons: An untenable premise of psychiatric genetics? *Acta Genet Med Gemellol*, 45, 349-360.

Pezdek, K., & Banks, W.P. (1996). *The Recovered Memory/False Memory Debate.* New York: Academic Press.

Pincus, H.A., Rush, A.J., First, M.B., & McQueen, L.E. (2000). *Handbook of Psychiatric Measures.* Washington, DC: American Psychiatric Association.

Piper, A. (1997). *Hoax and Reality. The Bizarre World of Multiple Personality Disorder.* Northvale, NJ: Jason Aronson.

Ploghaus, A., Tracey, I., Gati, J.S., Clare, S., Menon, R.S., Matthews, P.M., Rawlins, J.N.P. (1999). Dissociating pain from its anticipation in the human brain. *Science*, 284, 1979-1981.

Pope, K.S. (1996). Memory, abuse, and science: Questioning claims about the False Memory Syndrome epidemic. *American Psychologist*, 51, 957-974.

Pope, K.S. (1997). Science as careful questioning: Are claims of a false memory epidemic based on empirical evidence? *American Psychologist*, 52, 997-1006.

Pope, H.G., & Hudson, J..I. (1992). Is childhood sexual abuse a risk factor for bulimia nervosa? *American Journal of Psychiatry*, 149, 241-248.

Pope, H.G., Oliva, P.S., Hudson, J.I., Bodkin, J.A., & Gruber, A.J. (1999). Attitudes towards DSM-IV dissociative disorders diagnoses among Board-certified American psychiatrists. *American Journal of Psychiatry*, 156, 321-232.

Putnam, F.W. (1989). *Diagnosis and Treatment of Multiple Personality Disorder.* New York: Guilford.

Putnam, F.W. (1995). Resolved: Multiple personality disorder is an individually and socially created artifact. Negative. *Journal of the American Academy of Child and Adolescent Psychiatry*, 34, 960-962. Rebuttal, 963.

Putnam, F.W. (1997). *Dissociation in Children and Adolescents.* New York: Guilford.

Ross, C.A. (1984). Diagnosis of multiple personality during hypnosis: A case report. *International Journal of Clinical and Experimental Hypnosis*, 32, 222-235.

Ross, C.A. (1985). DSM-III: Problems in diagnosing partial forms of multiple personality disorder. *Journal of the Royal Society of Medicine*, 75, 933-936.

Ross, C.A. (1986). Biological tests for mental illness: Their use and misuse. *Biological Psychiatry*, 21, 431-435.

Ross, C.A. (1989). *Multiple Personality Disorder. Diagnosis, Clinical Features, and Treatment.* New York: John Wiley & Sons.

Ross, C.A. (1991). Epidemiology of multiple personality and dissociation. *Psychiatric Clinics of North America*, 14, 503-517.

Ross, C.A. (1994). *The Osiris Complex: Cast Studies in Multiple Personality Disorder.* Toronto: University of Toronto Press.

Ross, C.A. (1995). *Satanic Ritual Abuse: Principles of Treatment.* Toronto: University of Toronto Press.

Ross, C.A. (1997). *Dissociative Identity Disorder. Diagnosis, Clinical Features, and Treatment of Multiple Personality. (2nd ed.).* New York: John Wiley & Sons.

Ross, C.A. (2004). *Schizophrenia: Innovations in Diagnosis and Treatment.* New York: Haworth Press.

Ross, C.A. (2006). *The C.I.A. Doctors: Human Rights Violations By American Psychiatrists.* Richardson, TX: Manitou Communications.

Ross, C.A. (in press). The dissociative disorders. In Million, T., Blaney, P., & Davis, R. (eds.). *Oxford Textbook of Psychopathology.* New York: Oxford University Press.

Ross, C.A., & Joshi, S. (1992). Schneiderian symptoms and childhood trauma in the general population. *Comprehensive Psychiatry*, 33, 269-273.

Ross, C.A., & Matas, M. (1987). A clinical trial of buspirone and diazepam in treatment of generalized anxiety disorder. *Canadian Journal of Psychiatry*, 32, 351-355.

Ross, C.A., & Pam, A. (1995). *Pseudoscience in Biological Psychiatry.* New York: John Wiley & Sons.

Ross, C.A., Miller, S.D., Bjornson, L., Reagor, P., Fraser, G.A., & Anderson, G. (1990). Schneiderian symptoms in multiple personality disorder and schizophrenia. *Comprehensive Psychiatry*, 31, 111-118.

Ross, C.A., Miller, S.D., Reagor, P., Bjornson, L., Fraser, G.A., & Anderson, G. (1990). Structured interview data on 102 cases of multiple personality disorder from four centers. *American Journal of Psychiatry*, 147, 596-601.

Sargant, W. (1957). *Battle For the Mind.* Garden City, NY: Doubleday.

Simpson, M. (1995). Gullible's travels, or the importance of being multiple. In Cohen., L., Berzoff, J., & Elin, M. (eds.). *Dissociative Identity Disorder: theoretical and Treatment Controversies.* Northvale, NJ: Jason Aronson.

Spanos, N.P. (1996). *Multiple Identities and False Memories. A Sociocognitive Perspective.* Washington, DC: American Psychological Association.

Speigel, D. (1997). *Repressed Memories.* Washington, DC: American Psychiatric Press.

Steinberg, M. (1995). *Handbook for the Assessment of Dissociation. A Clinical Guide.* Washington, DC: American Psychiatric Press.

Steinberg, M., Rounsaville, B.J., & Cicchetti, D.V. (1990). The Structured Clinical Interview for DSM-III-R Dissociative Disorders: Preliminary report on a new diagnostic instrument. *American Journal of Psychiatry*, 147, 76-82.

Stone, M.H. (1989). The course of borderline personality disorder. In Tasman, A., Hales, R.E., & Frances, A.J. (eds.). *Review of Psychiatry, Volume VIII.* Washington, DC: American Psychiatric Press.

Taylor, M.A., Berenbaum, S.A., Jampala, V.C., & Cloninger, C.R. (1993). Are schizophrenia and affective disorder related? Preliminary data from a family study. *American Journal of Psychiatry*, 150, 278-285.

Tsuang, M.T., Stone, W.S., & Faraone, S.V. (2000). Toward reformulating the diagnosis of schizophrenia. *American Journal of Psychiatry*, 157, 1041-1050.

Van der Kolk, B.A., McFarlane, A.C., & Weisath, L. (1996). *Traumatic Stress: The Effects of Overwhelming Experience On Mind, Body, and Society.* New York: Guilford.

Walker, J.R., Norton, G.R., & Ross, C.A. (1991). *Panic Disorder and Agoraphobia: A Comprehensive Guide for the Practitioner.* Pacific Grove, CA: Brooks/Cole.

Waller, N.G., & Ross, C.A. (1997). The prevalence and biometric structure of pathological dissociation in the general population: Taxometric structure and behavior genetic findings. *Journal of Abnormal and Social Psychology*, 106, 499-510.

Waller, N.G., Putnam, F.W., & Carlson, E.B. (1996). The types of dissociation and dissociative types; A taxometric analysis of dissociative experiences. *Psychological Methods*, 1, 300-321.

Williams, L.M. (1994). Recall of childhood trauma: A prospective study of women's memories of child sexual abuse. *Journal of Consulting and Clinical Psychology*, 62, 1167-1176.

Whalen, J.E., & Nash, M.R. (1996). Hypnosis and dissociation:

Theoretical, empirical, and clinical perspectives. In Michelson, L.K., & Ray, W.J. (eds.). *Handbook of Dissociation. Theoretical, Empirical, and Clinical Perspectives.* New York: Plenum.

Zanarini, M.C., Frankenburg, F.R., Dubo, E.D., Sickel, A.E., Trikha, A., Levin, A., & Reynolds, V. (1998). Axis I comorbidity of borderline personality disorder. *American Journal of Psychiatry*, 155, 1733-1739.

REFERENCES

AUTHOR AND TITLE INDEX

A

B

N

O

P

Putnam, F.W.
Development, reliability, and validity of a dissociation scale, 62, 142, 330, 348
Diagnosis and Treatment of Multiple Personality Disorder, 141, 330, 343, 354
Dissociation in Children and Adolescents, 141, 330, 343, 354
Resolved: Multiple personality disorder is an individually and socially created artifact. Negative, 347, 354
The types of dissociation and dissociative types; A taxometric analysis of dissociative experiences, 338, 356

R

W

Y

Z

Subject Index

Tables are indicated by t; figures by f.

D

N

O